Library of
Davidson College

MANAGEMENT ACCOUNTING SIMPLIFIED

MANAGEMENT ACCOUNTING SIMPLIFIED

WILMER WRIGHT
President, Wilmer Wright Associates, Inc.

McGRAW-HILL BOOK COMPANY
New York   St. Louis   San Francisco   Auckland   Bogotá
Düsseldorf   Johannesburg   London   Madrid   Mexico
Montreal   New Delhi   Panama   Paris   São Paulo
Singapore   Sydney   Tokyo   Toronto

Library of Congress Cataloging in Publication Data

Wright, Wilmer.
 Management accounting simplified.

Includes index.
1. Managerial accounting.   I. Title.
HF5635.W967   658.1'511   79-14609
ISBN 0-07-072080-0

Copyright © 1980 by McGraw-Hill, Inc. All rights reserved. Printed in the United States of America. No part of this publication may be reproduced, stored in a retrieval system, or transmitted, in any form or by any means, electronic, mechanical, photocopying, recording, or otherwise, without the prior written permission of the publisher.

1 2 3 4 5 6 7 8 9 0   DODO   8 9 8 7 6 5 4 3 2 1 0

The editors for this book were W. Hodson Mogan, William R. Newton, and Celia Knight, the designer was Elliot Epstein, and the production supervisor was Thomas G. Kowalczyk. It was set in Baskerville by KBC/Rocappi.

Printed and bound by R. R. Donnelley & Sons Company.

To
James W. McCauley, M.D.
and
Roy S. Cohen, M.D.
and
Mary Wright, R.N.

Whose professional skill and dedication above and beyond the call of duty during my recent medical crisis made this book possible.

CONTENTS

	Preface	ix
1.	**The Origin and Development of Management Accounting**	1
2.	**Flexible Budgeting Made Easy**	9
3.	**Zero-Base Budgeting Streamlined**	37
4.	**Determination and Control of Direct Material Costs**	49
5.	**Determining True Product Costs**	61
6.	**The Exception Principle of Reporting to Management**	75
7.	**Models for Automation of Management Accounting**	87
8.	**Control of Capital Expenditures**	93
9.	**Profit Guidelines for Marketing Decisions**	101
10.	**Practical Long-Range Planning**	119
11.	**Meeting External Reporting Requirements**	137
12.	**The Future of Management Accounting**	147
	Appendix I *Typical Functional Specifications for Automation of Routing Files, Bills of Material Files, Product Costs, and Management Accounting Reports*	151
	Appendix II *Glossary of Accounting Terms*	231
	Appendix III *The Wright Comparative Ratios for U.S. Manufacturing Industries, 1961-1977*	235
	Index	247

PREFACE

This book is designed to help take the mystery out of accounting for nonfinancial executives by making it simple for them to understand management accounting. Since management accounting is designed to be clear to nonfinancial executives, this is not nearly so ambitious an undertaking as making it simple for them to understand general accounting for external reporting, as Wilson Seney has done in the many American Management Association seminars he has conducted on this subject.

Throughout this book direct standard costs have been utilized as the foundation of the simplified systems of management accounting because direct costing makes price-cost-volume relationships crystal clear and helps managers make difficult decisions where volume of production and sales is the variable factor. For example, in long-range planning and pricing, as well as make-or-buy decisions, volume is the most important variable.

Flexible budgeting in the direct standard cost system is made easy by making it mandatory that no period or mixed accounts may be charged to a productive department. Regression analysis to separate the fixed and variable portion of mixed accounts therefore becomes unnecessary, and the flexible budget system is much easier for first-line supervisors to understand. Thus the emphasis is rightly placed on improving productivity.

By integrating the zero-base budgeting procedure with the long-range planning procedure and feedback, the paperwork burden found in most zero-base systems is streamlined.

Through the full automation of the general ledger, routing file, and bills of material file, the problem of keeping standard costs current in periods of inflation becomes relatively simple.

Our experience has shown that standard cost systems are abandoned most frequently because of the clerical work required for manually revising the individual standard product costs each year. This annual revision places such a burden on the accounting staff that there is a great temptation to carry on with the old standard costs (factored for inflation) for another year, and this goes on year after year until the standard costs become so obsolete they lose their credibility and so lose their value as a management tool.

By maintaining a frozen and a current file of standard prices for material and purchased components, current replacement standard costs can be run at any time for a selected group of products. Then at the beginning of each fiscal year the current file, along with the new flexible budget standards, can be used to update all standard product costs. This run usually requires only a few hours of computer time. Thus there is no temptation to use obsolete standard costs year after year, and the standard product costs retain their credibility with operating executives.

Finally, this book presents a simplified procedure for adjusting operating profit and inventory values as determined by direct standard costs to the same value as would have been determined by absorption standard costs. The results are acceptable to public accountants for external reporting.

The techniques presented in this book have been tested in over 100 actual installations in a wide variety of industries.

The author wants to express his deep appreciation to his business colleagues and clients over the past several years, whose thinking and experience are reflected in this book. He is particularly indebted to his wife, Mary, who was his arms and legs after he was released from the hospital and until he became ambulatory, and also to Howland Dudley, former Executive Vice President of Wilmer Wright Associates, Inc.; to Michael Cunney and Donald P. Sweetser, long-time partners in Wright Associates, Walter Gentes, Controller of Cincinnati Time Recorder Company, and Brian Sickler, Financial Vice President of the Edwards Company, who furnished material for a number of the figures; to Paul Atwood, retired President of Union Bay State Chemical Company, an early convert to direct standard costs; to Henry Hoffman, retired Chief of Internal Auditing, the Nestle Company; to Ray Longenecker, Vice President and Controller of Armstrong Cork Company, and Logan Cheek of Xerox, author of *Zero-Base Budgeting Comes of Age*; to James Collier, Director of Publications of the National Association of Accountants (NAA); and last but certainly not least to Edythe E. Sweetser, who typed the entire manuscript and contributed many helpful suggestions.

Wilmer Wright

MANAGEMENT ACCOUNTING SIMPLIFIED

1
THE ORIGIN AND DEVELOPMENT OF MANAGEMENT ACCOUNTING

In the typical small company, the original internal accounting system was designed when the company was very small and the chief executive was intimately familiar with product costs and personally established budgets and objectives. The first accounting systems, therefore, were designed to provide reports for banks. Here the objective was to show how much profit was being made and how valuable were the inventories.

Next the accounting system was used to provide reports to the Internal Revenue Service, and the purpose became one of showing how little profit had been made, and, in doing that, inventories were priced at the most conservative level.

As the business grew in size and complexity, the chief executive no longer was able to maintain intimate knowledge of production costs or profit objectives. At this point the manager would request the accounting department to provide cost and profit data in order to do a better job of running the company.

The accountants would then try to use this dualistic accounting system to provide cost data and timely reports of what was actually happening. In recent years more and more managers have refused to take third place in this numbers game. They want their management accountants to provide them with a system of internal accounting that will furnish timely reports for decision making and optimization of profits, and to show how each executive has performed in meeting or beating objectives.

The chief executive then looks to the practicing public accountants to provide the bridge between these reports and requirements for external reporting.

Experience has shown that whenever a company has a good internal management accounting system it is a simple matter to provide any additional information needed for external reporting.

The historical development of modern management accounting systems began in the nineteenth century.

In 1875 John Walker of Liverpool, England, devised and published a monograph under the title, *Prime Costs Keeping for Engineers, Ironfounders, Boiler and Bridge Makers, et cetera, Practically Explained with the Method of Arriving at All the General Averages Required.* He explained methods of recording the weights and prices of material and the average cost of labor and material for each quarter of a year. Overhead was added as a percentage of the total prime cost and included management and commercial, trucking, storekeeping, engine drivers, and interest on capital.

Although Walker's system was the first formal system, it was still just a method of averaging actual past experience. In 1910 Harrington Emerson, who was one of the fathers of the scientific management movement, presented a paper before the American Society of Mechanical Engineers in which he criticized the accountants' method of looking backward. He said costs should be stated in terms of "what they should be" and executive performance should be measured against these cost standards.

In 1919 the National Association of Cost Accountants was formed in the United States and the *NACA Bulletin* was devoted to describing new approaches to providing managers with better accounting information for decision making and control.

In 1922 G. Charter Harrison designed the first cost system on the principles expressed by Harrington Emerson. He called it the system of *standard costs*. His first actual installation was at the Boss Manufacturing Company in Kewanee, Illinois.

In 1928 the Westinghouse Company decided to adopt standard costs for their management accounting, but they were not satisfied with Harrison's system because it was based on cost ratios which did not distinguish the effect of volume changes. The reports of executive performance were therefore confused by the unknown effect of volume.

Ralph E. Case, who had been trained by G. Charter Harrison, working with a task force of Westinghouse accountants and engineers, solved the problem by developing what they called the *flexible budget*. Budget allowances were tied into the standard cost system by means of a *volume variance,* so that the effect of volume changes could be shown separately when measuring a given executive's performance.

As more and more companies adopted standard costs, practicing public accountants began to accept this method for external financial reporting provided the standard costs were reasonably close to the actual average costs.

Management accountants, however, experienced great difficulty in explaining to operating executives, the effect of these volume variances on net profit, so that managers became very critical of accountants. Dialogues such as the following became more and more common:

> *Chief:* Suffering catfish! Do you mean to tell me that, with sales up more than $300,000, our profit is $20,000 less than last month?
>
> *Controller:* Yes, Mr. Scrooge.
>
> *Chief:* You're crazy, Cratchett, or else our confounded accounting system isn't worth blasting powder! Why, that sales increase should have boosted net profit by at least $30,000 and yet here you show a decrease of $20,000! I know for a fact that we haven't cut our selling prices, and the statement shows that selling expenses are not out of line.
>
> *Controller:* That's true, but in October we produced just about half as much as we sold, with the result that the charge for unabsorbed factory overhead ate up the gross margin increase, and some more to boot.
>
> *Chief:* Well, all I can say is your standard cost system is all cockeyed if it produces results like that! Why do we have to recognize unabsorbed overhead anyhow?
>
> *Controller:* Good accounting recognizes it as a regular thing! It's according to Hoyle; make no mistake about that!
>
> *Chief:* Then to hell with good accounting practice and Hoyle too! I want a profit and loss statement that shows a profit increase when we make sales like these, and I don't give a damn what production is. I'm sick and tired of trying to explain comparisons like this to our directors.[1]

This type of criticism was particularly valid in highly seasonal business with great variations in inventory levels and high period costs. The experience of the Continental Can Company is an outstanding example. As explained by Controller Gregg Barry at an AMA seminar in 1958, it was this company's practice to produce and store cans just prior to the packing season because, when the season started, it did not have production capacity to meet demand. Under the standard absorption cost system, standard costs were set on the average planned level of production for the year. Thus, when production was

---

[1] Jonathon N. Harris, "What Did We Earn Last Month," *NACA Bulletin*, section 1, Jan. 15, 1936, p. 501

at the capacity level for inventory, large volume variance gains resulted and were carried directly to profit and loss. As a consequence, operating profit could and sometimes did exceed net sales. The accountants certainly had trouble explaining that to their plant managers.

In order to avoid these distortions and so eliminate the problem of explaining volume variances to operating executives, Jonathon Harris and G. Charter Harrison devised a technique they called *direct costing*.

Their developmental work was completely independent but parallel. Harris was the first to install the new method at Dewey & Almy Chemical Company in 1934. Harrison made his first installation at Spool Cotton Company about a year later.

The first technical paper on direct costing was written by Harris, who submitted it to the National Association of Cost Accountants. At that time Dr. Raymond Marple was in charge of screening articles for publication in the *Bulletin*. He fully realized how hard the leaders of the accounting profession had been working to get acceptance of standard ground rules for matching costs against revenue on the absorption cost basis and that Harris's new concept attacked the very foundation of these ground rules. But Dr. Marple immediately recognized the value of the new method for management accounting and, with considerable trepidation, approved the manuscript for publication in the January 1936 *NACA Bulletin*.

G. Charter Harrison published his monograph about a year later as one of a series of monographs in a booklet entitled *New Wine in Old Bottles*. The subtitle was *Why Most Profit Statements are Wrong*.

In its early days direct costing attracted converts faster than did standard costs in its early days. The cost-plus-fixed-fee contracts of World War II put the spotlight on costing methods, and the contract termination negotiations after the war kept the spotlight on them.

In 1947 C. Robert Fay, who had been a member of the Westinghouse Task Force that developed the original flexible budget system, installed a direct standard cost system at the Pittsburgh Plate Glass Company, which was the first large company to adopt this method.

As president of the Controllers Institute in 1947-48, Bob Fay gained converts rapidly. One of the most important was I. Wayne Keller, controller of Armstrong Cork Company, who had a very sophisticated standard cost system with flexible budgets. He made a number of improvements in the system that had been installed at Pittsburgh Plate Glass, particularly in the handling of flexible budgets. He devised the method of charging only variable costs to production departments, whereas at Pittsburgh Plate Glass many mixed accounts had been used where the variable factors had been determined by the method of least squares, and explained to first-line supervisors by means of scattergraphs which showed volume vs. expense for a number of months based on actual records. This method was not only very time-consuming but assumed that in actual past experience expenses had been controlled as volume changed, which was an erroneous assumption.

It was found that about the only mixed account which needed to be charged to production departments was electric utilities. Here it was a simple matter to analyze the fixed part of the electric bill and charge it to a nonproductive department at the time of original entry. Since the fixed part of the expense was mainly due to the demand charge, this expense was usually charged to the chief electrical engineer who was responsible for handling negotiations with the electric power company. Then the direct charge was based on either metered kilowatt-hour (KWH) usage, as in the melting tanks, or on estimated KWH based on connected load, as in the grinding departments, which were not metered.

Following these two installation, direct costing rapidly gained converts. The pressure for conversion came largely from operating management. Public accountants were solidly against its use for external reporting, so that, with the exception of Robert Beyer (past president of the NAA), they did very little to promote it for internal management accounting. The commissioner of Internal Revenue and the Securities Exchange Commission (SEC) took this same attitude, unless, like Pittsburgh Plate Glass, the company had a long previous record of excluding fixed costs from inventory.

Continental Can Company, Fostoria Glass Company, American Can Company, Universal Cyclops Steel Company, and Farrell Steamship Lines were among the early converts to this system of management accounting, and, like Armstrong Cork Company, most of them continued to use full absorption costs for valuing their inventories in their external reporting. The accounting labor for making the closing journal entries was found to be negligible. For example, Wayne Keller told an AMA seminar on direct costing that preparing the accounting data for making the journal entry for this annual adjustment required less than one *work-hour*. (A work-hour, formerly called a man-hour, is defined as the unit of one hour's work by one full-time worker working at normal efficiency.)

On February 15, 1956, the Research Institute of America published a staff report, "Direct Costing—Short-Cut to Executive Decisions," which began:

> In too many companies, traditional business records are obscuring, not highlighting, the true state of affairs. But accountants and executives, working together, have found a way of bridging the gap between conserv-

ative accounting and management's needs. Here's how direct costing can make tough operating decisions easier for you. . . .

The Institute is convinced that the potential value of direct costing as a management tool is such that Members will at least want to give it a hearing. This Report focuses on the main advantages to the executive user, and shows how in tackling a number of key business problems the direct costing approach can make existing accounting records a great deal more revealing.

There are some drawbacks to direct costing where accounting records must be used for purposes other than making operating decisions. Complete adoption of direct costing, for example, would require finished goods to be carried in inventory at direct cost value only—which today would not be acceptable to the Revenue Service for tax purposes.

Unfortunately, the Research Institute was talking about management accountants such as Jonathon Harris and G. Charter Harrison, who were working with managers to bridge the gap, not the accounting authorities in public accounting firms or in the American Accounting Association who resented the speeches and writings of Harris and Harrison. Certainly no one would accuse either of these two gentlemen of using the "soft sell" in putting direct costing systems forward or in criticizing proponents of absorption costing.

Then, in 1973, the government ruled that some fixed accounts must be included in costs when valuing inventories for tax returns. This ruling had little effect on companies that had converted to direct costing because most of them had followed the Armstrong Cork Company example and had devised a simple method of adjusting their inventory valuation to absorption cost values.

In 1967 McGraw-Hill published, as part of their *Accounting* series, a book by I. Wayne Keller entitled *Management Accounting for Profit Control.*

About that time the National Association of Accountants changed the name of their publication from *NAA Bulletin* to *Management Accounting,* and, since that time, have directed their continuing education efforts to management accountants. They have established a Certificate in Management Accounting (CMA) program to provide recognition of professional competence and educational attainment in management accounting.

In February 1977, President George D. Gee reported:

The initial examination for the Certificate in Management Accounting was held in 1972 for 410 applicants. Four years later, in June 1976, more than 1,030 applicants took the five-part exam—almost a threefold increase. Sixty-one candidates successfully completed the first examination; 265 passed all parts of the latest one.

Sponsored, by NAA, the CMA program has exceeded our expectations, justifying the initial start-up costs. In fact, it should become NAA's most notable educational activity. The response from professors, students, businesses and CPAs alike has been very enthusiastic. "Help Wanted" ads now frequently include CMA holders among the qualifications for a position. The program has indeed filled a vacuum in the field of accounting.

The Institute of Management Accounting, which was organized by NAA to administer the program, has identified and structured the body of knowledge underlying the concepts of management accounting. In doing so, it has rendered a great service for all men and women in the accounting field.

Now we appropriately can recognize excellence in the development of professional accounting skills. The Robert Beyer Medal awards presented annually honor those with outstanding grades and also the national president who was so instrumental in the development of the program.

As scholars and management accountants build upon this foundation, the discipline will grow in usefulness and value to corporate management. A pioneer in the development of the program, NAA will continue to work toward its improvement and growth to full maturity.

2
FLEXIBLE BUDGETING MADE EASY

In American industry there are two basic methods of budgetary control. They can be compared to two diametrically opposed philosophies, dictatorship and free enterprise.

In the "dictatorship" approach, there is rigid budgetary control by a "budget czar," and no one can spend outside the budget without prior approval.

Under the "democratic" method, flexible budget standards are established. Control of each item of overhead is assigned to the most appropriate key person whose performance is measured against these budget standards.

The budget czar is one person wielding a big stick. The rest of the organization makes certain that they spend all the money in the allocated budget, whether wisely or not. If they don't, they know that the next year's budget will be cut.

Cost improvement is accomplished by periodic cost reduction drives. There is a certain arbitrariness and drama about a cost reduction drive that fires the imagination and stirs the hearts of some people, especially those who like to keep the staff guessing as to where the ax will fall next.

Not too many years ago cost reduction programs were industry's equivalent to spring housecleaning. In their worst form they were economy drives, and the typical directive would be to cut everything 20 percent. It usually took people about 6 months to recover, if they ever did fully recover, but more and more companies have seen the folly of their ways and cost reduction programs conducted on a shotgun basis to achieve some short-term objectives are about as out-of-date now as technocracy. In the end most of them cost far more than they save.

When fixed budgets are applied to productive departments, there is no incentive for improvements in productivity. In many cases, the budget reports do not even show direct labor as an item on the budget report—only overhead items, such as indirect labor, operating supplies, and fringe benefits. Also each expense item is usually shown as a percent of direct labor, if direct labor is shown at all. Thus, when productivity improves, direct labor is reduced, so that it looks as though the supervisor is doing a poor job of controlling overhead when he or she has actually saved many dollars by improving productivity for which no credit is given.

On the other hand, assume that sales of the items of a given department have increased dramatically beyond the expected level so that the budget for direct labor is small. In order to meet demand the supervisor must add and train new employees for which there is no budget allowance. As a result, the budget report makes the supervisor look bad, even though he or she has beaten all records on productivity per employee.

In another department sales have slipped from the forecast and it is easy to meet shipping requirements. Supervisors in such departments show large favorable variances because their budgets have been based on a much higher expected sales and production level. Such a system provides a negative incentive for improving productivity.

These are the reasons for failure of the dictatorship approach to budgetary control.

On the other hand, the democratic approach makes each member of the management team try to find sound ways of reducing costs, knowing full well that such contributions will show up in budget reports to top management.

Of the two systems it has been found that the democratic or free-enterprise system gives the better results. Who, then, should control costs? The answer is each key person in the organization for accounts assigned to his or her responsibility. How should they be controlled? The answer is by measuring each item against flexible performance standards before the money is spent. The "who" is called *responsibility accounting* and the "how" is called *flexible budgetary control.*

There are three different methods of utilizing flexible budgets.

Simple flexible budgets

Absorption standard costs with flexible budgets

Direct standard costs with flexible budgets

Simple flexible budgets, which are budget reports that are not tied into the general ledger, are the simplest application and, with a capable budget director, can be very effective. Their primary weakness is that the budget director often shows outstanding cost reductions only to have the profit results of the period show completely the reverse. The result is lack of confidence in the budget reports and a general letdown in enthusiasm for the budgetary control program.

Absorption standard costs with flexible budgets, i.e., the Westinghouse system, result in a complete reconciliation of the budget performance with the general books of account. The link that ties the two systems together is the volume variance accounts. This costing procedure is difficult to explain to nonaccounting executives. Also, with this system it is often difficult to assign responsibility for control of costs to the most appropriate key executive. On the other hand, authorities who have had experience with both state that direct standard costs do everything that absorption standard costs do and they are easier to install than flexible budgets with absorption standard costs. They are easier for nonaccounting executives to understand. They make the application of responsibility accounting more accurate and flexible.

The first step in setting up the flexible budget system is classification of accounts and their assignment to the key person who is in the best position to control them. A careful study is made of each account, and the basis for fair measurement is determined. Past performance is plotted on a scatter chart and an analysis of performance made at different levels of activity. Finally, in consultation with the key supervisor responsible for controlling the accounts, the budget standard is established which should be an attainable target. This is written up on a budget data sheet and is approved by the person responsible. Similar budgets are set up for all accounts under the key person's responsibility.

BUDGET DATA SHEETS

In building the labor and expense standards, information is assembled on budget data sheets for each account under each key person as established in the chart of accounts. Some companies use spread sheets by source of the expense items. Others use a separate sheet for each account under each key person with a budget summary sheet summarizing all the accounts assigned to a given key person. The latter method has the advantage of providing a complete budget manual in terms of responsibility accounting.

Well-designed budget data sheets are most effective in securing intelligent participation in the establishment of flexible standards for each key person. A well-designed budget data sheet shows the cost center name and number and the account name and number. It shows the unit of measure and the selected activity level. It shows by expense source the items that are charged to the account. Past performance data and the computations on which the selected

12 Management Accounting Simplified

budget standards are based are shown in enough detail to facilitate future revisions and to make easy the analysis of variances. Finally, the budget data sheets provide for approval signatures that ensure participation by the key person responsible and proper review by top supervisors.

Figure 2-1 shows a budget data sheet for the ABC Manufacturing Company. It was used in an initial direct standard cost installation where a new chart of accounts had been in effect for a full year before the flexible standards were established. The normal activity level and the performance level were selected as the actual average for the previous 12 months. The account shown

---

BUDGET DATA SHEET

DATE 6/1/	COMPILED R.O.S.	ACCT. CLASS Mixed	COST CENTER NAME Machine shop	COST CENTER NO. 02
DATE 7/15/	ACCEPTED C.A.G.	PERIOD Month	ACCOUNT NAME Material handling	ACCOUNT NO. 206
DATE 7/28/	APPROVED R.G.O.	UNIT Standard Direct Labor Hours		UNITS IN PERIOD 1960

DATE	REASON FOR REVISION OF BUDGET	AMOUNT	TOTAL REVISION
		$	$
		$	$
		$	$
		$	$

THIS ACCOUNT IS CHARGED WITH

All wages paid to the following occupations:
1. Occupation No. 304, Cranemen
2. Occupation No. 306, Lift Truck Operator

BUDGET WAS DETERMINED AS FOLLOWS:	TOTAL	PERIOD	DIRECT

Analysis of year 19___ and consultation with Department Foreman, Mr. Smith

Occupation No.	Name	Hours	Rate per Hour	Total
304	Craneman	850	$2.55	$2,167.50
306	Lift Truck Oper.	534	2.38	1,270.92
		1,384		$3,438.42

Average Rate per Hour: $\frac{\$3,438}{1,384} = \$2.48$

Budgeted Fixed Hours = 600
Average Rate per Hour = $2.48
Budgeted Fixed Expense = $1,488

TOTAL STANDARD BUDGET	$3,438	$1,488	$1,950

Figure 2–1 Budget data sheet for the ABC Manufacturing Company.

Flexible Budgeting Made Easy **13**

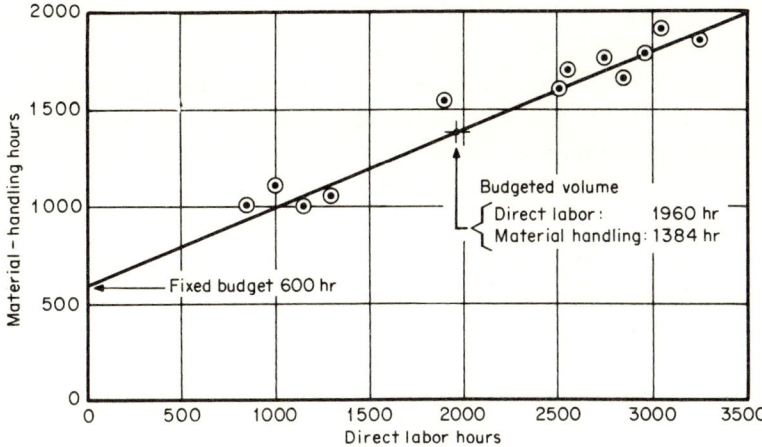

Figure 2-2 Scattergraph analyzing material-handling hours in terms of direct labor hours.

here is material handling, which was classified as a mixed account. Accordingly, a scattergraph was prepared for J. M. Brown, the forewoman of the department, to use in selecting the budget standard. (See Figure 2-2.) When the actual data points shown on the budget data sheet are plotted, Brown can easily see that a line running from 600 material-handling hours at zero production to 1334 material-handling hours, when 1960 standard direct labor hours are produced, fits the performance for the past 12 months (see Table 2-1). She then figures from a practical standpoint how many people she would

Table 2-1
ABC MANUFACTURING COMPANY
Performance over 12-Month Period

Month	Direct labor hours	Material handling hours
January	3050	1902
February	2852	1655
March	2548	1697
April	2953	1798
May	3250	1856
June	2750	1750
July	2506	1610
August	1898	1545
September	1150	1010
October	850	997
November	1006	1099
December	1300	1048

have at the two distinct levels of production, 1000 and 3000. This method confirms the selected line, so she is satisfied with the budget standard. These standard data are then converted to dollars of expense by applying the applicable hourly rate as shown on the budget data sheet.

It should be noted that if the flexible budget system had been in effect for a number of years and the above data sheet represented a revision for the coming year, the experience section would show actual, standard, and variance for the prior 3 years. This practice provides a long-range measure of cost control performance and avoids "cozy" budgeters.

Figure 2-3 shows the budget summary sheet wherein all of Brown's accounts are summarized. For each account on this sheet there is a budget data sheet similar to the one for account 206, with the exception of allocated expense, which is used for product costing rates and is not Brown's responsibility.

APPROVAL OF STANDARDS

One of the most frequent mistakes of control officers in directing the installation of a flexible budget system is failure to program adequate time for securing approval of the flexible standards before they are put into effect. Here is where all the talk about having each key person participate in setting the standards comes into sharp focus. Yet, too often, the schedule for installation fails to allow sufficient time to ensure that all the operating people understand the standards and are in complete agreement with them. The pressure of meeting the time schedule for installation is often interpreted by the operating people as simply railroading the standards through for approval.

With sound planning, however, this approval feature can be the most effective part of the whole standards program. Here is an opportunity to give each key person a complete understanding of the entire flexible budget system as well as of the behavior and control of the accounts for which he or she is responsible. Handled with care and patience, the operating people come away from these conferences with a feeling that they were given certain data by the accounting group and that they themselves determined the budget standards.

Furthermore, the review and approval by top supervision can be the basis for complete indoctrination of the operating people in the use of the flexible standards to eliminate waste and to provide better profits. This is the point at which the data is being presented in terms the operating people understand. This is the time to be sure that all levels of supervision understand the standards and how they fit into the management accounting system.

BUDGET SUMMARY SHEET

Cost Center No. 02	Cost Center Name MACHINE SHOP					Compiled R.O.S Accepted C.A.G Approved R.G.O.	Date 6/1/ Date 7/15/ Date 7/28/	
Units in Period 1960	Period Month	Unit Standard Allowed Hours						
ACCOUNTS			CLASS	STANDARD BUDGET			DIRECT RATE PER UNIT	
NO.	NAME			TOTAL	PERIOD	DIRECT		
100	DIRECT LABOR							
101	Lathe Operators							
102	Punch Press Operators							
103	Grinding Machine Operators							
	TOTAL DIRECT LABOR		D	5,292		5,292	2.70	
200	INDIRECT LABOR							
201	Supervision		P	650	650			
202	Clerical		D	310		310	.16	
206	Material Handling		M	3,438	1,488	1,950	.99	
207	Rework		D	175		175	.09	
210	Misc. Indirect Labor		D	260		260	.14	
	TOTAL INDIRECT LABOR			4,833	2,138	2,695	1.38	
300	OTHER EXPENSES							
301	Direct Operating Supplies		D	465		465	.24	
302	Expense Supplies		D	440		440	.22	
	TOTAL OTHER EXPENSES			905		905	.46	
	TOTAL DIRECT EXPENSE			11,030	2,138	8,892	4.54	
	ALLOCATED EXPENSE			2,595		2,595	1.32	
	GRAND TOTAL BUDGET			13,625	2,138	11,487	5.86	
	GRAND TOTAL BUDGET			13,625	2,138	11,487	5.86	

Figure 2—3 Budget summary sheet for the machine shop of the ABC Manufacturing Company.

Each key executive receives a monthly report showing progress in controlling costs and improving profits. The report shown in Figure 2-4 is a cost-and-variance statement for the machine shop of the ABC Manufacturing Company. The accounts shown are the responsibility of J. M. Brown, the forewoman of this department.

COST AND VARIANCE STATEMENT

VARIANCES					ACTUAL	THIS PERIOD		
THIS PERIOD	Aug. TO DATE	NO.	ACCOUNT		Aug. TO DATE	EXT. BUDG. ALLOWANCE	CURRENT ALLOWANCE	ACTUAL
		100	**DIRECT LABOR**					
(30)	100	101	Lathe Operators		6,018		2,972	3,002
(62)	(70)	102	Punch Press Operators		5,108		2,500	2,562
(10)	74	103	Grinding Machine Operators		201		85	95
(102)	104		TOTAL DIRECT LABOR		11,327		5,557	5,659
		200	**INDIRECT LABOR**					
(9)	(3)	201	Supervision		1,303		650	659
(5)	4	202	Clerical		666		326	331
(370)	(702)	206	Material Handling		7,890		3,535	3,905
(120)	(192)	207	Rework		570		184	304
70	154	210	Miscellaneous Indirect Labor		407		273	203
(434)	(739)		TOTAL INDIRECT LABOR		10,836		4,968	5,402
		300	**OTHER EXPENSES**					
20	23	301	Direct Operating Supplies		981		488	468
60	143	302	Expense Supplies		808		462	402
80	166		TOTAL OTHER EXPENSES		1,789		950	870
(456)	(469)		GRAND TOTAL		23,952		11,475	11,931
THIS PERIOD		PRODUCTION UNIT	Standard Hours				**YEAR TO DATE**	
1,960		PRODUCTION	BUDGETED UNITS				3,920	
2,058			ACTUAL UNITS				4,234	
105%			ACTIVITY (Volume) – PERCENT				108%	
96%			EFFICIENCY – PERCENT				98%	
104%			TOTAL COST RATIO				102%	
Sept. 1958 PERIOD		COST CENTER	MACHINE SHOP		NO. 02		KEY PERSON J. M. Brown	

Figure 2–4 Cost-and-variance statement for the machine shop of the ABC Manufacturing Company.

Brown can see at a glance that her performance for September should be improved. Her direct labor accounts have dropped from a $206 favorable variance in August to a $102 unfavorable variance in September. This was the result of interruptions in production due to a shortage of tools and grinding wheels. Brown then broke into jobs already in progress to be sure orders were shipped on time. Therefore, she decreased the efficiency of her direct labor and put a larger burden on her materials handling crew.

With this report, it was obvious to Brown that she must improve her planning in order to reduce these variances. Similar reports for all other key persons make it simple to keep the whole team on its toes with a minimum of top executive attention.

However, the most important point is that the flexible budget provides for controlling expenses before the monies are spent. A sudden change in schedule or an emergency breakdown is immediately covered by the key person on the job because adjustments can be made at once. He or she doesn't have to wait for budget orders to come from the "budget czar"; that's why it is called a "flexible budget." It measures how well each member of the management team is able to meet cost standards regardless of volume changes.

However, it has been found that the simplest way to set up flexible standards is to classify all expense accounts that are charged to productive departments as if they were 100 percent variable rather than use scattergraphs and mixed accounts. In this way the whole flexible budget system is made so simple that any first-line supervisor can understand it. This accounting system, however, requires that no mixed accounts be charged to a productive department. When an account is truly a mixed account, such as electric power, it is broken into two parts. The fixed part, which is largely the demand charge, is charged to the supervisor in charge of utilities. Only the variable portion is charged to productive departments. This is based on the theory that the principal method the head of the production department can use to reduce cost and improve budget performance is to improve productivity.

The potential for improving productivity was demonstrated in the famous productivity study that was made at the Hawthorne Plant of the Western Electric Company in 1927 and 1928. In this study a number of operators from the relay assembly department were set up in a separate laboratory and their production was measured very carefully. Each morning they were interviewed to determine whether or not any outside factors had occurred that might affect their production that day. Also, they were made to feel a part of the experiment so they had a direct interest in the results and were informed of the results as they developed. Then certain working conditions were changed. For example, they were given short rest periods in the morning and again in the afternoon, and it was found that their production level increased. Also, lighting was improved, and production increased. Each time conditions were changed, it was found that production increased until, at the end of several months and many changes in working conditions, they had increased their production by about 40 percent over the level at which they were operating when the study started.

At that point, one of the operating superintendents said: "Why don't we return the conditions back to the same as they were before we started the experiment?" This was done, and, with this change, production increased again. This result completely baffled the research engineers who were conducting the experiment, so they analyzed all the variable factors that were involved and decided that the main factor that had resulted in this increased production was the attitude of the workers. They were now a part of the management team and they looked forward to going to work each morning and being interviewed and hearing the results of what was happening. This demonstrates the potential a production supervisor has for creating an atmosphere for productivity.

In order to measure productivity, it is important that you have a common denominator of production. In the case of the relay assembly, this was a completely assembled relay. As it was completed it dropped onto a conveyor belt and a production unit was automatically recorded.

When you have many different types of products flowing through a given cost center, it is important that you arrive at a common denominator which measures the amount of human effort involved in producing this part or that product.

Following are the common denominators ordinarily used:

Standard work-hours

Standard machine-hours

Pounds

Square feet

Completed units

When a sufficient amount of scientific measurement is available, it is possible to know how much human endeavor is needed for a given operation on a given product. *Basic time standards* mean that engineers have developed proper methods, proper layouts, and proper tools so that, for example, in a drill press operation the worker has definite things that have to be done from the time he or she starts to drill a piece until that piece is finished and another one is ready to be drilled. The time study designates this as "elements of a given operation."

Machine-hours may be used when many operators are working together at a machine or on a production line. For instance, consider a drop hammer operation. This operation requires three workers. One does the shaping, one the feeding, and one tends the furnace. In these instances, it is better to use standard hours in the terms of the machine rather than the worker. The determining factor, therefore, is how many units are turned out per hour by the whole crew.

Most importantly, productivity should be measured only on good work completed.

STANDARDS FOR MEASURING PRODUCTIVITY

After determining the classification of accounts and the common denominator for measuring productivity to be used for each cost center, the next step is to determine the basic standards for measuring productivity in that cost center. This step may be accomplished by preparing engineered time standards or engineering estimates, or by analyzing past performance.

When a wage incentive plan is in effect, it is important to tie the unit of measure into the incentive rate structure so that the incentive pay computation can be used as the basis of the budget performance report. If incentive rates are accurate and a high degree of coverage is maintained, this method is by far the most efficient. In any event, it is at this point in the installation that the management accountant must have the active support of the industrial engineers and production supervisors. It should be their function to set the standards and to revise them as conditions change. The management accountant is responsible for applying dollar values to these standards and for testing them against actual performance in order to determine whether they are consistent and attainable.

Even where complete direct labor standards are in effect, there are usually many revisions that must be made in the basic measure of productivity in order to convert to sound flexible budgets.

In departments where sound wage incentive plans are in operation, the use of the wage incentive rates as the productivity measure provides the most efficient and accurate method of developing flexible budgets. The method of handling them depends on the type of incentive plan in effect.

Straight Piecework

It is frequently stated that piecework is the oldest form of wage incentive and the most abused. However, with good administration, sound methods standardization, and engineered time standards as bases of the piece rates, this wage plan should be the most effective and inexpensive system to operate from the standpoint of both incentives and flexible budgets.

Assume a piecework plan where only good work is paid for and each operator performs the necessary rework without compensation credit. This plan, a form of incentive that was in effect in the garment industry for many years, utilizes piecework dollars as the basic unit of measure for product costs. Since material is usually on consignment, all that it is necessary to know in order to determine the standard cost for making a given garment are the piecework rates for all operations on that garment and the overhead rate. This procedure will be explained more completely in the discussion of product costing. However, the simplicity of the old piecework system makes the fundamental principles of accounting for direct costs so easy to understand that a preliminary explanation of the piecework procedure is presented at this point. Explanations covering more complex systems will be found in subsequent chapters.

The mechanics of this procedure is shown graphically by Figure 2-5. The piecework payroll multiplied by the overhead rate becomes the charge to work-in-process for each period. Each garment that is finished and shipped is credited to work-in-process at the individual piecework rate times this same costing rate. The actual overhead expenses are compared with the standard, and the difference is closed to profit and loss for the period. All period costs are charged to profit and loss at actual cost.

Under modern systems of piecework, however, the application is not quite so simple. Guaranteed minimum hourly rates are established which require separating the makeup allowances from the straight piecework earnings. New models or operations usually are handled on average until piece rates have been established and accepted. In other words, the workers are paid an hourly rate equal to their average hourly earnings while on regular piecework until the rates are officially installed. For standard costing these nonrated jobs must be covered immediately by a temporary standard so that standard costs can be computed and variances due to delay in getting the new rate accepted can be shown. The new products or revised processes can then be evaluated for merchandising and pricing decisions. In other words, the production piecework reports must show an estimated standard value of work done on average or day work so that the excess cost can be charged to a separate account. Excess costs for rework, extra operations, or special allowances for nonstandard conditions must also be computed. Finally, the standard piecework dollars produced are determined, and the excess actually paid for any of the above reasons is charged to appropriate variance accounts. Handling this report on a

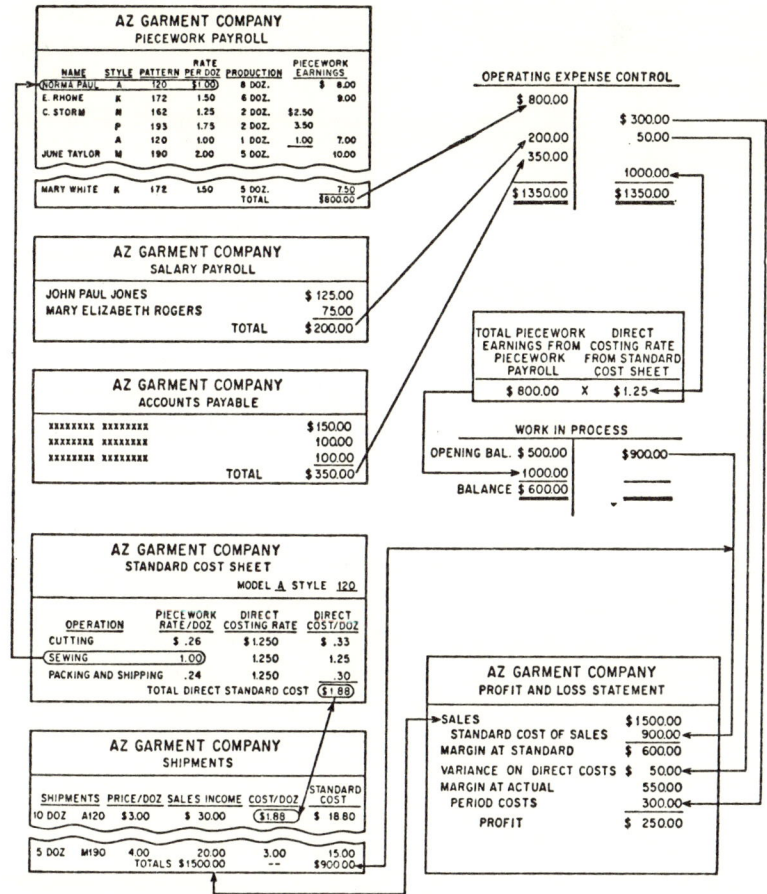

Figure 2—5 Example of a flowchart for direct standard cost accounting system in a piecework shop.

daily or weekly basis provides management with an excellent control report for maintaining the wage incentive plan. At the same time the accounting data for the standard cost system are immediately available for the monthly cost-and-variance reports.

Bedaux Plan

The Bedaux incentive plan calls for use of a B as the basis of measuring performance. The B represents one work-minute at a selected acceptable performance level. Standard B values are determined by speed-rating actual time-study observations and adjusting them to this level. When an operator produces more than 60 *B*'s of work per hour, a bonus is given which is equal to three-fourths of the savings due to production above the minimum acceptable level. An average, fully-trained incentive worker is expected to produce 80 *B*'s per hour. For this performance, the bonus computation is as follows:

$$\frac{80 - 60}{60} \times \frac{3}{4} = 0.25 \text{ or } 25 \text{ percent bonus}$$

The most outstanding characteristic of the Bedaux plan is the emphasis on increased effort rather than on improved and standardized methods. Rates usually are set on operations rather than on good products completed. Only the manual part of a machine operation is rated, so that an operator cannot earn an incentive bonus on the machine portion of the production cycle.

The net effect is to make it extremely difficult to use the Bedaux plan as a basic unit of measure for flexible budgets. Nevertheless, the use of *B*'s is practical where good coverage is maintained, if adequate precautions are taken against inflated production reports, and standards are developed for the machine segment of production cycles. Failure to do this can result in serious inventory discrepancies.

An outstanding example of such failure occurred a few years ago in a manufacturing plant producing imitation leather cloth. The Bedaux plan had been in operation for a number of years and good coverage was maintained. The industrial engineering department provided the cost group with the operation descriptions and the number of *B*'s to produce a yard of finished leather cloth for each grade, style, and finish. The standard cost per *B* was determined, and this was charged to work-in-process based on the *B*'s which were reported by each operator in each department. As products were shipped, work-in-process was credited with the amount per yard determined by multiplying the *B*'s shown by the industrial engineers by the standard costing rate. At the end of 6 months, the work-in-process accounts seemed to be growing out of proportion to the physical stock in the plant, so it was decided to take a physical inventory. When the physical inventory was priced at standard, a very serious shortage was found. Investigation showed wholesale overreporting on the part of operators with no adequate supervisory check of their reports. As a result, each operation was set up from a cost standpoint on the standard *B*'s that should be used to produce a good yard of product through that operation. The performance each day on the incentive plan was then measured against the standard cost of good leather cloth produced, and the differences were explained. The results were elimination of the inventory discrepancies, honest incentive reports, and better operator performance.

Halsey Plan

The Halsey plan is based on splitting the savings with the operators as under the Bedaux system. Usually this is done on a 50-50 basis. The principal difference between the Halsey plan and the Bedaux plan is that, under the former, standard allowed hours are used instead of B's, and incentive performance reports are based on good products completed rather than on operations performed.

As a result, the Halsey plan is much easier to apply as a basic measure of activity level than is the Bedaux plan. However, both plans have become somewhat obsolete because the workers are no longer content to get only a share of the savings due to their increased effort. Consequently, most Halsey plans have been converted and a high percentage of Bedaux plans modified to give the workers 100 percent of these savings.

Under these plans the principal effort must be directed toward making sure that nonstandard operations and rework are reported and evaluated in terms of cost standards.

Rowan Plan

A study of the Rowan plan reveals that it is simply a Halsey plan in disguise. As workers increase their performance level, they receive a smaller and smaller share of the cost savings. This result is accomplished as follows: the bonus is computed by dividing hours saved by actual hours worked: whereas under the Halsey plan, standard allowed hours are used as the base.

For example, assume the following: Operation X has a rate of one standard allowed hour per 100 units produced. Worker A produces 150 units in 1 hour, Worker B produces 200 units in 1 hour, and Worker C produces 300 units in 1 hour. (See Table 2-2.)

Thus, it can be seen that under the Rowan plan the bonus would reach 100 percent only when the hours saved reached infinity. This characteristic is considered by the proponents of the Rowan plan as its principal advantage. It is contended that when loose rates are established they will never get out of hand because of the mathematical limit. In actual practice the result has been that the workers have limited their production to secure a bonus of about 30 percent, and management has paid the price in low productivity.

In applying the Rowan plan incentive rates to standard costs, the standard allowed hours are used in the same way as in the Halsey plan. However, care must be taken to avoid using rates that distort the true cost. In other words, in cost centers where incentive rates are out of line and these rates fail to reflect

Table 2-2
BONUS COMPUTATION FOR HALSEY 50–50 PLAN

Performance data	Worker A	Worker B	Worker C
Standard hours produced	1.50	2.00	3.00
Actual hours worked	1.00	1.00	1.00
Hours saved	0.50	1.00	2.00
Halsey 50-50 plan			
Bonus computation	0.25 / 1.00	0.50 / 1.00	1.00 / 1.00
Bonus as percent of base pay	25%	50%	100%
Rowan plan:			
Bonus computation	0.50 / 1.50	1.00 / 2.00	2.00 / 3.00
Bonus as percent of base pay	33%	50%	67%

the true time required for work on different products, accurate budget standards must be developed and applied to determine true productivity.

Standard-Hour Plan

The standard-hour plan is by far the most widely accepted wage incentive plan. It may be regarded as the Halsey plan with 100 percent of the savings being paid to the workers.

The incentive calculation is made as simple as possible so that payroll errors are avoided and the worker has complete confidence that the pay is correct. With the standard-hour plan there is no need to convert the rates to the *B* hour developed and then to dollars earned. The calculation is simplified even further when applied to group rates.

The following illustration demonstrates the ease of calculating rates which are incorporated into the one-for-one standard-hour plan. It is important to remember that the standard allowed hour rate includes the basic time to do the job, allowance for normal personal fatigue and delay time, plus the incentive factor.

Assume

Base minutes for operation (per unit)	= 1.75
Allowance for personal fatigue and delay	= 10%
Incentive factor	= 25%

then

    Standard allowed hour per unit equals:

$$\frac{1.75 \times 1.10 \times 1.25}{60} = 0.04/\text{unit}$$

Assume

Worker's production in 8-hr day	=	250 units
Base rate of job	=	$2.00/hr

then

Standard allowed hours produced: 250 × 0.04	=	10 hrs
Worker's pay for the day: 10 × $2.00	=	$20.00

    The most significant fact in the above calculation is that the number of units actually completed exceeded the standard production by 25 percent, and the operator received 25 percent more than the base pay. This direct relation of production to earnings is the factor that makes the one-for-one standard-hour plan so easy to explain.

    The application of the one-for-one standard-hour plan to group incentives is even more effective in simplifying the computation of rates and earnings. The rate for a production line is determined by balancing the work assignments and determining the controlling factor or operation. It usually turns out that some machine process time is the controlling factor. The time per unit of production at the control point times the standard number of people on the line gives the base work-hours per unit of production. Conversion to standard allowed hours is then the same as illustrated above for individual rates. The computation of group earnings is as shown in Table 2-3. This percent bonus is

Table 2-3
COMPUTATION OF GROUP EARNINGS

Item	Units produced	SAH* per unit	SAH* produced
P-2073	2000	0.21	420
P-2197	500	0.30	150
P-3792	800	0.25	200
Total SAH produced			770
Hours worked (77 workers; 8 hrs each)			616
Hours saved			154
Percent bonus			20%

*Standard allowed hours.

then applied to the base pay of each of the workers in the group for the hours worked.

The standard-hour plan is generally set up with adequate safeguards against overreporting and is based on standardization by prior methods. However, the use of average incentive earnings on nonrated jobs and special rates for nonstandard operations makes it imperative that in performance reports these variances be seperated.

USE OF STANDARD DATA

The most efficient and accurate method of establishing basic standards for both wage incentives and flexible budgets is through the use of element time-standard data as developed by the industrial engineers.

Element time standards consist of tables, charts, formulas, and allowances by means of which the time for an operation or process may be determined without recourse to stopwatch timing, to detailed methods time measurement (MTM) analysis, or to other individual time measurement techniques. The standard data are evolved by making studies of a broad range of operations and products for the cost center in question and by reducing each operation to its component parts. These elements are then studied to determine the laws of variation between the conditions for a given class of work and the time required to perform the work. These laws of variation are finally developed into formulas, tables, and charts from which the total standard time may be computed for any operation in connection with the particular class of work being studied.

The obvious advantages of using time-study data in this way are that considerable time is saved in establishing the basic standard by formula rather than by individual time study, that the values are more consistent, that they can be determined from working drawings and other manufacturing information before the job is actually performed in the shop, and that a high-salaried industrial engineer is not needed to apply the standard data. A comparatively small number of representative time studies or MTM analyses provides sufficient material from which to make a formula which will apply to an entire class of work. It is possible, therefore, by the use of element time standards to develop standard costs for jobs and products for which it would be completely impractical to develop basic standards by individual time study. Figure 2-6 shows a case study from a large manufacturing company making telephone equipment. The cost of setting basic standards from element time-standard data is compared with the cost of setting the same rates from individual time study. The savings in clerical and engineering time are self-evident. The intangible savings due to having more accurate predetermined costs before an

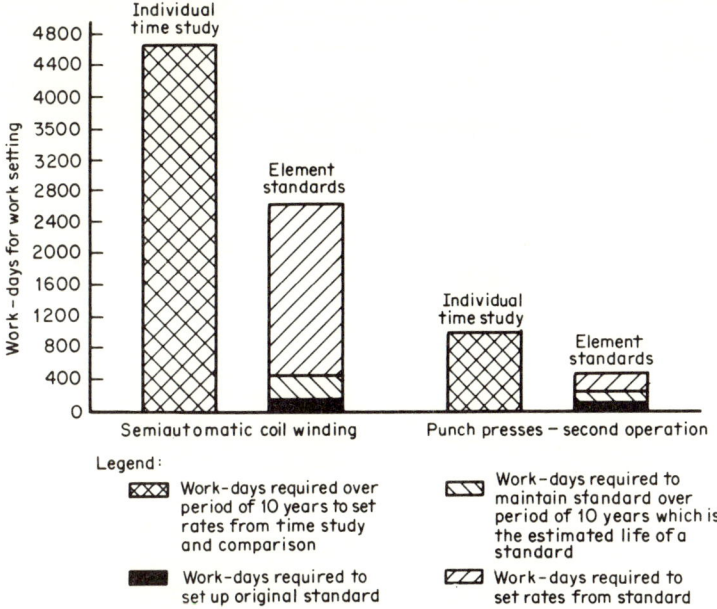

Figure 2-6 Comparative cost of setting rates, from a company manufacturing telephone equipment.

item is run in the shop are believed by many to be even greater than the tangible savings.

In setting up sound standard-time data, the industrial engineers assigned to the task force must become intimately familiar with all the work that is handled by each cost center being studied. For example, if the activity to be covered is the Avey drill press department, the assigned industrial engineer becomes a specialist on Avey drill presses. The first task is to make sure that operating conditions are standardized and that the operators are instructed in the best way to perform the work. After the operators have become proficient, a complete time analysis is made of a wide variety of the work, using stopwatch, MTM, or other time measurement techniques. Element time values are entered on master data sheets, which are designed to show how various conditions of the work affect the time values. It is then relatively easy to determine the standard-time values for the constant elements and the more simple variables. Sometimes more complex variables require special experimental studies in order to develop the standards. Figure 2-7 shows the results of such a study for Avey drill presses.

After all the element time values and their laws of variation have been established, necessary allowances are determined by means of production studies or work-sampling techniques. The engineer then develops formulas,

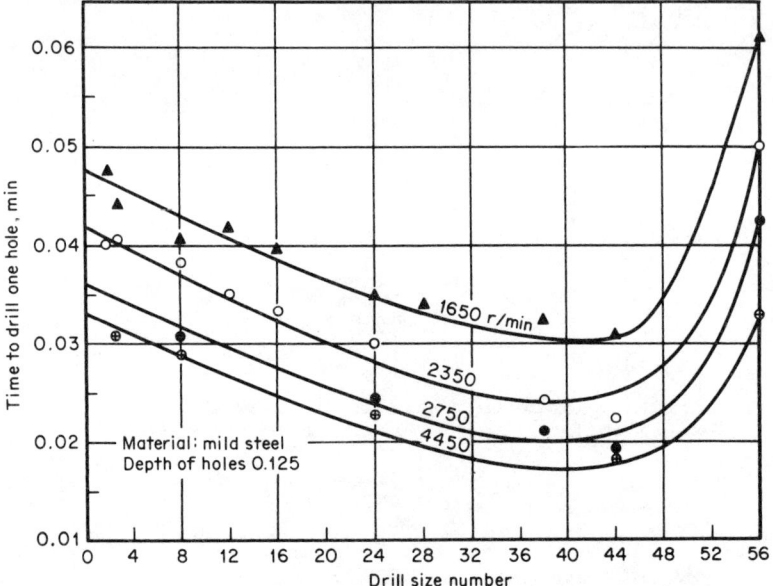

Figure 2—7 Avey drill press standards.

charts, and tables in order to present the whole group of time data in a form that can be used by the accounting group in establishing basic time standards for standard costs and flexible budgets.

Temporary Standards

In many cases, where accurate standard-time data are not available, temporary cost standards can be established by work sampling, past performance reports, and rough time studies. These can be very effective as a first step. Later they can be refined when engineered time standards become available.

An outstanding example of this technique occurred during the original installation of the direct standard cost system at the Pittsburgh Plate Glass Company.

At that time the manufacture of the "Twindow" had just passed the pilot plant stage and was rapidly increasing in sales. Manufacturing methods were in a constant state of flux, and improvements in methods and even in design were being made constantly. There were no time standards on the operations, and cost accounting was being accomplished with a conventional job cost system.

In view of the lack of standard-time data, it was decided to set up standard direct overhead rates for this activity and to determine direct labor cost by the existing job cost system until the process was standardized and engineered time standards were available. However, on closer investigation of the operation of the job cost system, it became evident that it could never provide management with the necessary information either for controlling costs or for determining pricing and merchandising policies. It was simply a means of matching costs against revenue to provide a monthly profit-and-loss statement.

The principal reason the job cost system was so ineffective was the tremendous number and variety of orders. The units were custom-made to fit architects' specifications, and few units were ordered in the same size. One order might represent fifteen items of one unit each and a wide range of sizes and types.

Consequently, accumulation of the total cost of a given order was unsatisfactory because it could not be correlated with the size and type of product. An attempt was made to keep the job costs by individual line item on each order. However, this minute distribution of time resulted in so many inaccuracies that the results were of no value and it was abandoned.

In addition, these data failed to show merchandising executives how far they could expect costs to be reduced, because, at best, they were simply historical figures. No basis was provided for projecting the realizable costs on which selling prices and sales policies should be based.

It was therefore decided to set up this activity on standard direct costs based on rough time standards, with the intention of revising the standards every few months as technological improvements indicated an important shift in costs.

An analysis of the direct labor operations showed that the primary factor affecting the time per unit was the perimeter of the Twindow. This was so because the principal work consisted of applying a stainless steel rim and sealing the edge of the twin pieces of glass that provided the thermal insulation.

Work-sampling and stopwatch time studies provided time standards for a selected number of sizes. These time values were then plotted against perimeter inches (see Figure 2-8). These studies disclosed that the time required to perform most operations contained a constant element per unit regardless of the size of the unit. In addition, the work-hours per unit increased at a constant rate on a straight line from zero to x inches of perimeter. Beyond that point the line increased at a greater rate per inch because more operators were required to handle the larger sizes. Thus, the single formula shown in Figure 2-8 based on eight data points provided the standard direct labor hours for an infinite number of sizes.

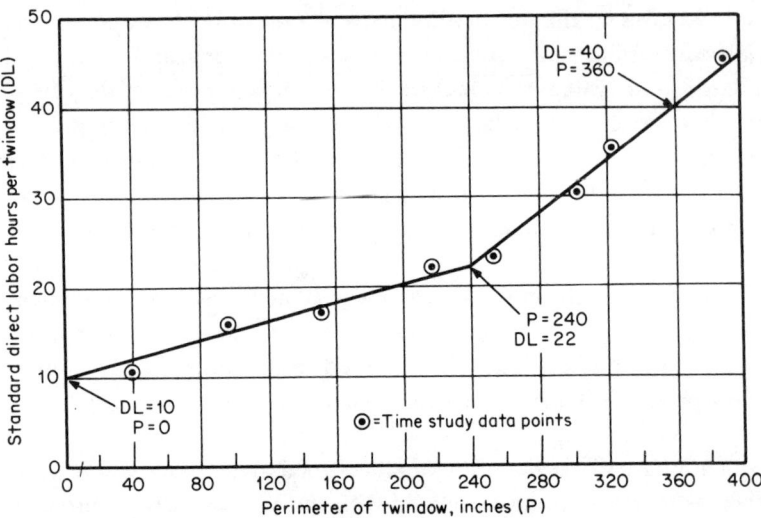

Figure 2—8 Standard data for assembly of Twindows.

This procedure was followed for each of seven cost centers. With these simple standards, a daily report for each center was provided showing hours worked, number of units completed, total perimeter inches, and perimeter inches over x per unit. These production quantities were extended by the formula, and the production supervisors were given a report on their direct labor effectiveness each day. At the end of the month these standard work-hours were totaled and extended by the standard cost per work-hour to determine the charge to work-in-process for labor and expense.

Due to the infinite variety of sizes and types, setting predetermined standard cost cards was impractical. The formulas, therefore, were used to prepare tables for all sizes of units, so that the standard cost for any unit could be selected directly from the tables. The tables then were used to compute the direct standard cost of each line item on each order at the time the order was received. Using the tables, the total time to determine the direct standard cost for a line item was from 2 to 4 minutes. The clerical cost of handling this standard cost system was approximately one-half the cost of operating the previous job cost system.

The application of rough and simple standards to each process provided a benchmark for management to measure progress in improving manufacturing methods. The daily reports provided shop supervisors with the means of developing a high level of productivity. Finally, the direct standard costs brought to light certain types and sizes that were unprofitable. The job cost system never could have achieved these results.

Engineering Estimates

In a large number of instances where individual cost estimates are required for bidding on each individual order, it has been found that the cost data for the engineering estimates can be arranged so as to provide a basis for measuring productivity of direct labor.

For example, in a lithographing company, it was found that by redesigning the form of the cost estimate, the estimated time could be shown by control centers and multiplied by direct standard costing rates to provide the data needed for applying the pricing formulas. On jobs where the company was successful and received the order, the performance in each cost center on all jobs going through each day was measured against the engineering estimates. The actual time was accumulated against each job and compared with estimates for each operation and cost center. In cases where the method planned in the engineering estimate had to be revised in actual production, this variance was shown and the responsibility was assigned. As a result, the cost estimates became more realistic and the plant performance improved to meet or even beat these realistic estimates.

Another company manufacturing special electronic equipment to order found that they bid on many orders which they failed to get. Therefore, they used a shortcut method of cost estimating for purposes of bidding. However, as soon as they were awarded a contract, they immediately developed a detailed engineering estimate in terms of operations and cost centers. This estimate became the standard cost and was compared with the estimate used in the bid.

In cases where the shortcut bid resulted in a profit margin at standard that was too small, intensive methods work was applied to reduce the cost so that an adequate margin at standard could be expected.

The revised and detailed estimates were used to measure performance in each cost center each day and then accumulated by each job so that margin at actual could be forecasted on each job as it progressed through the shop.

PERFORMANCE REPORTS

As soon as the basic standards for measuring activitity in a given cost center are completed, procedures should be instituted for providing operating supervisors with timely reports showing actual performance against those standards. These reports accomplish three things. First, inaccurate rates on certain products or processes are brought to light so that corrections can be made before standard costs are established. Second, accumulating data on basic standards provides the base for establishing variable costing rates. Third, timely performance reports result in cost savings through more effective supervision.

The first cost centers to be studied should be selected in terms of potential savings through better productivity. The entire cost of the installation, then, can often be less than the reduction in cost of direct labor in a few of the first departments covered. From that point on, the installation can pay its way.

The timing of these performance reports is most important. Many direct labor performance reports are issued each day to cover the previous day's production. In other cases a weekly performance report is utilized in order to reduce the clerical cost and still provide a good measure of control. In some cases, however, even an hourly report may be justified.

For example, in a large distilling company the problem of controlling the direct labor cost in the bottling department was found to change so quickly that a daily report was deemed inadequate. In fact, the first 2 months' flexible budget reports showed an unfavorable variance of $35,000 per month even though the report was delivered to the supervisors by 9:00 a.m. the next day and showed performance for each hour of the previous day.

The bottling department employed about 500 operators and used seven lines. Each brand and size required a certain number of operators corresponding to a certain line speed. When a given brand number was completed, the operators were shifted to a new line. An attempt was made to have lines set up at night and to plan a run that would last at least half a shift. Since many changes occurred during each shift, however, the problem of ensuring that each line was operating at the proper speed and was staffed by the proper number of operators required hourly surveillance.

To accomplish control, an "executone" intercommunication system was installed. The supervisor of each line could communicate directly with the time clerk who was located in a glass-enclosed room high above the bottling floor where each line could be seen. At the beginning of the day the supervisor was given the planned runs and the operators' starting assignments. When a line was changed to another brand or size, the supervisor would call the clerk and relay the changed assignments of operators who had been on the line.

If the total number assigned to the line was different from the standard, the clerk would immediately inform the supervisor. At the end of each hour the total cases produced on the line were compared with the standard, and the supervisor was informed as to the performance level.

At the end of the day, a summary report was made for each line. This report showed the variance from standard due to staffing (number of people assigned), line speed (bottles per minute at filler), and performance level (number of good bottles filled, labeled, and packed compared with the theoretical number based on line speed). Figure 2-9 shows a sample of this report. With this reporting system, the supervisors were able to eliminate the $35,000

Flexible Budgeting Made Easy 33

	LINE PRODUCTION REPORT										
BRAND	Old Scratch			SIZE	Quart			DATE	Dec. 10, 19—		
LINE SUPERVISOR	J. Smith							LINE #	2		
STANDARD FILLER SPEED	60 B.P.M.								Full - Half		
STANDARD CASES PER OPERATING HOUR	300										
EXCISE NO.	251	STAMP	Pa.	CASES	2053	START	8:05	FINISH	4:20		
EXCISE NO.	251	STAMP	Ohio	CASES	32	START	4:20	FINISH	4:25		
EXCISE NO.		STAMP		CASES		START		FINISH			
EXCISE NO.		STAMP		CASES		START		FINISH			

	CLOCK TIME	8-9	9-10	10-11	11-12	12-1	1-2	2-3	3-4	4-5	
LINE	ALLOWED MINS. DOWN	55		15		30		15		30	
A	STANDARD OPERATING MINS.	60	60	45	60	30	60	45	60	30	
B	ACTUAL FILLER SPEED	60	60	60	60	60	60	60	60	60	
C	STANDARD CREW	47	47	47	47	47	47	47	47	47	
D	ACTUAL CREW	50	50	50	50	50	50	50	50	50	
E	NO. CASES STANDARD	275	300	225	300	150	300	225	300	150	2200
F	NO. CASES PRODUCED	180	300	225	300	150	300	215	270	150	2085
G	% PRODUCTION EFFICIENCY	66%	100%	100%	100%	100%	100%	93%	90%	100%	94.3%
H.	OVER MANNING										
	RECONDITIONING	2	2	2	2	2	2	2	2	2)	3
	PRESSURE-SENSITIVE STAMPS	1	1	1	1	1	1	1	1	1)	
I	DELAYS										
	BLOWER			3					3	)	10 Min.
	CAPPER	3							1	)	
J	CUMULATIVE PRODUCTION	180	480	705	1005	1155	1455	1665	1935	2085	

MECHANICAL OPERATIONS AND OTHER INFORMATION	YES	NO		STD. MANNING				DOZENS	UNITS STANDARD	UNITS EARNED
				38						
				9	TOTAL DOZENS PRODUCED			2085	15.4/100	321.1
CASE CODER	X			MOVE TO OTHER LINE						
CRIMPING MACHINE		X		TANK CHANGE ON LINE						
MOVED TO LINE NUMBER		X		EXCISE CHANGE ON LINE						
CAPPING OR CORKING	X					TOTAL UNITS EARNED				321.1
DIVIDING BOTTLES		X				ACTUAL LINE LABOR HOURS				287.8
LABELLER MACHINE	X					TOTAL VARIANCE				33.3
PONY LABELLERS		X				DELAY VARIANCE				6.6
SPOTTING BOTTLES		X				MANNING VARIANCE	3 x 8			24.0
NECKWRAP		X				PRODUCTION RATE VARIANCE				2.7
CAPSULING MACHINE		X								
POT DEVIN MACHINE		X								
#HAND LABELS OPERATION		X								

Figure 2—9 Line production report for a large distilling company.

unfavorable variance in less than 1 month. In the third month they showed a favorable variance and continued to improve in later months.

ABSORPTION STANDARD COSTS VS. DIRECT STANDARD COSTS

The flexible budgets shown in Figures 2-2 and 2-3 were based on the Westinghouse system of absorption standard costs with flexible budgets. With direct standard costs using the Wayne Keller system for flexible budgets there would have been no mixed accounts or fixed accounts charged to Brown's department. The material handling account number 301 would have been classed as 100 percent variable, and supervision would have been charged to the general supervisor so that Brown's budget summary sheet would have been as shown in Figure 2-10. This charge reemphasizes the importance of improving productivity as a means of reducing costs for first-line supervisors. It also simplifies the work of establishing the flexible standards. No scatter charts are re-

BUDGET SUMMARY SHEET							
COST CENTER NO. 02	COST CENTER NAME MACHINE SHOP				COMPILED R.O.S.	DATE 6/1/	
					ACCEPTED C.A.G.	DATE 7/15/	
UNITS IN PERIOD 1960	PERIOD Month	UNIT Standard Allowed Hours			APPROVED R.G.O.	DATE 7/28/	
ACCOUNTS			CLASS	STANDARD BUDGET			DIRECT RATE PER UNIT
NO.	NAME			TOTAL	PERIOD	DIRECT	
100	DIRECT LABOR						
101	Lathe Operators						
102	Punch Press Operators						
103	Grinding Machine Operators						
	TOTAL DIRECT LABOR		D	5,292		5,292	2.70
200	INDIRECT LABOR						
201							
202	Clerical Electric Power		D	310		310	.16
206	Material Handling		D	3,438		3,438	1.75
207	Rework		D	175		175	.09
210	Misc. Indirect Labor		D	260		260	.14
300	OTHER EXPENSES						
301	Direct Operating Supplies		D	465		465	.24
302	Expense Supplies		D	440		440	.22
	ALLOCATED EXPENSE			2,595		11,487	1.32
	GRAND TOTAL BUDGET			12,975	1,488	10,380	6.95

Figure 2–10 Budget summary sheet, based on direct standard costs, for the machine shop of the ABC Manufacturing Company.

quired and no analysis by the method of least squares is needed. To dramatize the simplicity achieved by eliminating mixed accounts, we include an explanation of the least squares method, which is an example of the type of analysis required with the absorption standard cost method where mixed accounts are used.

Method of Least Squares

Given accurate cost and activity data under controlled conditions, the method of least squares will give the most precise result. However, if an abnormal figure appears, it will often distort the result. Such abnormal data should therefore be excluded from the computation.

The method of least squares assumes that the line is best fitted to a series of data points when the sum of the squares of the deviations of the observed points from the line is less than that for any other line which may be drawn. It is derived from the theory of normal frequency distribution. While understanding the mathematical development requires a thorough knowledge of differential calculus and the mathematical theory of probability, application of the formulas derived from the mathematics is comparatively simple. Briefly, the theory shows that the constants M and B for the straight-line

Table 2-4
ANALYSIS OF 12-MONTH DATA

Month	Tons produced	Indirect labor	X^2	XY
January	280	490	78,400	137,200
February	340	592	115,600	201,280
March	420	646	176,400	271,320
April	360	606	129,600	218,160
May	300	494	90,000	148,200
June	320	530	102,400	169,600
July	250	368	62,500	92,000
August	400	600	160,000	240,000
September	500	700	250,000	350,000
October	350	554	122,500	193,900
November	200	400	40,000	80,000
December	240	422	57,600	101,280
Totals	3,960	6,402	1,385,000	2,202,940
$N=12$	ΣX	ΣY	ΣX^2	ΣXY
Average	$X'=330$	$Y'=533.5$		
$(X')^2$			108,900	
$X'Y'$				176,055

formula may be determined by solving two simultaneous equations which are known as normal equations. These are:

$$\Sigma Y = M\Sigma X + NB$$
$$\Sigma XY = M\Sigma X^2 + B\Sigma X$$

where N is the number of data points and the Greek letter Σ is the sum of the quantities to be taken. Solving the simultaneous equations,

$$M = \frac{\Sigma XY - NX'Y''}{\Sigma X^2 - N(X')^2}$$

where

$$X' = \text{average value of } X \text{ or } \frac{\Sigma X}{N}$$

$$Y' = \text{average value of } Y \text{ or } \frac{\Sigma Y}{N}$$

Table 2-4 gives sample data for a 12-month period and names the variables for computation by the least squares method.

The computation is as follows:

$$M = \frac{2{,}202{,}940 - 12\,(176{,}055)}{1{,}385{,}000 - 12\,(108{,}900)}$$

$$M = \frac{90{,}280}{78{,}280} = 1.154/\text{ton}$$

$$B = 533.5 - (330)(1.154) = 152.7$$

In summary, this chapter shows that the democratic method of budgetary control with flexible budgets is more effective than the dictatorship approach with fixed budgets which are dictated by a budget czar. It shows how to dispel the complexities of the traditional flexible budget system by eliminating mixed accounts. As a result, first-line supervisors focus their efforts on creating a climate for improved productivity rather than pinchpenny economy. Elimination of mixed accounts makes it possible to use simple arithmetic and common sense in lieu of advanced mathematical theory.

3
ZERO-BASE BUDGETING STREAMLINED

With President Carter's announcement that zero-base budgeting would be applied to the federal budget, the concept mushroomed overnight. While its most enthusiastic supporters recognized its limitations, manufacturing organizations began trying to adapt it to their budgeting procedures, even in production departments.

Chairman Arthur Burns, who originally suggested the concept to the president of Texas Instruments, was talking only about the control of government expenditures—Jimmy Carter's success with it was for the government of the state of Georgia. Even Peter Pyhrr of Texas Instruments, who wrote the *Harvard Business Review* article that triggered Jimmy Carter's conversion to zero-base budgeting, states that zero-base budgeting "cannot be straightforwardly applied to decisions to increase or decrease expenditures in the manufacturing area."

DEFINITION OF ZERO-BASE BUDGETING

Zero-base Budgeting is a system of budgeting that helps management allocate its limited dollars more effectively by relating expenditures to benefits to be realized. This is accomplished by having each unit manager prepare budget requests (decision packages) in a form that shows the results to be achieved and the consequences of not approving the budget request.

According to the Research Institute of America, in its "Manager's Guide to Zero-Base Budgeting" (*Management Alert,* June 15, 1977):

> The name Zero-Base Budgeting is misleading, especially when the media discuss the concept in relation to government. The implication is that

37

zero-base budgeting is a tool for finding and eliminating unnecessary functions. This is not the case. . . .

Zero-base budgeting is usually a tool for helping management decide whether each function will make its maximum contribution to the overall effectiveness of the organization at its present level of expenditure, a lower one or higher one. . . .

Any budget system is designed to help management allocate a limited resource (money) among the various activities of the organization. Zero-base budgeting aims to help management make these decisions more effectively by relating expenditures to the results expected to be achieved. This is accomplished by asking each manager to present separate budget proposals for each function of the unit for which that manager is responsible.

For example, under conventional line-item budgeting, a personnel manager would specify expected departmental expenditures for salaries, supplies, payments to employment agencies, etc. The total of these costs would be reviewed and approved by top management. Under Z.B.B., the personnel manager would present separate sets of decision packages for each of the department's functional activities, such as recruiting and hiring, E.E.O. compliance, benefits, administration, etc. Each of these functions is broken down into the accounts usually applied to the whole Cost Center.

Another popular misconception about zero-base budgeting is that the present level of expenditures has no influence on the amount of funds requested for the coming year. Since the application of zero-base budgeting to activities for which scientific work measurement is not practicable, the ranking of decision packages has to be subjective. The present level of spending is one of the few factual data that is available to guide the ranking process. Thus it is found that in most decision packages under zero-base budgeting the present level of expenditure is given a prominent role.

Decision packages are usually ranked by a committee consisting of the unit manager's peers. As a result, "fat-filled" packages are spotted and are given a lower rank so that managers are discouraged from submitting fat-filled packages.

Some managers feel that zero-base budgeting is too cumbersome to do every year even though it provides an excellent mechanism for taking the fat out of an organization.

However, as Jimmy Carter proved in his application of zero-base budgeting to the administration of the state of Georgia, by integrating the planning organization with the budgeting organization the result can be a reduction in clerical effort required for the annual budget. He reported a 50 percent reduction in the administrative work load through use of zero-base budgeting.

HOW TO INTEGRATE PLANNING AND ZERO-BASE BUDGETING

In companies that have developed the most effective management accounting systems, profit planning in depth is considered to be the most important feature.

These companies have three types of plans: the long-range plan, the master profit plan, and the monthly report on profit plan.

The monthly report on profit plan presents the forecast for the current month, the next month, and the remainder of the year and is covered in detail in Chapter 6. The long-range plan is covered in some depth in Chapter 10.

The master profit plan, which is oriented in terms of products and executive responsibility, covers the current year and is discussed in detail below. Here is the place where integration with zero-base budgeting can be most effective in streamlining procedures.

Here's what Logan Cheek says about the need to streamline these procedures:

> Restricting your efforts to one or two key objectives also facilitates a more businesslike relationship among the staff. In this regard, two of my earlier zero-base budgeting experiences come to mind.
>
> The first case involved developing a long-range personnel department plan. Toward the end of the process, the vice president asked if all the submissions could be readily converted into next year's budget. The answer was no: Since developing a budget was not the original intent of the study, the forms did not require account-level detail. . . .
>
> The second case occurred a year later in putting together a staff budget. Right in the middle of the process, the controller came under pressure to allocate staff overhead more equitably among product lines. Naturally, I was asked whether the necessary analytical information was available in the zero-base decision packages. Again, the answer was no: The [decision package] forms did not contain allocation detail.[1]

By designing the decision packages (budget data sheets) to show this allocation by product lines, the ranking process is facilitated (see Figure 3-1). The end result of the zero-base budgeting effort provides a master profit plan which shows profitability by product line and establishes the framework for profitability guidelines as discussed in Chapter 9.

THE MASTER PROFIT PLAN

Since financing plans are essentially long-range, the master profit plan is set up in terms of *return on capital employed* rather than *return on net worth*.

[1] Logan Cheek, *Zero-base Budgeting Comes of Age*, AMACOM, New York, 1979, pp. 21–22.

DECISION PACKAGE FORM AND BUDGET DATA SHEET						
DATE	COMPILED	ACCT. CLASS	COST CENTER NAME		COST CENTER NO.	
DATE	ACCEPTED	PERIOD	ACCOUNT NAME		ACCOUNT NO.	
DATE	APPROVED	UNIT MANAGER					
THIS ACCOUNT IS CHARGED WITH:							
DESCRIPTION OF GOALS AND OBJECTIVES:							
						ALLOCATIONS TO PRODUCT LINE	
BUDGET WAS DETERMINED AS FOLLOWS:					TOTAL	PRODUCT LINE	AMOUNT
TOTAL STANDARD BUDGET							

Figure 3—1 Decision package form and budget data sheet.

The most effective way to select an objective return on capital employed is to compare your company with a number of companies in the same industry. By making an appraisal of the relative strengths of each of the selected competitors in terms of executive talent, product quality, production facilities, and distribution methods, your company may be slotted quite accurately. It is then a simple matter to select an objective return on capital employed that is ambitious enough to challenge management, yet realistic enough to be attainable. Table 10-3 shows a record of such an appraisal.

After selecting the overall objective, the basic framework for building the master profit plan is the analysis of return on capital employed by product line.

Sales Forecast

Having selected broad objectives, the first step in the preparation of the master profit plan is the sales forecast. The forecast should be as detailed as is practicable. In seasonal industries, it should be by product line and by months, so that the impact of volume and sales mix can be incorporated in the master profit plan.

Beyond any question, sales forecasting is the most difficult task in profit planning. This is particularly true when the forecast involves a number of specific products, sales areas, and seasonal factors. Here again, it is better to have a rough forecast than no forecast at all. In fact, most companies start with a forecast of total sales and then each year refine the procedure and techniques until a satisfactory program is achieved.

One of the simplest methods of sales forecasting in a seasonal business is to chart the 12-month moving average sales. A somewhat more sensitive method is the computerized application of exponential smoothing.

Most companies make the top sales executive responsible for preparing the sales forecast. Others have the sales department prepare the preliminary forecast, and then the controller or the planning committee reviews it and adjusts it to correct for inherent sales optimism. This adjustment is made by comparison with historical trend charts such as the 12-month moving average, general economic indicators, and indicators by end use. Other methods of testing the sales department forecasts include industry and share of market forecasts, new product plans, market surveys, and production or financial capacity.

In large organizations, the sales manager usually bases the forecast on estimates from the field force. A typical procedure is as follows.

The planning committee of the XYZ Company meets each September with all divisional sales managers. They present data on historical trends, economic indicators, product plans, and share of market data. This group formulates a tentative total sales forecast for the next calendar year with tentative totals for each division. They also develop a revised forecast by years for the succeeding 4 years.

Each divisional sales manager then meets with the regional sales managers, reviews the overall picture, and gives them the tentative divisional quotas. Tentative regional forecasts are developed that add up to the divisional quota.

Each regional sales manager then works with the sales representatives and develops a detailed sales forecast. The regional sales forecasts are submitted to the division managers by the end of October. These forecasts are reviewed and consolidated, and the division managers' forecasts are submitted to the planning committee by the middle of November. They are reviewed by the controller and the planning commttee and adjusted in consultation with each division manager.

The final consolidated sales forecasts covering the next calendar year by months and by product lines and totals for the succeeding 4 years by year.are issued by the first of December.

Preliminary Statement of Objectives

Within the framework of the long-range plan and based on the preliminary sales forecast for the coming year, a statement of objectives should be issued to all key executives. With this statement of objectives each key executive is in a position to prepare a decision package which shows a statement of capital expenditures needed, personnel recruitments, price increases to be expected, methods improvements, and cost reduction programs. In short, the key executives can present a preliminary plan of operation designed to achieve the overall objectives, provided these objectives are clearly stated and pinpointed by executive responsibility.

The form of the preliminary statement of objectives is dependent on the size and complexity of the organization. In a small, compact organization, the controller or chief financial officer usually holds a number of briefing sessions and discusses in depth the broad objectives, product and facility plans, sales outlook, and cost trends. These sessions are then followed by conferences with each individual executive to assist in developing plans and decision packages for his or her area of responsibility.

In large companies having complex organizational structures, the communications are more formal and specific time schedules are required. In the case of the XYZ Company mentioned above, the division managers are responsible for preparing detailed monthly operating budgets for the following year and tentative annual estimates for the succeeding 4 years. This work is initiated immediately following the September conference of sales managers and must be in the controller's hands not later than December 1. These plans also include requests for increased personnel, capital expenditures, and estimates of anticipated price increases.

Format

One of the most frequent criticisms of direct costing, by the advocates of absorption costing, concerns the failure to include *fixed* or *period* manufacturing costs on standard product cost sheets. The critics say, "How do you know that each product is carrying its fair share of burden if you don't allocate fixed charges to products?"

Here is a widely held misconception about direct costing. In a well-designed direct standard cost system, not only period manufacturing costs but all other period expenses are allocated to products in the decision packages as part of the master profit plan. Since period costs are usually committed for a relatively long time, they are important in profit planning and long-term decisions. The marginal contribution and profit-volume relationships provide the data required for day-to-day decisions, so the inclusion of allocated period expenses on product cost cards only confuses short-term decision making.

In developing the master profit plan, period costs are allocated in total dollars for the planned volume and sales mix. They should never be unitized. It is the unitizing of period costs on product cost cards that makes absorption costs so confusing to operating executives. This confusion is avoided by showing the allocation, in total, on the master profit plan, along with the forecasted volume and mix. Operating management can then see clearly the price-cost-volume relationships and make mental adjustments for possible deviations from the forecast.

The key to the simplicity of allocating period costs to product lines is the design of the profit plan. Table 3-1 shows the profit plan for the ABC Company. It can be seen that both period expenses and capital employed are allocated to product lines.

The selection of a logical product grouping is one of the most important features of a simple and effective profit-planning procedure. By carefully selecting product groups, the profit plan can be easy to prepare and still show whether each product line is carrying its fair share of burden. But of even more value, this form of profit plan shows management whether each product is providing an adequate return on capital employed. Thus the selection of logical product groups must also take into account the problem of allocating capital employed.

One of the most important features of this form of profit plan is the column for idle plant. Use of this column permits the evaluation of each product line

Table 3-1
ABC MANUFACTURING COMPANY
PROFIT PLAN

Description	Total	Line A	Line B	Line C	Idle plant
Sales forecast	$70,000	$10,000	$20,000	$40,000	
Direct cost:					
Material	$30,000	$ 2,000	$ 8,000	$20,000	
Direct labor and expense	23,000	3,000	6,000	14,000	
Total	$53,000	$ 5,000	$14,000	$34,000	
Margin	$17,000	$ 5,000	$ 6,000	$ 6,000	
Percent of sales (P/V)	24%	50%	30%	15%	
Planned period	12,100	2,500	4,000	5,500	$ 100
Net operating profit (loss)	$ 4,900	$ 2,500	$ 2,000	$ 500	$ (100)
Percent of sales	7%	25%	10%	1.3%	
Capital employed	$33,000	$10,000	$12,000	$10,000	$1,000
Percent return	15%	25%	16.7%	5.0%	(10%)

NOTE: $000 omitted.

on a long-range volume basis while providing an overall realistic profit plan for the coming year. Based on the degree of seasonal fluctuations in production, a percent of theoretical capacity is selected as the long-term level for normal facility utilization. In a year when the planned volume is below this level, the period costs and capital employed for unused capacity are shown under idle plant. In years when the planned volume exceeds this normal level, the abnormal utilization of facilities is shown as a credit in this column.

In addition to presenting the profit plan in terms of product line, a similar analysis by market or channel of distribution provides a further insight into areas where sound planning can stimulate profit and growth. Also, in multi-plant operations, analysis by each production unit is often effective in pinpointing areas for profit improvements.

In product lines or markets where an unsatisfactory return is indicated, planning in depth is required to correct the situation. For example, in the profit plan shown by Table 3-1, product line C presents a very unsatisfactory picture. While it helps the short-range plan because of the $6-million profit contribution, return on capital employed is so low that long-range corrective plans must be formulated.

There are a number of methods of study that can be made to select plans for solution of this problem. First, the position of the line in its life cycle must be evaluated. Have the short-line competitors moved in on this product and penetrated the market on the basis of price? What design modifications can be made to support a premium price? What new items can be added to the line to provide product-line balance? Can manufacturing methods be improved? Can material substitutions be made? Can capital turnover be accelerated? Can distribution costs be reduced? If the result of this study of line C is negative, then long-range plans must be made to replace the line with one that has a good potential return on capital employed.

The important point, however, is that with such profit planning in depth, a product line should never reach this hopeless stage, because, as each individual product moves through its life cycle, it will be followed by other new items which will ensure product-line balance.

Allocation of Decision Package Costs

The allocation of costs to product lines on each decision package is dependent upon the selection of product groups, the complexity of the manufacturing process, and the form of organization. When product lines are departmentalized, much of the assignment is direct. However, when joint use of facilities is involved, the techniques of standard absorption costs should be utilized.

The best procedure is first to determine all items that can be assigned specifically to a product line. A good method to follow is to pick the items of expense that would not be incurred if the product line were discontinued. These can be summarized as specific period expenses. Then for items that use joint facilities, the costing rates per machine-hour can be developed and assigned to product lines in proportion to the machine-hours each product line should use to produce the planned sales volume and mix.

The most important thing to remember, however, is that period expenses with zero-base budgeting have a different logic of distribution than do overhead costs with a standard absorption cost system. Therefore, it is important to review carefully the basis of distribution for each period expense that must be allocated. In addition, engineering research and development, and selling and administrative expenses must be analyzed and allocated to product lines on a logical basis.

In short, the same arbitrary decisions have to be made for allocating decision package costs as are required to determine burden rates with any standard cost system. However, with zero-base budgeting and direct standard costs these arbitrary allocations are set forth in total, and management can see clearly the relative amount of arbitrary allocations involved in each case. With absorption standard costs they are buried in the cost center burden rates, which will always remain a mystery to operating executives.

Allocation of Capital Employed

The allocation of capital employed to products or product lines follows the same general philosophy as the allocation of period expenses. In fact, many of the bases used for allocating period costs can be used directly for allocating related classes of capital employed.

One example is the allocation of depreciation on machinery and equipment. Once a sound basis is established for such allocation, the capital employed in machinery and equipment can be similarly distributed.

The basis for distributing rent and occupancy period costs (square feet) can also be used for the distribution of capital employed in such facilities.

Inventories and accounts receivable can usually be identified by product line. Cash is often taken as a given percentage of a month's expenditures for each product line.

Review and Approval

An effective profit plan is the end product of the combined thinking and participation of all key persons in the entire organization. With zero-base budgeting, the degree of participation provides a perspective of the business and a realization of the interdependence of each operation with all other factors of the business.

It is a customary procedure to screen, revise, and approve profit plans at several levels of management. In most companies, the controller is responsible for consolidation and final preparation of the profit plan for top management approval.

In cases where this consolidation shows an unsatisfactory picture, the controller will generally go to the key executives and ask them to sharpen their pencils and come up with a more satisfactory plan. Or the controller may go to top management and suggest that all key executives be called together for an intensive review of the situation and subsequent revision of the plan.

Finally, the profit plan is officially approved. In most companies this is done by the president, although in many companies the executive committee or the board of directors gives final approval. At this point the official profit plan is distributed and becomes the basic measuring stick for top executive performance and the means of integrating planning and control at all levels of management. How this integration of planning and control is achieved is explained in Chapter 6 under monthly report on profit plan.

A FINAL WORD

In conclusion, it is appropriate to quote the concluding remarks of Jimmy Carter in his speech to the National Governors Conference in 1976.

> Zero-base budgeting has proved its value for those organizations endowed with a will to manage, to engage in a productive dialogue founded on mutual trust during tough planning and budgeting decisions, and to find new and better ways to serve their constituents or customers. But like most new management tools, success requires balancing the approach with classic, common sense human-relations and creative problem-solving techniques.
>
> Where that balance is achieved, however, the hard efforts required have indeed generated more light than heat, with greater efficiency and resource allocation to boot. In the public sector, there is no inherent conflict between careful planning, tight budgeting, and constant management reassesment on the one hand and compassionate concern for the deprived and afflicted on the other. Waste and inefficiency never fed a hungry child, provided a job for a willing worker, or educated a deserving student. Similarly, in the private sector, misdirected or redundant staff efforts never paid a dividend, provided a meaningful, rewarding job for a competent employee, launched a successful product on time to specification, or satisfied a demanding customer.[2]

[2] Jimmy Carter, in a speech delivered at the National Governors Conference, June 1976, reprinted in ibid., p. 303.

4
DETERMINATION AND CONTROL OF DIRECT MATERIAL COSTS

One of the most important elements, and one that is most often neglected in determining product costs, is the cost of direct materials. Here is one of the greatest potentials for cost control and product development through accurate standards for material price and accurate measurements of use. Yet many cost accountants use a "broad brush" in this area for purposes of accounting and then make special estimates of current prices and yields when accurate product costs are needed for marketing decisions. Such decisions have no real bases of reference, and the usage and yield data most often are simply optimistic guesses with no background of measurement or adequate statistical control. The mechanics for handling material costs with standard costs are as follows:

Standard prices are set for each direct material that is purchased. At the time the material is received, the actual price is compared with the standard price. The difference is charged or credited, as the case may be, to profit and loss for the period as purchase price variance. Thus the material is put into inventory at standard price at time of acquisition. Yields and scrap are measured at each operation and compared with standard usage and yield. The variances are then used to adjust the inventory so that the inventory of work-in-process at any time will contain material at standard prices and usage, no matter at what stage of processing the various products may be. When the finished product is shipped, the total material as shown on the cost sheet for that product is credited to the proper inventory account and charged to cost of sales.

STANDARD MATERIAL PRICES

In most companies the purchasing agent is held responsible for establishing standard prices. The timetable for requiring these standard price schedules is usually set as late as practicable in the installation or revision schedule. In other words, standard prices are scheduled just before they are required for computing direct standard product costs and for pricing inventory.

The purchasing agent should consider trends and explore long-term price behavior before forecasting the expected price for each item during the coming year. Estimates should also be based on normal quantities purchased and on realistic trade discounts. All contract prices are per se the standard prices.

Differences of opinion exist as to how to handle cash discounts. Some companies consider this item as a financial transaction and include it under the other income and deduction section on the income statement. Others consider that cash discounts will always be taken, and they figure the cash discount as a reduction in the price of the material. The trend seems to be toward the latter treatment, and any lost cash discounts are charged to purchase price variance.

Incoming freight paid for by the purchaser should be included in material cost and should be figured on normal delivery quantities, sources, and methods of shipment. Consequently, the direct standard price for a given item is the estimated invoiced price per unit, less discounts, plus incoming transportation costs.

It is extremely important that each item of material be clearly identified. Use of parts' or materials' specification numbers, as well as standard nomenclature description, is recommended. A card index for each item showing the number, name, and complete description of the item, along with the complete history of computation of the price standards, has been found very effective in providing control of price standards. Figure 4-1 shows such a price index card.

In any event, standard prices are furnished to the accounting department on either specification sheets or individual cards for all direct materials that are to be purchased. When new types of material items are added, it is the responsibility of the purchasing agent to immediately determine the standard prices and to forward the data to the accounting department. Moreover, when important changes in price trends occur, the purchasing agent should notify the accounting department so that a determination can be made as to whether or not the standard prices and direct standard product costs should be revised immediately in order to reflect the changed market conditions.

PURCHASE PRICE VARIANCES

The simplest method of handling purchase price variances is the one described above where only one inventory account is used. The purchase price variance is taken at the time the material is received and is charged (unfavorable variances) or credited (favorable variances) to profit and loss for that

		STANDARD MATERIAL PRICE INDEX CARD						
Description _____				Spec. or Part No. _____				
				Unit _____				
EFFECTIVE DATE	NORMAL QUANTITY	INVOICED COST	DISCOUNTS	INCOMING FREIGHT		NET COST	COST PER UNIT	
				CLASS	AMOUNT			

Figure 4—1   Standard material price index card.

period. Special methods of handling this variance are covered later in this chapter.

Under the conventional method, all material in inventory, whether raw material, work-in-process, finished parts, purchased parts, or finished goods, is included in the one control account and priced at standard.

As new items are received, the invoices are matched with the purchase orders and the receiving reports. The standard prices are then entered on the invoices or the voucher jackets. The standard prices are multiplied by the quantities received, and the difference is charged or credited to the proper variance account for each item purchased. The purchase price variance accounts may be set up either by type of material or by end use of material or both. Where materials are common to more than one product line, material price variances are prorated to product lines.

When the incoming freight bill is received, it is broken down by purchase price variance account number and charged entirely to purchase price variance. In other words, for simplicity of accounting, most companies do not compare incoming freight actual with standard and get a separate incoming freight variance. Instead, they look at the entire material price variance, and whenever a given item gets out of line, they go back and check the reason from included invoices and all freight bills. Figure 4-2 shows a typical purchase price variance summary set up by type of material.

PURCHASE PRICE SUMMARY

__4__ WEEK PERIOD ENDED _9/30_ 19 __

CURRENT PERIOD				DESCRIPTION OF MATERIALS	YEAR TO DATE		
VALUE		VARIANCE	CURRENT RATIO		ACTUAL VALUE	VARIANCE	CURRENT RATIO
STANDARD	ACTUAL						
				BATCH MATERIALS			
1,439	1,434	6	100	SAND	3,794	25	100
1,980	1,903	77	96	SODA ASH	6,097	247	96
1,680	1,718	(38)*	(102)	SNY. CALCIUM CARBONATE	3,436	(76)	(102)
				POTASH, CALCINED	4,164	148	97
1,200	1,140	60	95	NITER	2,280	120	95
				ALUMINUM HYDRATE			
				ZINC OXIDE	775	50	94
				BARIUM CARBONATE			
42	49	(7)	(116)	FLUORSPAR	49	(7)	(116)
				ARSENIC	532	(67)	(114)
				ANTIMONY OXIDE	560	(36)	(107)
				BORAX			
				MANGANESE (Black)	69	3	96
184	183	1	100	SODIUM SILICA FLUORIDE	183	1	100
				NEODYMIUM OXIDE	215		100
				POTASSIUM BICHROMATE			
				POWDER BLUE			
				MANGANESE CAUCASIAN			
				COPPER OXIDE			
				TITANIUM OXIDE	2,650	20	99
				COBALT HYDRATE			
21	20	1	94	MOLD OIL	40	3	94
				MAGNESITE, CALCINED			
				TETRASODIUM PYROPHOSPHATE			
				LITHARGE	5,721	79	99
67	28	39	41	SODIUM SULFATE	55	79	41
1,400	1,300	100	93	SELENIUM	2,600	200	93
				NICKEL SULFATE			
				CALUMITE	15	–	100
				PETALITE			
				MANGANESE CARBONATE	56	7	89
				BARIUM SULFATE	238	(10)	(104)
314	334	(20)	(106)	CADMIUM SULFIDE	668	(40)	(106)
				TRISODIUM PHOSPHATE	275	37	88
				DOLOMITE	221	290	45
135	173	(38)	(128)	FELDSPAR	173	(38)	(128)
262	249	12	95	LITHIUM CARBONATE	249	12	95
8,724	8,529	195	98	TOTAL BATCH MATERIALS	35,113	1,037	97

*Parentheses denote unfavorable variance.

Figure 4—2 Purchase price summary.

MATERIAL USAGE VARIANCES

For tight control of materials, a good storeroom for raw materials and parts is a prime necessity. Best results are secured when the area is under a competent storekeeper and only the storekeeper's staff has access to it.

Good perpetual inventory records are another prerequisite. Where materials are carried at standard prices, it is not necessary to keep them by valuation, but only by quantity. When book values of total items or class breakdowns are needed, they may be calculated quickly by multiplying the physical balances by the standard prices.

The location of the inventory records, as well as the responsibility for maintenance, should be in the production control departments. If possible, the records should be located next to the accounting department. They must be maintained in such a way that the accounting department can compute a standard inventory valuation at any time.

Bin tickets and frequent verification of balances on hand are considered necessary by most authorities. Use of "cycle count" physical inventories and verification of balances on hand whenever the bin stock is at a low point are effective.

Control of work-in-process is usually the responsibility of the production control department, and it is also desirable to have these records maintained so that the accounting department may calculate a book inventory of work-in-process at any time. Otherwise, a physical inventory of work-in-process showing the last operation completed is required in order to check the standard book valuation.

Finished goods should be kept on perpetual inventory records similar to those for raw materials. Responsibility for maintaining these records is usually vested in the production control or marketing department.

Requisitions or bills of material for withdrawing raw material for processing should specify the standard quantity. These standard quantities should take into account standard yield and scrap. Whenever excess spoiled or defective work requires issuance of additional material, the requisition should be charged to the material usage variance account.

For each productive operation where scrap or rejects are produced, provision should be made to measure the amount produced and to compare it with the standard allowances previously established. The difference provides an adjustment to inventory value and a charge (unfavorable variance) or credit (favorable) to material usage variance. Table 4-1 shows a typical material usage variance report.

PROCEDURES TAILORED TO SPECIAL NEEDS

Although the above procedure meets the requirements of many companies, there are special situations in certain industries where the procedures must be tailored to provide management with additional control information about material costs. For example, in a specialty steel company it was found that the large inventories and fluctuating market prices did not permit taking the price variance at the time the material was received. In addition, management

Table 4-1
ABC MANUFACTURING COMPANY
MONTHLY VARIANCE REPORT
Material Usage and Scrap

Description	Standard	Actual	Variance
Plate shop:			
Product line A	$ 12,200	$ 9,500	$ 2,700
Product line B	10,300	10,400	(100)
Product line C	43,700	48,800	(5,100)
Total plate shop	$ 66,200	$ 68,700	$ (2,500)
Machine shop:			
Product line A	$ 11,900	$ 8,700	$ 3,200
Product line B	40,400	31,200	9,200
Product line C	51,600	53,900	(2,300)
Total machine shop	$103,900	$ 93,800	$ 10,100
Assembly department:			
Product line A	$ 6,200	$ 6,700	$ (500)
Product line B	9,400	8,400	1,000
Product line C	7,200	10,100	(2,900)
Total assembly department	$ 22,800	$ 25,200	$ (2,400)
Total product line A	$ 30,300	$ 24,900	$ 5,400
Total product line B	60,100	50,000	10,100
Total product line C	102,500	112,800	(10,300)
Grand totals	$192,900	$187,700	$ 5,200

NOTE: Parentheses denote unfavorable variances.

needed to know how good a job the melting department superintendent was doing in using low-cost materials and scrap. The case of an industrial paint company provides another example of such a special application. These two examples demostrate how flexible the application of standard material costs can be within the framework of a standard cost system.

A Specialty Steel Company

To meet the requirement of a company manufacturing special alloy steel, the following procedure is used:

Purchase Price Variance All purchased material is put into raw material inventory at actual cost. At the time the material is withdrawn for an electric furnace charge, the purchase price variance is recorded. Thus, the material is charged to work-in-process at standard cost, which represents normal market value since standard prices are changed with important shifts in market prices.

For example, if a 10,000-pound lot of ferrochrome assaying 20 percent Cr (chromium) and 80 percent Fe (iron) is withdrawn for a furnace charge, it is valued at standard prices.

2000 lb Cr @ $0.20	$400
8000 lb Fe @ $0.03	240
	$640

If the cost of the lot had been $600, a favorable purchase price variance of $40 would be calculated and credited to profit and loss, and $640 standard value would be charged to work-in-process.

Metallurgical Practice Variance For each grade, the standard value of metals input per heat is predetermined for a standard mix. For materials that are purchased as a specific element, such as nickel, the standard quantity of nickel for the standard mix for a given size heat is extended by the standard price (which is the current market price). However, for items such as revert scrap, the percent recovery and the standard price of each element are applied to the analysis of the scrap to determine its standard value per pound. The standard tapped weight and the good ingot yield per charge are established, and the standard cost per pound at standard mix and yield is determined for each grade.

Each day, the standard cost of input materials is computed and compared with the cost of the good ingot yield at standard mix value for each heat. The difference is the metallurgical practice variance. Table 4-2 shows this computation for one heat. These variances are summarized by grade both daily and monthly, the causes for substantial variance are analyzed, and corrective steps are taken.

Yield Variance Product weights are reported at various stages of manufacture and are recorded on the heat card. The good product weight for each grade and heat is summarized for each operation or group of operations, and, by subtracting this weight from the previously recorded weight, the actual total scrap loss is determined. Scrap is picked up daily throughout the plant and is accumulated and weighed by grade. The total actual loss minus the accumulated weight of scrap gives the unrecoverable loss. The difference between this figure and the standard unrecoverable loss for the operations performed represents the material part of the yield variance. The difference between the total scrap produced at each operation and the standard allowance shows the labor and expense portion of the yield variance. (See Table 4-3.)

Table 4-2
METALLURGICAL PRACTICE VARIANCE REPORT
Grade No. 1743   Heat No. M 14709   Date 3/16/60

		Actual			Standard allowance		Variance gain or (loss)		
Code	Material	Pounds used	Standard cost/ pound	Cost of melt	Rate/ pound*	Value	Value	Formula variance, percent standard	Yield variance
152	A	2230	$0.296	$ 660					
156	B	200	0.024	5					
159	C	300	0.124	37					
207	D	400	0.375	150					
256	E	500	0.250	125					
295	F (revert scrap)	6000	0.130	780					
	Tapped weight	9630		$1757	$0.161	$1550	$(207)†	(13.4)	
	Revert scrap credit	2530‡	0.130‡	329	0.130	44	285		
	Good ingot yield	7100§	0.162§	1150	0.162	1506	(356)	—	($71)
	Total variance						$(278)		

*Supported by a standard melt formula sheet.
†Parentheses denote unfavorable variances.
‡Actual quanity put into revert inventory at standard rate.
§Actual quanity put into ingot inventory at standard rate.

Table 4-3
ANALYSIS OF YIELD VARIANCE
Production of a Small Bar from Melt

Operation	Description	Actual weight, lb	Standard weight, lb	Variance, lb	Variance, dollars
Charge electric furnace		41,000	41,000		
Melt and pour ingots	Good production	36,000	36,000		
	Recovered scrap	1,000	1,000		
	Loss metal (up stack)	4,000	4,000		
Roll (large mill)	Good production	30,600	30,600		
	Recovered scrap	5,300	5,300		
	Loss (scale)	100	100		
Condition billet	Good production	26,928	26,940	12	(36.00)
	Recovered scrap	3,672	3,600	(72)	15.00
	Loss (scale)	0	60	60	
Roll (small mill)	Good production	23,535	23,000	(535)	
	Recovered scrap	3,330	3,900	570	427.00
	Unrecovered loss	63	40	(23)	23.00
Finish bar	Good production	21,393	21,393		
	Recovered scrap	2,100	1,565	(535)	525.00
	Unrecovered loss	42	42		
Inspection	Passed	20,516	21,000	484	
	Rejects (recovered scrap)	877		(877)	(439.00)
Ship (stock)	Good Product	20,516	21,000	484	
				Total yield variance	515.00

57

An Industrial Paint Company

In this company, bids are prepared for 95 percent of the orders received. These bids are based on current market prices for raw materials. Since raw material represents 85 percent of the cost of manufacture and market prices fluctuate widely, close control of material costs and quotations is vital.

Standard Prices at Current Market In preparing quotations, the cost estimator uses the latest prices received if they are not over 30 days old. For items received prior to the past 30 days, the cost estimator obtains a current price from the purchasing agent. Furthermore, it is the responsibility of the purchasing agent to inform the cost estimator promptly of all price changes.

Quotations Become Standard Cost The estimator prepares the quotation showing a separate total for the replacement material cost. If the order is received within 30 days of the estimate, the quotation cost is used as standard material cost. If it is received later, a new standard replacement material cost is computed on the basis of the current replacement prices.

Formulas for varnishes and other intermediates that are normally used as part of a paint formula are changed with each change in the market price of the materials used in such intermediate formulas. There are approximately 250 such formulas, with an average of approximately seven raw material items per formula. The standard costs for all intermediates are figured on the computer each time there is a change in the price of ingredients.

Purchase Price Variance The inventory of raw materials, including incoming freight, is carried at actual cost and, when it is applied to a given batch, is charged out at a residual average price. In other words, the quantities and valuation of the opening inventory, plus the purchases made during the period, are used to get an average price. This price is applied to all transfers out of inventory.

Gallons produced are then multiplied by the quotation material cost per gallon. The difference between the residual average actual material cost and standard replacement (quotation) material cost is charged or credited to a replacement price variance account, which is then either charged or credited to profit and loss each period.

Thus the direct standard cost of sales represents the profitability of the items sold at current market value; and the replacement price variance account, over the long period, shows just how good a job the purchasing agent is doing in anticipating price trends.

The following two cases represent typical special usage measurement procedures.

Telephone Wire and Cable Manufacturing Company

In this company the cost of materials represented such a large part of the total cost that the yield and scrap control was of paramount importance. Thus usage standards were established for copper wire and insulating compound, and it was found to be practical to set up procedures to measure yield and scrap on a daily basis. These daily reports revealed some important facts. The gauge of the wire being used was larger than required because, as the coating machines were first designed, the take-up reel mechanism stretched the wire so that it was reduced in gauge. Later, when better take-up mechanisms were designed, the larger gauge wire was still used. This resulted in use of extra compound for insulating, which increased the overall size of the cable. When the proper gauge of wire was used, material usage was substantially reduced and the end product improved. This close control resulted in a savings of $300,000 per year in the cost of wire and insulating compound.

Upholstered Furniture Manufacturing Company

One of the largest cost elements in upholstered furniture is the cost of cloth and its excess usage. Here again it was found that a daily usage control report was needed to pin down responsibility. Each year there were large unexplained inventory discrepancies in the upholstery cloth inventory account, although perpetual inventory accounts were kept by cover grade and location.

It was, therefore, determined that a daily report of usage in the cutting room was practical. It was also decided to keep the perpetual inventory on each roll. Thus when rolls were received from the vendors, they were run over an inspecting and measuring machine and a measuring tape was interleaved when the roll was rerolled. In the first place, the cost of this inspection and measurement was immediately repaid through better performance from the vendors because they knew their defects and errors would be caught. Also, the comparison of performance in one cutting room to another developed a keen competition in terms of avoiding waste, which resulted in substantial savings in material costs. Finally, a computer program was purchased which determined the optimum layout of patterns for a given cover on a certain style of sofa or chair. Without the close daily control the computer program could not have been justified because the inventory discrepancies would have voided the savings claimed.

The above two cases demonstrate that the added cost of inspection and control of material usage on a daily basis is paid for many times over through direct savings in material costs.

5
DETERMINING TRUE PRODUCT COSTS

It is a fundamental principle of accounting that appropriate costs be matched against revenues to determine period income. Many management accountants make the mistake of assuming that true product costs can be determined by a job cost system and that this system clearly matches costs against revenues since the job costs can be closed out at the time of shipment. In actual experience, however, the job cost system seldom results in accurate costs. This inaccuracy is entirely due to the difficulty of floor control and inaccurate input. For example, when the lots of the same products are being processed through the shop at the same time, it is almost impossible to avoid wrong charges. Also, when the job is shipped and the job costs are closed out before late invoices have been processed, the job cost is understated.

As Harrington Emerson stated in 1910, costs should be stated in terms of what costs should be and variances from these costs should be assigned to executive responsibility. Thus, if a job cost is based on an engineering estimate and actual charges are matched against this estimate, wrong charges are easily detected before the books are closed for the period. In other words, to get true costs you should use standard costs and variances from standards so that the true cost is the standard cost adjusted by the variances. This procedure not only avoids errors but pins down responsibility for achieving the performance level on which the standards are based. In other words, there is no reason why standard costs cannot be set on all products even though they be only rough engineering estimates. The comparisons of actual costs against these estimates not only improves the accuracy of the estimates but provides an incentive to improve the actual performance.

STANDARD PRODUCT COSTS

The key to the accounting mechanics of standard cost is the measurement of input to inventory by responsibility (producing departments) and the measurement of output from inventory to cost of sales (shipments) by products. This means that the basic standards used to measure performance in a given cost center must be used to establish the direct standard value added to each product going through that cost center. Likewise, the same standard prices and material requirements used to measure input and yield variances must be applied to the individual product cost sheets. In addition, the standard cost sheet must be designed to show not only the total standard cost of finished products as they are shipped, but also to reveal the total accumulated standard cost at any stage of manufacture. This is shown graphically by Figure 5-1.

At the beginning of any accounting period, the opening inventory showing the quantity of product at each stage of manufacture is priced at the standard cost shown on the cost sheet for that stage of processing. Production for each cost center during the current period is also costed and measured against the same standards used in the product cost sheets. The standard cost is charged to inventory, and the period costs and the variances are charged to profit and loss. Shipments during the period are credited to inventory at standard cost, as shown on the cost sheet for the finished product, and are charged to direct standard cost of sales. A physical inventory taken at the end of the period and priced from the same cost sheets as the opening inventory should equal the balance in the inventory account. Any difference between the two figures means there was an error in measuring variances or in taking the physical count. This balancing feature is very important; it means inventory discrepancies can't be swept under the rug. They must be investigated and explained.

Material Specifications

Since, in most cases, material cost represents the major portion of the product cost, the importance of having accurate material specifications and bills of material cannot be overemphasized. Good standards for the calculation of yield or shrinkage are also vital.

For assembled products, the bills of material should be based on an adequate numbering system for parts, subassemblies, and complete assemblies. There should be detailed drawings and specifications for each of these. In addition, there should be a well-organized engineering change control that will keep the bills of materials up to date and signal the accounting depart-

Determining True Product Costs **63**

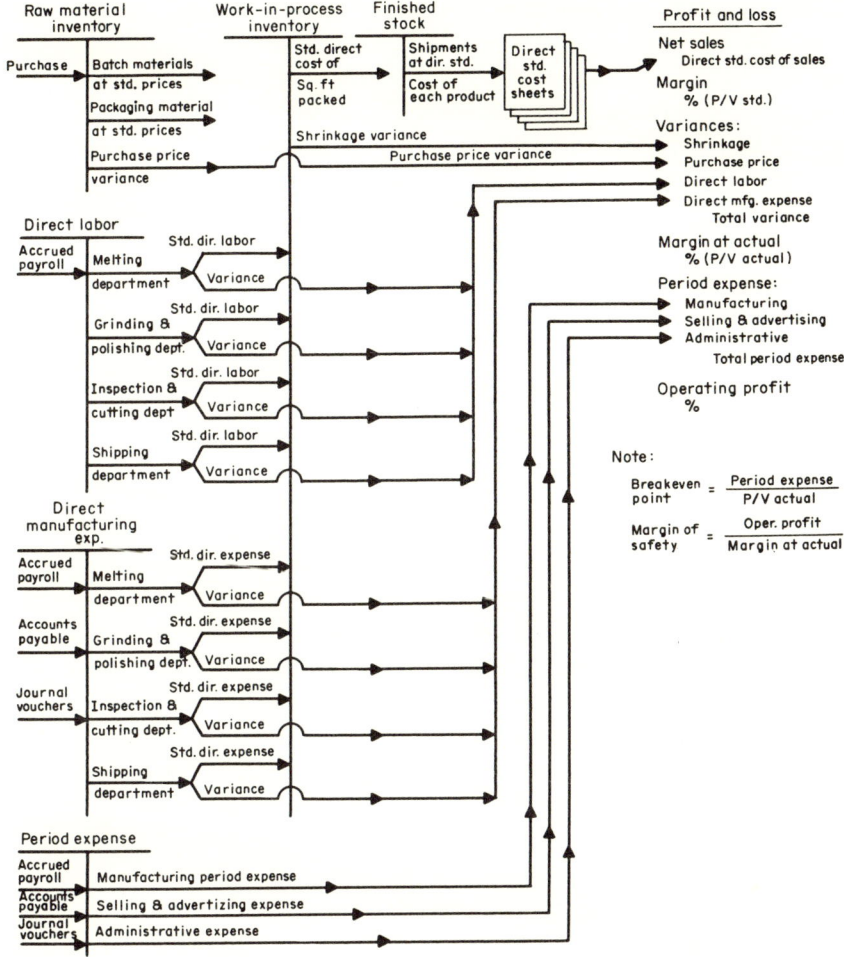

Figure 5—1 Standard cost system.

ment when standard cost sheets should be revised to reflect a given engineering change.

When practicable, standard economic lot sizes should be established and the standard quantities of material for these lot sizes should be shown on the bills of material and route sheets.

As described in Chapter 4, these material usage and yield standards should be checked against actual performance daily, weekly, or monthly, depending upon the degree of control required. In cases of large variances, corrective measures should be instituted and the standards should be adjusted before they are applied to the product cost sheets.

The requirement of complete material specifications and the measurement of actual usage against standards are sometimes difficult where secrecy is desired. For example, in a pharmaceutical company it was necessary to have the chief chemist extend the formula sheets by the standard prices for each ingredient and provide the accounting department with the standard material cost per batch. This was all that appeared on the cost sheet for basic materials. Another example occurred in a textile finishing plant. The dyemaster refused to divulge his formulas. A chemical engineer was assigned to record all usages of material and to develop the dye formulas from actual experience. The dyemaster finally realized that the written formulations saved a lot of color adjustments and waste of dyestuffs. He then cooperated completely in putting down on paper his "secret" formulations, which aided in the development and control of costs.

Standard Process Sheets

As pointed out in Chapter 2, industrial engineering must be represented on the installation task force. Its responsibility is the development of standard processing methods and standard times for each operation or process. The accountants then determine the dollar cost for the time required for each operation on each product, summarizing both conversion cost and material cost information on the standard cost sheets. Thus the standard process sheets, along with the material specifications and bills of material, become the basic framework on which the standard product costs are constructed.

In cases where alternate processes are used, the most common practice is to select the lowest-cost process as standard. Whenever an alternate process is used, the excess is shown as a nonstandard practice variance. In this way, management is apprised of the amount of money being spent because adequate facilities are not available to employ the optimum processes.

In chemical plants, the process sheets generally are in the form of flowcharts, with the yield data an integral part of the flowchart. In machining operations, the process sheet usually consists of the route sheet that determines the sequence and tooling for the various operations. In any event, the time standards entered on the process sheets by the industrial engineers for computing standard costs must be the same as those used for computing productivity as described in Chapter 2.

Just as the purchasing department is required to keep the cost department informed of price changes, so must the industrial engineering department notify the cost department of changes in standard process, along with the effective date of change. The general practice is to make the change in standard cost of sales and direct measurement of input as soon as the change is effective. Adjustment of inventory valuation is then based on an estimate of the quantity of inventory on hand that is affected by the change. On the other hand, some companies maintain their standard product costs and show the difference as a revision of standards variance until the next cost revision. At that time, the physical inventory is priced with the new standard product costs, which are maintained until the next revision time—usually not longer than a year.

DEVELOPMENT OF COSTING RATES

There are two basic types of cost centers: productive and nonproductive. Productive centers add value to each product that is processed through them. Nonproductive cost centers consist of service centers and general factory expense centers.

Depending upon the way the responsibility chart of accounts is set up, there may be a sizable proportion of direct costs in nonproductive cost centers. For example, in companies that charge all maintenance and repair costs to the plant engineer, the direct cost of maintenance and repair of machinery and equipment in each productive cost center should be allocated to that center. Where fringe benefits and payroll taxes are assigned to general factory expense centers, these direct costs must be distributed to the productive cost centers to cover the direct labor and variable indirect labor in each productive cost center. Utilities, such as electricity for power and steam for processing, must also be allocated to productive cost centers on the basis of their standard usage, even though the responsibility for control of these costs remains with the plant engineer.

As explained in Chapter 2, the trend in recent years has been to charge more and more of these costs to the productive departments. Maintenance is now frequently charged on a sold service basis. Payroll overhead is shown on the departmental cost-and-variance statement because it is desirable to have line supervisors aware of the real total hourly labor cost. Utilities are frequently metered, so that accurate charges for usage can be developed for the principal users of these services and charged directly to their accounts. In any event, after the allocation of service and general factory charges, the grand total costing rate per unit for a given cost center is shown on the budget summary sheet in the right-hand column.

In some cases, responsibility reporting does not provide a breakdown of cost centers detailed enough for accurate product costing. Rather than disturb the responsibility reporting, a method has been devised to compute subcenter rates. This method can be tailored to meet almost any special situation and

COST DISTRIBUTION SHEET

COST CENTER NO.: 38   COST CENTER NAME: X Y Z PROCESS   PERIOD: 19 ___

ACCT. NO.	ACCOUNT NAME	NORMAL DIRECT BUDGET	SUB CENTER NO.	38-1	38-2	38-3	BASIS OF DISTRIBUTION
			SUB CENTER NAME	MIXING	PELLETIZING	PACKING	
			UNIT OF MEASURE	CREW HOURS	MACHINE HOURS	CREW HOURS	
			NORMAL UNITS	75	187	93	
01	MIXING LABOR	$ 696		$696			Direct
02	PELLETIZING LABOR	301			$301		"
03	PACKING LABOR	856				$856	"
10	INDIRECT LABOR	218		218			"
19	EMPLOYEE BENEFITS	310		137	45	128	Labor Dollars
85	POWER	281		99	163	19	Machine Ratings
86	STEAM	515		172	343		" "
32	MAINTENANCE - REPAIRS	1,060			1,060		Direct
	TOTAL COST	$4,237		$1,322	$1,912	$1,003	
	COST PER UNIT			$17.63	$10.22	$10.78	

Figure 5—2 Cost distribution sheet.

still keep the responsibility reporting intact. Figure 5-2 shows a typical cost distribution sheet where subcenters were used to improve accuracy in standard product costs.

It should be noted also that this technique provides a method for using two activity measures for the same cost center. For example, in a plant manufacturing large forgings it was found that the forge shop had two primary direct cost factors: work-hours and machine-hours. The work-hours determine the direct overhead cost for such items as fringe benefits and other payroll overhead, and the machine-hours provide a much more accurate measure of the direct cost of gas and tooling. By setting up this department on a cost distribution sheet with one subcenter based on work-hours and another based on machine-hours, product costs were refined and more accurate cost and control reports were provided.

Design of the Cost Card

In designing the cost card, the magnitude of the job of computing and revising standard product costs is the controlling factor. In companies where there are only a few standard product costs, the standard cost card can be designed to provide as much detail as desired. On the other hand, when a tremendous number of product cost cards are required, a special study should be made to streamline or automate the assembly of information and computation of costs.

Figure 5-3 shows a typical standard product cost sheet based on the ABC Company and the costing rates and standards described in Chapter 2. It can be seen that the same costing rate as shown on the budget summary sheet (Figure 2-10) is used to determine the standard conversion cost of part number Y-320 being processed through the machine shop.

Similar cost summary sheets provide the costing rates for operations performed in the other departments. The material specifications and the standard purchase price schedule provide the material cost data.

In processes where there is substantial shrinkage, it is good practice to develop standard economic lot sizes and then compute the cost for completing a standard lot. Thus, the starting quantity takes into account the amount of shrinkage that will normally occur at each operation during the manufacturing process. The standard cost per unit at each stage includes the net cost of shrinkage up to that point and therefore provides the unit standard cost for pricing in-process inventories. Figure 5-4 shows a cost sheet that utilizes this type of procedure.

PRODUCT COST SHEET

UNIT – Per Piece

220 GROSS WT/PIECE PRODUCT Spare Part
218 NET WT/PIECE ITEM Y-320

COST CTR. NO.	MATERIAL OR OPERATION DESCRIPTION	MATERIAL & LABOR STANDARDS			STANDARD COST RATES		DIRECT COST	
		UNIT OF MEASURE	STD QTY. USED – UNIT		DIRECT		MATERIAL VALUE	LABOR & EXPENSE
			MATERIAL	LABOR	MATERIAL	L. & E.		
(2)	(3)	(4)	(5)	(6)	(7)	(8)	(9)	(10)
	MATERIAL	Pounds	220		075		16 50	
01	PLATE SHOP	D L Hr		18		4 97		89 46
02	MACHINE SHOP	D L Hr		3		5 86		17 58
04	ASSEMBLY	D L Hr		4		4 80		19 20
	TOTAL						16 50	126 24
		DIRECT	TOTAL PRODUCTION COST (PER PIECE)					142.74
			SELLING, GENERAL AND ADMINISTRATIVE					23.89
			TOTAL DIRECT COST TO PRODUCE AND SELL					166.63

Figure 5—3 Product cost sheet.

STANDARD PRODUCT COST SHEET

PRODUCT DESCRIPTION: 36 x 6 x 15" Ring
PRODUCT CODE: No. 56789
UNIT: Per Piece
TYPE OF STEEL: Elco Carbon
STANDARD COST: $0.030 Material 0.015 Conversion

C.C. NO.	MATERIAL OR OPERATION DESCRIPTION	UNIT STANDARD	UNIT OF MEASURE	PIECES FINISHED	FINISH WEIGHT PER PIECE	TOTAL FINISH WEIGHT, LB	SCRAP PRODUCED, LB HEAVY MELT @$40.00/TON	SCRAP PRODUCED, LB TURNINGS @$20.00/TON	UNITS USED	COSTING RATE PER UNIT OF MEASURE	TOTAL STANDARD COST MATERIAL	TOTAL STANDARD COST CONVERSION	COST PER UNIT MATERIAL	COST PER UNIT CONVERSION
01	Elco Steel					144,000					$4,320	$2,160	$35.80	$24.17
08	Slicing Lathe	0.300	Machine Hrs.	105	1,100	115,500	27,500	1,000	31.50	12.00	(560)	378	34.50	42.88
11	Forge	0.050	Crew Hrs.	100	1,000	100,000	15,500		5.00	350.00	(310)	1,750	34.50	54.88
13-1	Heat Treat	1.500	Furnace Hrs.	100	1,000				150.00	8.00		1,200	34.50	79.21
12-1	Machine	3.500	Machine Hrs.	98	700	68,600		31,400	350.00	6.50	(314)	2,275	32.00	82.21
13-2	Heat Treat	1.000	Furnace Hrs.	98	700				98.00	3.00		294	32.00	90.77
25	Inspect	0.300	Man-hrs.	90	700	63,000	5,600		29.4	3.80	(112)	112	33.60	91.22
26	Ship	0.100	Man-hrs.	90	700				9.0	4.50		41	33.60	
	TOTALS			90	700	63,000	48,600	32,400	—	—	$3,024	$8,210	$33.60	$91.22

STANDARD DIRECT MFG. COST $124.82

Figure 5—4 Standard product cost sheet.

Figure 5-5 shows another method for figuring shrinkage that has been used in a number of glass-manufacturing plants. Here, percent shrinkage is used because, since the process is continuous, there are no economic lot sizes.

In companies where there are only a small number of product costs, extremely elaborate cost sheets are sometimes considered practical. In fact, some companies allocate both period costs and capital employed to each product so as to develop return on capital employed as a guide to pricing decisions. Figure 5-6 shows such a cost sheet. However, many authorities on costing dislike this form of presentation because it unitizes period costs and capital employed. These authorities usually prefer to compute the standard direct cost per unit on the cost sheet and then allocate the period costs and capital employed in total as part of the profit-planning procedure.

COMPUTATION OF STANDARD PRODUCT COSTS

As stated above, the design of the product cost sheet should be tailored to fit the relative quantity of cost sheets involved. By the same token, a method of programming the computation should be devised that will provide a complete set of new or revised cost sheets when needed without requiring excessive overtime for their preparation.

In an installation for a company having a large number of product costs and with complex processes, standards and bills of material, it is vital that each department perform its part in providing the basic data. The industrial engineering department generally provides the process sheets and enters the basic time standards. These are the same standards used to measure activity levels for each cost center, as described in Chapter 2. The product engineering department provides the material specifications and bills of material. These are the same standards used to measure the material usage variance. The purchasing department provides the standard purchase prices, which are the same prices used to measure purchase price variance. The budget department establishes the flexible budget standards and measures labor and expense against these standards. Finally, the cost department computes the standard direct costing rates, assembles the data for each product, computes the costs, and then verifies their accuracy. In most companies, the cost department transcribes the data from source documents to product cost forms and completes the computation. In some companies where there is a tremendous quantity of product costs, the industrial engineering department or production control department produces the process detail and time standards on the cost form as a by-product of their departmental function. The cost department then adds the material cost data, the costing rates, and completes the computation. In other cases, electronic data computers have provided the

STANDARD PRODUCT UNIT COST CARD

GROSS WT/PIECE _____
NET WT/PIECE _____
AVERAGE MOVE _____
DATE _____

TYPE OF WARE BLOWN
LINE NO. 9460/2   DEC. NO. _____
SALES DESCRIPTION JUICE
FACTORY DESCRIPTION CRYSTAL
TABULATING CODE NO. _____

UNIT: M PIECES

Cost Ctr. No. (1)	MATERIAL OR OPERATION DESCRIPTION (2)	MATERIAL & LABOR STANDARDS UNIT OF MEASURE (3)	STD QTY. USED-UNIT MATERIAL (4)	STD QTY. USED-UNIT LABOR (5)	STD COST RATES VARIABLE MATERIAL (6)	STD COST RATES VARIABLE L. & E. (7)	MATERIAL VALUE (8)	LABOR & EXPENSE (9)	STANDARD VARIABLE COST LOSS/UNIT SCRAPPED (10)	SHRINKAGE % (11)	SHRINKAGE VALUE (12)	INVENTORY VALUE (13)
	BATCH MATERIAL	Batch	.74		34 09		25 23					
01	MIXING & HAULING (1.2568)	DL $	.93			2 5938		2 41				
04	MELTING	Per Hrs		37 76		1 7536		66 22				
21	FURNACE ROOM	DL $	237 00			1 3395		317 46				
08	LEHRS	B's Prod		50 00		1679		8 40				
22	FINISHING-SEL. CRACK-OFF	Std B's	140 00			06371		8 92	428 64	29.9	128 16	
	" -BAD WORK	"							111 18	19.4	21 57	
	"	"										
	"	"										
	" SMOOTHING	"	180 00			06798		12 13				
	" INSIDE BEVEL & OUTSIDE	"	220 00			06388		14 05				
	" OUTSIDE BEVEL	"				06388						
	" SAND BLAST LABEL	"	80 00			06146		5 08				
	" WASH-GLAZE-SELECT	"	305 00			06363		19 41				
	" PAPERING	"	230 00			06346		14 69	643 64	8.7	56 00	
	SUB TOTAL						25 23	468 68	751 72	0.6	205 73	699 64
	ORDER FILLING THRU SHIP.	3 Dz/Carton						52 08			4 51	
	TOTAL INVENTORY COST – VARIABLE PER M PIECES						25 23	520 76	XXX	XX	210 24	736 23

REMARKS	VARIABLE	TOTAL PRODUCTION COST – (PER DOZEN)	
		SELLING & ADVERTISING EXPENSE (%)	4.73
		ADMINISTRATIVE & GENERAL EXP. (%)	2.46
		TOTAL VARIABLE COST TO PRODUCE & SELL	.81
		NET SELLING PRICE (LIST PRICE $3.00)	1 30
		PROFIT CONTRIBUTION AT STANDARD	.69

(P/V = 46.0 %)

Figure 5-5 Standard product unit cost card.

STANDARD PRODUCT COST

Plant: OSHKOSH Product: YARN Date: MAY 1, 19

COST CENTER	NORMAL OPERATING INVESTMENT PER POUND	VARIABLE COSTS						FIXED COSTS			TOTAL COST	
		RAW MATERIAL	PACKAGING MATERIAL	DIRECT LABOR	DIRECT PAYROLL RELATED	OVERHEAD	WASTE	TOTAL	OVERHEAD	WASTE	TOTAL	OPERATION	CUMULATIVE
Pulp Preparation	$ 2.1557	$.23.9877	$	$.3321	.0697	.0435		24.4330	$.4198		$.4198	$24.8528	$ 24.8528
Steep. & Plfeid.	17.6206	3.63.67		2.4757	.5195	.7659	.0078	7.4056	3.8628	.0011	3.8639	11.2695	36.1223
Mercerizing	3.0054					.0469		.0469	.4690		.4690	.5159	36.6382
Churning	4.9472	4.0167		1.6333	.3427	.1886	.0094	6.1907	1.1615	.0015	1.1630	7.3537	43.9919
Mixing	11.5195	2.8479		.9998	.2098	.3290	.0323	4.4188	1.8804	.0059	1.8863	6.3051	50.2970
Viscose Cellar	13.1420			1.2037	.2526	.4448	.0055	1.9066	2.5159	.0013	2.5172	4.4238	54.7208
Total Per Steep	52.4804	34.4890		6.6446	1.3943	1.8187	.0550	44.4016	10.3094	.0098	10.3192		54.7208
Total Cost/Lb – Viscose	.2285	.1502		.0289	.0061	.0079	.0003	.194	.0448	.0001	.0449		.2383
Box Spinning	.7659	.0163		.0409	.0086	.0377		.1035	.1856		.1856	.2891	.5274
Cake Strip. & Wrap.	.0262			.0073	.0015	.0046	.0018	.0152	.0104	.0014	.0118	.0270	.5544
Cake Washing	.0940	.0072				.0118		.0190	.0247		.0247	.0437	.5981
Cake Drying	.0778					.0039		.0039	.0094		.0094	.0133	.6114
Cake Coning	.2105		.0052	.0219	.0046	.0085	.0072	.0474	.0526	.0064	.0590	.1064	.7178
Cone Inspect. & Pack			.0075	.0033	.0007			.0115				.0115	.7293
Shipping	.1098					.0004		.0004	.0115		.0115	.0019	.7412
Total Lot Cost	1.5127	.1737	.0127	.1023	.0215	.0748	.0093	.3943	.3390	.0079	.3469		.7412
Quality Adjustment								.0087			.0077		.0164
Adj. Inv. Value								.4030			.3546		.7576

Type: 150-40 Bright – 1st Quality
Profit + Fixed Cost / Sales = (.1281) + .4178 / .6840 = 42.35%

Package: 4.3 Lb Cone
Profit / Sales = (.1281) / .6840 = (18.73%)

M/M 70.60
Box Size 7 × 6
Doff 12
T.P.I. 2.5
Sales / Investment = .6840 / 1.5127
Freight/Lb .0110
S.A.R./Lb .0709
Profit / Investment = (.1281) / 1.5127 = 45.22%

Realizable Value .6131
Sales Price .6950
= (8.47%)

Figure 5—6 Standard product cost.

means of assembling the data from the originating sources and have produced completed cost sheets on high-speed printers.

Regardless of the method of assembly and computation of the product costs, the need for verification of accuracy cannot be overemphasized. Inaccurate basic data, misplaced decimal points, and computational errors end up as inventory discrepancies and wrong merchandising and pricing decisions. Therefore, in addition to the cross-checks vital to the transcribing and computing work, an overall review by informed management has been found very effective. This review is accomplished by providing operating executives with a list of the product costs showing net sales realization, direct standard cost, margin, and *profit/volume* (P/V) *ratio* (see Chapters 9 and 10). In cases where the full list is too cumbersome, control limits may be set so that the executives receive a list of products in each product line where the P/V ratio is outside certain control limits. Each executive goes over the list and checks the items that appear to be in error. Cost sheets for items so checked are then reviewed by the industrial engineering department, the process engineering department, and the accounting department to verify their accuracy.

MAINTENANCE OF STANDARD PRODUCT COSTS

Most companies follow the practice of reviewing and revising standard product costs once a year. This revision is usually made effective at the beginning of the fiscal year. A few companies use their standard product costs from 2 to 5 years before revising them. They handle the difference between current budget standards and product cost standards as a revision of standards variance. However, it is generally believed by most managers who have converted to direct standard costs that an annual review and revision of standard product costs is necessary for informed decision making and control.

CASE OF THE XYZ COMPUTER COMPANY

A dramatic demonstration of both the failure of job costing and the advantages of direct standard costing for determining the true cost of a product occurred during an installation of the direct standard cost system at the XYZ Computer Company.

The XYZ Company manufactured a high-speed printer. One of their customers indicated an intention to purchase a large number of the high-speed printers if the company would reduce their previous billing price by 30 percent. The cost data compiled by their job cost system indicated that their costs had increased substantially since they had completed the previous order for this customer. Their first decision was to refuse to reduce the price. Since Wright Associates, Inc., was in the process of installing a direct standard cost system for all their products, they asked our advice. Our review of their cost estimates for the printer indicated so many discrepancies that we were convinced that they did not know their true costs within a margin of error of 30 percent. We indicated that we would concentrate on the costing of the high-speed printer and have accurate costs for them within 3 months. We then developed a computer program for costing their printer which produced an indented bills of material record with a summary of costs for each major subassembly. This study showed that the research and development department had improved the design since the previous order so that the inflation in price was more than compensated for. Also, the cost analysis by major subassemblies showed some important potentials for further cost reductions. The printout had over 4200 line items and required less than 5 minutes to run on their computer with printout on their high-speed printer, so it could be continously updated for any change in price of components or materials. As a result, they decided to accept a large order at the reduced price. By the time this order was shipped, they had accomplished so many cost deductions that the cost printout at the reduced price indicated that it was one of the most profitable items in their line. Their manual method of costing a 4200 line-item bill of material was so time-consuming that it was impossible to keep it up to date with engineering changes, and the job cost system of feedback gave management no feeling of security in the cost data. With the new automated system they were able to feed each engineering change into the file and produce an up-to-the-minute printout of the completely costed bills of materials. They also simulated price inflation in some of their components and included that in a special cost run.

This case clearly indicates that to get true product costs you need standard costs, even though they be rough estimates, which are compared with the actual costs and the variances shown by individual responsibility. When job costs are used they must be compared with either a standard or an engineering estimate and compared to actual in order to be sure there are no gross errors in the cost accumulation.

6
THE EXCEPTION PRINCIPLE OF REPORTING TO MANAGEMENT

Today's managers are becoming swamped with masses of detail which have grown beyond their capacity to handle, no matter how many hours they work each day. As Henry Blackstone, president of Servo Corporation, has said:

> In our modern world of printing and data processing, there is a freight-car load of chaff for each single kernel of valuable and useful information. The successful executive must have a highly developed, fact-sorting and weighing faculty to bypass tons of chaff.[1]

Blackstone's point is demonstrated by the case of Jim Smith, the marketing manager of a very large corporation. His company has ten manufacturing plants, and he directs the activity of over 100 sales offices. Jim told us that they had just completed the installation of a large computer and that now he received a complete sales analysis each month by sales office and by individual salesperson. He then reached in his bottom drawer and pulled out a bound volume of tabulating sheets over 6 inches thick and proudly announced that he had received it within 4 days after the close. When asked what action he had taken as a result of information presented in the report, Jim replied, "None, because I haven't had time to study it yet."

As companies install larger and more sophisticated computers, the mass of data that must be transformed into meaningful information becomes more and more unwieldy. The managers have mountains of data, but not enough hours in the day to transform the data into clear and distinct patterns on which to base executive action.

---

[1] Henry Blackstone, "Gathering Information," *Top Management Handbook*, McGraw-Hill, New York, 1960, p. 203.

That is the reason why management by exception is a must in this era of computers.

What is management by exception?

Management by exception is a system of observation, measurement, and communication that signals the manager at each organization level when managerial attention is needed, and remains silent when the problem can be better handled by a subordinate.

This concept is not new. In fact, Frederick Winslow Taylor, the father of scientific management, built his system on this concept. In a paper presented to the American Society of Mechanical Engineers in 1903, he stated:

> What may be called the "exception principle" in management is coming more and more into use, although, like many of the other elements of this art, it is [only] used in isolated cases. . . . It is not an uncommon sight, though a sad one, to see the manager of a large business fairly swamped at his desk with an ocean of letters and reports on which he thinks he should put his initial or stamp. He feels that by having this mass of detail pass over his desk he is keeping in close touch with the entire business.
>
> The exception principle is directly the reverse of this. Under it, the manager should receive only condensed, summarized, and invariably comparative reports covering, however, all of the elements entering into the management, and even these summaries should all be carefully gone over by an assistant before they reach the manager and have all the exceptions to the past averages or standards pointed out, both the especially good and the especially bad exceptions, thus giving him in a few minutes a full view of progress which is being made, or the reverse, and leaving him free to consider the broader lines of policy and to study the character and fitness of important men under him.[2]

Taylor's *Shop Management* was based on scientific measurement of productive operations and the comparison of actual performance against these standards. Taylor also developed a system of production planning and control that utilized the exception principle to "flag" any job that was behind schedule. He established a control room that was the nerve center of planning and control for the entire shop.

As reported in Chapter 1, in 1916 Harrington Emerson, one of Taylor's disciples, suggested that accountants, too, should utilize the exception principle in cost finding. He said, "Costs should be stated in terms of what they should be rather than what they have been averaging." The accountants turned a deaf ear to Emerson, and it wasn't until 1922 that his idea was implemented. In that year, G. Charter Harrison installed what he called a

---

[2] Frederick Winslow Taylor, *Shop Management,* Harper & Row, New York, 1911, p. 126.

"standard cost system" at the Boss Manufacturing Company in Kewanee, Illinois.

Here was a great step forward in the application of the exception principle of management. When costs for any department were out of line as compared to standard, the manager of that department could quickly see the causes and take corrective action. However, this first standard cost system threw up false signals when costs were out of line because of the volume of production. Since this system set standards per unit of production for fixed costs such as rent and depreciation, departments with higher than normal production looked good while departments with lower than normal production looked bad.

In 1928, the Westinghouse Company installed the standard cost system of accounting, but, since they wanted to pay a "key-person" bonus to foremen and forewomen based on the control of costs, they decided to eliminate the false signals due to volume of production. Accordingly, they devised the flexible budget system which separated the variance from standard due to volume from the controllable variance, and they paid a key-person bonus on the controllable variance.

This system was a great step forward for exception reporting but, as explained in Chapter 1, it still threw up false signals about relative profitability of products and the profit results of building up or cutting down inventories. In 1935, Jonathan Harris of Dewey & Almy Chemical Company developed what he called a direct cost system which was designed to eliminate these false signals and to clearly separate the measurement of sales performance from production performance. It also provided a statement of income which was not distorted due to building up or cutting down on inventory levels.

APPLICATIONS OF MANAGEMENT BY EXCEPTION

In addition to direct standard costs, there are dozens of modern management practices that are based on the principle of management by exception. The following are some of the better-known applications.

The Critical Path Method (CPM)

This is also known as the program evaluation and review technique (PERT).

In 1962, "Rocky" Martino headed up a team for Olin Mathieson to control construction of a new brass mill. This team utilized the computer to update control data in a large chart room. Martino summarized the group's operation as follows:

This group supervised the plotting of network type arrow diagrams to:

1. Allocate the optimum number of construction workers on each job, by craft.
2. Watch closely over equipment venders' delivery dates.
3. Keep up with changes in customer requirements that affected the present mill's finished-goods inventories.
4. Adjust for last-minute design changes.

This group, working out of the chart room, used three key devices to keep projects moving foreward:

1. A color coding system to flag trouble spots. Green—work on schedule; yellow—work not started but float time unused; dotted red—work lagging but still expected to meet deadlines; solid red—work definitely behind schedule.
2. A weekly work-status report on which the analyst listed equipment and construction events that failed to meet deadline dates, with the reasons. It also itemized the events to be completed in the next two weeks. The report went to the project task force, construction personnel, engineers, and contractors. With this information, the task force planned moves to pull jobs back up to schedules.
3. A computer update that corrected the critical path as the final stages of construction quickened. As soon as the staff processed new punched cards indicating status changes, the computer was able to reroute a new path about every other week.[3]

Monthly Report on Profit Plan and Forecast of Variances

One of the most important exception reports from the standpoint of management accounting is the monthly report on profit plan. Figure 6-1 shows such a report. This form was first devised for a subsidiary of a large corporation. Wright Associates had just completed the installation of a direct standard cost system in this subsidiary, and, even though their executives had no experience in forecasting variances from the profit plan, we instituted the report as of the second month of operation. While we were preparing the statements for the first month, one of their prime competitors announced a reduction in price of 25 percent on their most profitable line. The decision was made at once to meet the competitor's prices, so that our first report showed a substantial unfavorable variance in the forecast for the remaining months of the year. In

[3] R. L. Martino, "Nerve Control Aids Modernization," *Factory,* October 1962.

fact, the planned profit for the year was wiped out. The board of directors accepted this forecast as realistic and called on all the key executives to find ways of making up this unfavorable variance through positive cost reduction plans and programs. We returned to the controller's office and were told that this was the same resolution that was made each year and that in 3 months' time it would be back to business as usual. We pointed out that we now had responsibility accounting so that we could pinpoint the ones who contributed

---

A one-page report tells the whole story.

ABC MANUFACTURING COMPANY   March 25, 19___

REPORT ON PROFIT PLAN
($000 Omitted)

ACTUAL		DESCRIPTION	March FORECAST	April FORECAST	12 MONTHS FORECAST
February	2 MONTHS				
		NET PROFIT FOR PERIOD			
$612	$1,347	MASTER PROFIT PLAN	$402	$550	$4,900
597	1,367	ACTUAL AND LATEST FORECAST	422	580	5,007
$(15)*	$ 20	VARIANCE	$ 20	$ 30	$ 107
		ANALYSIS OF VARIANCE			
		SALES			
$115	$ 150	Volume	$100	$ 75	$ 400
(85)	(70)	Price and Mix	(60)	(30)	(360)
(10)	(20)	Selling Expense	(5)	-	10
$ 20	$ 60	TOTAL SALES	$ 35	$ 45	$ 50
		MANUFACTURING			
$(58)	$ (62)	Labor and Expense	$(47)	$(40)	$ (250)
5	17	Material Usage and Scrap	8	10	85
10	11	Purchase Price	10	5	120
$(43)	$ (34)	TOTAL MANUFACTURING	$(29)	$(25)	$ (45)
		ADMINISTRATION			
		General Administrative			
$ 6	$ (8)	Expense	$ 10	$ 7	$ 66
2	2	Idle Plant	4	3	36
$ 8	$ (6)	TOTAL ADMINISTRATION	$ 14	$ 10	$ 102

*Parentheses denote unfavorable balance.

Advantages:
1. Sales responsibility is clearly defined.
2. Variance from planned profits is clearly shown by executive responsibility.
3. Supervisors at all levels look forward, not backward.
4. Promotes action, avoids alibis.

The report on profit plan integrates planning and control for all levels of management and results in improved profit and growth.

Figure 6–1   Report on profit plan.

to an improved profit picture. So we developed a plan to document the report on profit plan with specific detail as to how forecasted improvements were to be implemented and when they would be realized. The vice president of manufacturing, who was the junior member of the board, organized his group to work on this program, and they soon projected total savings equal to the loss due to the price cut.

With the follow-up system, these projections were realized and at the end of the year they not only achieved savings to offset the price cut but ended up with a profit greater than that projected by the original profit plan. Three years later this junior board member became the next president of the subsidiary. The effect of this attitude was repeated all down the line so that in meetings with first-line supervisors on departmental results the question was no longer, "Why did you have that unfavorable variance?"; but rather, "What are you doing to improve the variance and what is your forecast of the amount of improvement next month, and for the remainder of the year?"

Daily Report on Productivity

The next most important report from the standpoint of management by exception is the daily report on productivity, which shows how each individual in the direct labor force performed on the previous day. Here again, the volume of paper produced by the computer each day could swamp the first-line supervisors. On the other hand, if the management accountants provide a trend chart for each individual worker that shows the percent performance, percent coverage by standards, and the percent charged to indirect, it becomes easy for each supervisor to interpret the results each day for each individual. Figure 6-2 shows a sample of a daily computer printout, and Figure 6-3 shows a sample of a trend chart for an individual direct labor operator. As discussed in Chapter 2, the timeliness of such a report is of paramount importance and various methods of recognition can be used to reward good performances so that a direct wage incentive is not necessary. For example, posting a weekly list of operators whose performance showed improvement during the past week has been found very effective as a means for improving productivity.

ADVANTAGES OF MANAGEMENT BY EXCEPTION

1 Management by exception saves executive time. It avoids time-consuming work on trivia and details that can be handled just as well by subordinates. It avoids distractions by flagging critical areas and remaining silent on situations that are under control.

DAILY DIRECT LABOR PERFORMANCE REPORT

WORK DATE 04/14/
RUN DATE 04/14/
DEPT 403   SHIFT 01

CLOCK NUMBER	WORK ORDER NUMBER	PART NUMBER	SEQ NO	W/C NO	PIECES COMPL	EARNED HOURS SET UP	RUN	TOTAL	SET UP	RUN	TOTAL MEAS	ACTUAL HOURS PCT PERF	UNMEAS HOURS	TOTAL DIRECT	ACCT	TOTAL INDIR	TOTAL ELAP
001151	5715497	U01524	200	403067		.42			.35								
001151	5713866	U05603	200	403090		.42			.35								
001151	5715866	U05603	400	403090		.42			.44								
		EMPLOYEE TOTAL			65	3.19	.18	3.37	3.43	.84	4.27	78.92		4.27	17.80	.76	5.03
001170				403000											4163	.85	
001170	5701663	016124	500	403122	89	1.00	1.00		1.45						4163	.12	*
001170	5701663	016124	500	403122	208		2.33		1.07								*
001170	5706891	016125	500	403122	356		3.98		2.46								*
001170	5706891	016125	500	403122	89		1.00		4.14								
									1.02								
		EMPLOYEE TOTAL			653		7.31	7.31	7.62		7.62	95.93		7.62	3.54	.27	7.89
001216		U05797		403000	70										4157	.78	
001215		U06373		403000											4157	.72	
001216		U07952	400	403067		.42			.30								
001216	5689112	U08462	100	403090	24		.88		1.06								
001216	5710476	U07812	100	403064		.42			.32								
001216	5715565	U07923	600	403067		.42			.54								
001216	5716247	U07970	300	403067		.42			.52								
		EMPLOYEE TOTAL			94	1.68	.88	2.56	1.06	1.68	2.74	93.43	0.00	2.74	54.74	1.50	4.24
									100.00X	83.02X							
001343	5707492	017469	300	403083	701		7.85	7.85		7.89	7.89	99.49		7.89			7.89
		EMPLOYEE TOTAL			701		7.85	7.85		7.89	7.89			7.89			7.89
001354				403000									7.98	7.98			7.98
		EMPLOYEE TOTAL											7.98	7.98			7.98
001369				403000											4164	.16	
001369				403000											4163	.63	
001369	5713619	017462	100	403050	52		.54			.72					4163	.04	
001369	5713619	017462	100	403050	150		1.57			1.69							
		EMPLOYEE TOTAL			202		2.11	2.11		2.41	2.41	87.55		2.41	36.10	.87	3.28
001386		U09082	100	403090	177		.99	.99		.72	.72	137.50		.72			.72
		EMPLOYEE TOTAL			177		.93	.99		.72	.72	137.50		.72			.72
001544				403000											4163	.24	
001544				403000											4163	.22	

Figure 6–2 Computer printout reporting on daily direct labor performance.

82 Management Accounting Simplified

For example, Charles H. Percy, as board chairman of Bell & Howell, stated that under their system of management by exception executives were able to remove up to 90 percent of the routine work from their desks.

2 Management by exception maximizes the utilization of executive effort by concentrating managerial talent only where and when it is needed, and alerts management to opportunities as well as to difficulties. For example, at Smith-Corona-Marchant,

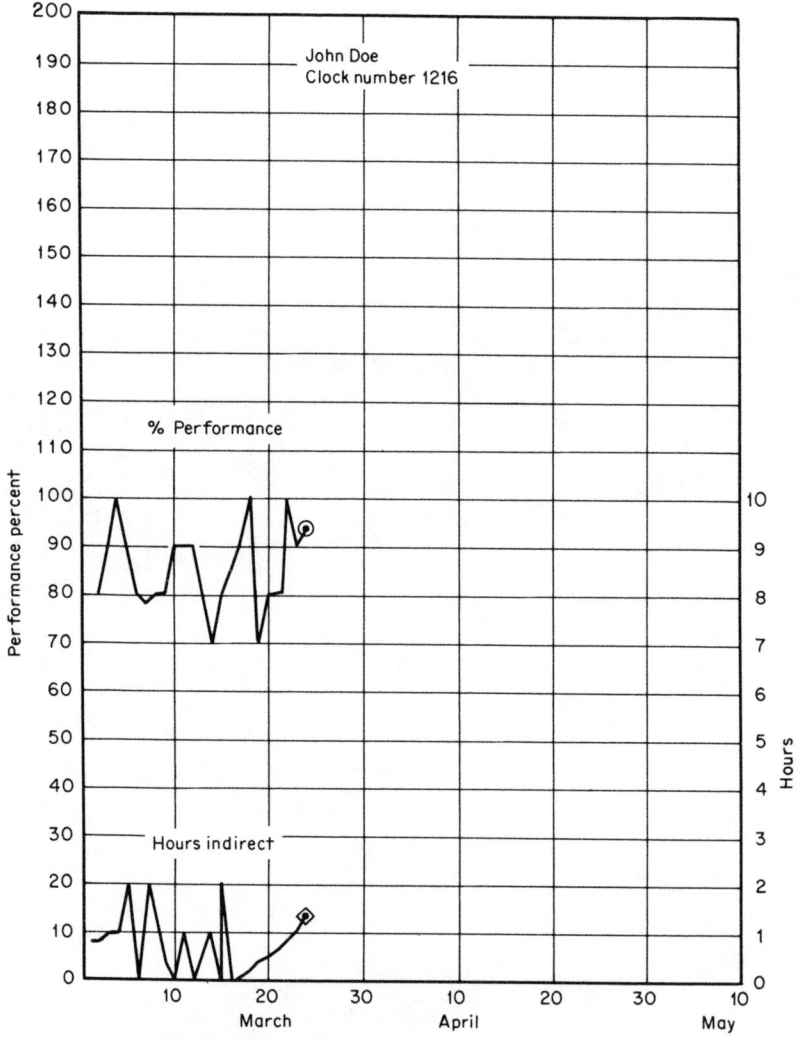

Figure 6—3 Daily performance report for individual worker.

Inc., executive attention is focused on exceptional marketing problems and potentials, by classifying products each year according to their sales potential. The first group, which includes those products that are expected to merely hold their own, gets little attention from top marketing executives. The second group, which includes those products that are adversely affected by a dwindling market, gets some attention from the standpoint of cost control and product improvement in order to secure a larger share of the market. The third group, however, gets intensive study by top management. This group comprises the products with the most immediate potential. Top management examines them from the standpoint of engineering, production, marketing, and finance to be sure that they do not fail to exploit all opportunities for improvement.

3 Management by exception requires qualitative and quantitative yardsticks for judging situations and people. Therefore, it takes much of the prejudice out of performance appraisals and stimulates communication between different levels of the organization. For example, Otis Elevator, in setting standards of performance for its many districts, holds up as a target the best performance achieved by any of its field units. Comparisons are then made on the basis of a composite target made up of the selected best features to be found in the entire field organization.

Pitfalls of Management by Exception

In this chapter we have seen what can happen when you feed management tons of data without sifting out the kernels from the chaff, and what can be accomplished by utilizing the potentials of the third generation of computers to signal management at each echelon whenever attention is required. However, it is important to caution you about some of the pitfalls of management by exception.

First, every executive must guard against the false sense of security that the concept of management by exception tends to develop. Standards of comparison tend to become obsolete, and some critical factors are almost impossible to measure. Management by exception is no substitute for thinking. In fact, the executive must be constantly alert to the failure of the signals to show the need for attention to a critical problem in time to take corrective action. For example, refer to the case of the bottling room discussed in Chapter 2 where hourly evaluation was required to prevent excess costs.

Second, the executive must not think that the company operates by a system of management by exception while he or she continues to call the shots, insulated from only the problems he or she doesn't like to handle.

Lester R. Bittel, in his excellent book, *Management by Exception*, tells of such a case:

> Jack Black, for instance, the executive vice president of a meat packing firm, divided up operational responsibility between four product-divisions assistant vice-presidents. On the advice of a management consultant, he surrounded himself with five functional managers heading up corporate personnel, engineering, public relations, finance and legal affairs. He also set up a planning and control section headed by a controller. Instead of gaining from this reorganization, the company slipped badly and Black, who formerly had been considered one of the top men in the industry, became completely ineffective. The trouble lay in the fact that Black couldn't resist over-the-shoulder supervising. His defection showed itself in a number of highly demoralizing forms:
>
> 1 He'd offer well-intended suggestions to those who were in charge of the divisions. Rather than permit his assistant vice presidents to learn from sad experience, Black regularly would issue a string of advice and cautions. To the division managers it had the effect of making them feel that whenever they made an independent decision that didn't work out well, Black would be in a position to say "I warned you against that."
>
> 2 He'd demonstrate impatience with the control system itself. Daily he'd pester his controller for interim reports. Often he'd call the divisions directly to have them put together a separate batch of figures or to verify data that had him worried. As a result, the assistant vice presidents gradually began to bypass the control system.
>
> 3 He'd anticipate suggestions from his functional staff. Instead of waiting for them to analyze monthly reports and to make recommendations, Black would come to his own conclusions first. Frequently he'd send his plans directly to the divisions before checking with the corporate staff specialists.
>
> 4 He'd jump into crisis problems before being invited. Black had an extremely keen mind. His business judgment was a proven commodity. When he sensed a crisis or the system turned up an exception, more often than not he would initiate action before his division managers could formulate their own decisions.
>
> Black typifies the competent executive who "buys" the management-by-exception idea intellectually but who is emotionally incapable of abiding by it. His reactions, of course, were exaggerated. But almost every executive can find real difficulty in submerging some of his own talent in order to strengthen the over-all effectiveness of his organization.[4]

[4] Lester R. Bittel, *Management by Exception*, McGraw-Hill, New York, 1964, p. 28.

The third pitfall is to be sure that the executive who is freed from demands of routine work fills the time with creative effort. He or she must expect to work harder and enjoy it more. When the red lights are not flashing, it's time for long-range planning to be sure the company is ready to exploit every opportunity as it unfolds.

MANAGEMENT BY COMPUTER

Now let's think back to Frederick W. Taylor's concept of management by exception. He and his disciples envisioned mammoth control centers into which data would flow at high speeds and be translated automatically into signals for action, or a green light would appear indicating that all was going according to plan. They dreamed of a system where the manager would sit at a console and make split-second decisions based on the data that flowed into the control center which had been automatically measured and evaluated.

Unfortunately, they were more than 50 years ahead of their time. The years that followed their pioneering in scientific management led to decentralization of profit responsibility because the technology of communication and evaluation was too time-consuming to accomplish their objective.

Today, as a result of the development of digital computers, Taylor's dream has become a practical reality.

Another type of visual control that is truly in the Taylor concept is at Hughes Aircraft Company in their El Segundo, California, plant:

> A plant-wide closed-circuit television system links the works manager's office with purchasing, receiving, stores, machine-load scheduling, two assembly departments, and finished stores. Telecasts alert interested functions to parts shortages on scheduled projects, for instance. And machine-loading progress is marked on a continuous strip chart that is photographed as it rolls past the camera. The company had formerly used electronic data processing to check on small parts shortages, but it found that the half a day, or more, needed to feed data into the machine and process it was too slow. Now one TV camera and fifteen monitors provide information almost instantaneously. Initial cost for installation was $8,000. Rental cost of cameras is $200. per month. In addition to providing management instantaneously with the variance data it needs, Hughes estimated its paperwork savings alone at $50,000. in sixteen months.[5]

In conclusion, computers make management by exception a must because, without it, the managers will drown in the oceans of paper belched out by these monsters. On the other hand, computers offer the means of realizing the

---

[5] "Plant-Wide TV System Keeps Eye on Production," *Factory*, June 1962, p. 114.

dream of every disciple of the scientific management movement. *Business Week* has described this system as almost a reality at Lockheed Aircraft Company.[6]

> In the not too distant future, minutes after top managers sit down in the control room, charts displayed on video screens will update them on all the company's operations. Computers, programmed with company policies, will take up-to-the-minute information, organize it into chart form, run it through a slide-making machine, and flash it to the waiting managers. Furthermore, if a project is in trouble, the computer can pretest solutions before manpower and materials are committed.

[6] "Millennium for Decision Makers," *Business Week*, August 10, 1963, p. 54.

7
MODELS FOR AUTOMATION OF MANAGEMENT ACCOUNTING

During the past three decades digital computers have been achieving the most rapid technological development of any product in modern industrial history. In fact, the evolution of computer hardware, since the silicon transistor replaced the vacuum tube in computer circuits, has been almost miraculous. Unfortunately, software did not achieve the same degree of progress so that managers became slaves of these computer monsters as they were led to believe they would enjoy fabulous rewards if they invested in the latest generation of hardware. Thus the entire automation program became dependent upon the systems and programming staff, and data-processing personnel, by training, were overly sensitive to the volume capabilities of the hardware and underresponsive to the needs of managers. It was a frequent, if sad sight to see a frustrated manager who had spent a fortune to secure the latest hardware, only to be told that he couldn't have a simple computer report because the systems and programming staff were booked up on vital jobs for as much as 2 years ahead. This was particularly true in the security industry where managers used the fact that they had the latest generation of computers as a status symbol even though they were receiving no benefit from the new computer because of lack of effective software.

Thus a vicious circle developed. The managing partner needed the advanced hardware to maintain status with peers. The electronic data processing (EDP) manager needed experience with the latest hardware, which would enhance a résumé and help secure a better job with another firm. The systems and programming staff had no incentive to create programs without "bugs" because any program that went "on stream" without trouble was not given credit since it was assumed that the new hardware was responsible. On the other hand, when a program was in trouble, the systems staff and programmers were in close touch with top management. They were given much credit for working around the clock which became a way of life for them. Finally they were given great credit for solving problems which should never have been in the system in the first place.

These facts were demonstrated by the quarterly analysis of costs and profits which Wright Associates made for many years for a number of securities firms. The firms with the most advanced computer systems consistently showed the highest cost per transaction and those with the oldest generation of hardware showed the lowest cost per transaction. In fact, at least two large firms can trace their failure to problems caused by installations of advanced automation systems.

The managing partners who finally got control of this EDP situation did so by using outside consultants to provide software on a "turnkey" basis. These fixed price contracts were risky for the consultants, but it was the only way they could demonstrate the tremendous waste that was occurring with the in-house systems and programming environment. As reported in Chapter 5, our first automated product cost system was for a computer manufacturer who was a victim of this same syndrome.

This company had an IBM 370-135 system in place and had been working for over 2 years to implement a material requirements planning system with little success. They had a bills of material processor in place and were trying to get their data base of bills of material up to date. We had them run an *ABC* analysis and took the position that for product cost purposes we could forget about *C* items, which represented 80 percent of the items in the bills of material but only 5 percent of the value. Also, they did not have a unique code number to identify the product as it was shipped, so we got them to assign unique code numbers to each item to be shipped, along with linkages to major subassemblies. Thus, sales forecasts could be exploded into parts and subassembly requirements which was vital for their materials requirement planning system and in turn was necessary for our automated product cost system.

With our limited objective and a 3 months' deadline, we proceeded to develop a simple systems design (see Figure 7-1), which utilized the bills of material data base that was in place, and, by developing standard direct labor and expense rates for the machine shop and the assembly department, we were able to provide accurate product costs for all of the parts and subassemblies needed for the high-speed printer. Thus, as soon as our coding was complete for entering the labor and expense rates and the material and purchased parts standard prices into the file, we were ready to proceed with the system, and, as stated in Chapter 5, it took less than 5 minutes to run the printout for a 4200 line-item indented bill of material with costs for each part and major subassembly.

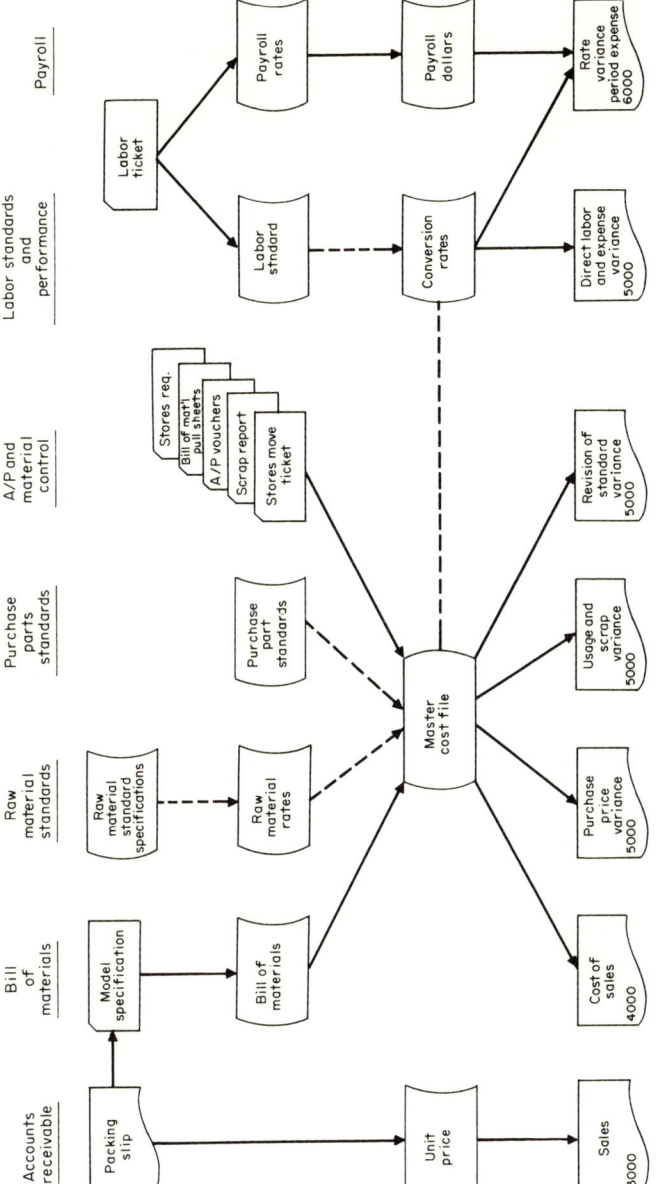

Figure 7–1 Process flow for standard cost system.

90 Management Accounting Simplified

One incident occurred which demonstrated the systems staff's attitude toward "bugs." When we were ready to run the first cost summary, the computer began printing out strange numbers and the systems staff began to "wring their hands in despair." Our specialist, however, identified the problem, at once, as bad input. We found that the keypunch operators had not followed instructions in preparing some of the file input data. As soon as this was corrected, the program ran without any further trouble.

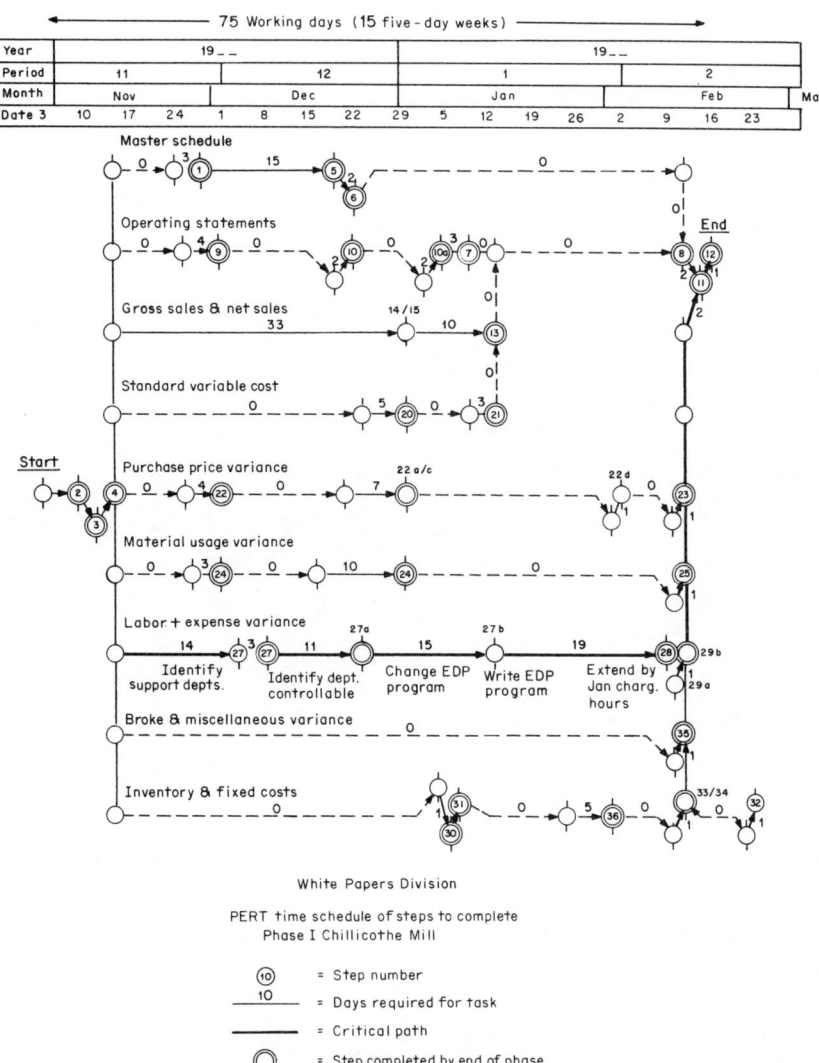

Figure 7–2 Critical path (PERT) arrow diagram.

TIME REQUIREMENTS FOR CRITICAL PATH SCHEDULING

PREPARED BY: ____________

DATE: ____________

PROGRAM: ____________ LOCATION: ____________ Page ____ of ____

	(1)	(2)	(3)	(4)	(5)	(6)	(7)	(8)	(9)	
	TASK NO.	DESCRIPTION	RESPONSIBILITY	SCHED. COMPLETION DATE	TIME REQUIREMENTS				REMARKS	
					MAN HOURS	NUMBER OF PEOPLE	HOURS PER DAY	CAL. DAYS 5÷(6x7)		
1										1
2										2
3										3
4										4
5										5
6										6
7										7
8										8
9										
										26
										27
28										28
29										29
30										30
31										31
32										32
33										33
34										34
35										35

Figure 7–3 Planning chart list time requirements for critical path scheduling.

By eliminating the C items from the bills of material requirements for our data base, we speeded up the completion of the data base. We then instituted a critical path or PERT chart for insuring the completion of the product cost system within 3 months. Our technique for planning and control of such projects is a combination of the critical path arrow diagram and the Gantt chart. Figure 7-2 shows a sample of such a chart with color codes, which is the same as the one Martino used in his Olin Mathieson Brass Mill application (see Chapter 6). The foundation of this chart is the planning sheet shown in Figure 7-3.

Appendix I shows a typical functional specification, which is the first step in the critical path schedule for any automation program for the automated product cost system. The accompanying statement of objectives in the appendix provides an important step-by-step procedure for utilization of this technique. The critical path technique has been found to be effective in helping managers get control of their in-house systems and programming staff.

In the application of automation to the management accounting system and operating statements, our first requirement was a chart of accounts designed to achieve true responsibility accounting with simple closing procedures. Here it was imperative that the design of the operating statements could be changed by managers without any blocking due to the lack of available systems and programming staff. The system was therefore designed so that changes could be made by filling out a simple instruction document with the keypunch operator's instructions for the computer. Thus no further programming was necessary to get the new format.

The system was also designed to provide a complete audit trail back to transactions of original entry.

This system replaces the traditional general ledger and trial balance and provides for flexible budgetary control reports to management, along with profitability by product lines and comparisons with profit plans by responsibility. It speeds up the closing so that within a few months after installation a full set of operating statements can be available within 5 days after the end of the period.

8
CONTROL OF CAPITAL EXPENDITURES

Control seems to imply that a company intends to be careful that it does not spend too much for plant and equipment. It must be recognized that such control should cause management to ask if it is spending enough so that it can produce a quality product at a reasonable cost and remain competitive with other companies in the same industry. The capital budget is important to the development of cash-flow projections and is a vital part of long-range planning. Evaluating specific proposals must require that each item in the capital budget be consistent with the long-range strategic plan.

In most companies this consistency is insured by the system of analysis and approval of specific items in the capital budget. For example, proposed capital expenditures are classified and specific procedures are established for each class.

CLASSIFICATION OF CAPITAL EXPENDITURES

The following are typical classifications of capital expenditures:

- Class I   Capital expenditures for providing facilities for "make" vs. "buy."
- Class II   Capital expenditures for achieving other cost reductions.
- Class III Capital expenditures for increasing plant capacity.
- Class IV   Capital expenditures required to comply with government regulations or to improve employee or community relations, such as devices for avoiding air pollution or a new cafeteria.

Class I

It is in the area of "make" vs. "buy" decisions that some of the fuzziest thinking has resulted from using full cost data. Many companies that do not have direct costing systems use rough estimates of out-of-pocket costs as a basis for make-or-buy decisions. Others take the position that if the outside purchase price is less than the estimated "whole" cost then the item should be bought. Such an assumption fails to provide precise data from which to compute incremental savings to be expected. Lacking accurate predetermined direct costs in the form described in Chapter 5, many companies let these "acres of diamonds" go by default. Responsibility is quite often delegated to process engineers and buyers who base their decisions on arbitrary ground rules and a crystal ball.

Using the management accounting system described in Chapter 5, the following four basic tools are provided for making these decisions.

1. Clean-cut separation between direct and period costs.
2. Accurate estimating procedures which predetermine true direct product costs.
3. An estimating procedure for determining the additional period costs that would be required to "make" vs. "buy" a given item.
4. Logical bases for measuring the additional capital investment that would be required to make a given item as compared to buying it from outside vendors.

A great deal of judgment and common sense is required in order to weigh all factors in such decisions. For this reason many companies have established make-or-buy committees with representatives from the principal interested departments. Concise data are prepared in advance for committee action at periodic meetings. In a well-organized committee, decisions are reached promptly and a minimum of such decisions require top management review or approval. A typical procedure is as follows:

1. Design engineers and process engineers specify processes, operation, tooling, and tolerances.
2. Production control estimates quantity requirements.
3. Industrial engineering develops preliminary time standards and a rough estimate of direct conversion and material cost.
4. Purchasing provides estimated outside vendors' proposals with prices.

5 Cost analysis section of controller's department rough-screens vendor proposals by applying appropriate pricing formulas. Items that are not clearly "buy" are returned to the process engineers.

6 Process engineers prepare more detailed specifications, routing sheets, and tooling requirements for items returned by cost analysis section.

7 Production control makes more accurate usage forecast and evaluates production capacity for manufacturing these items.

8 Industrial engineering makes more accurate application of standard data and material requirements and provides a careful estimate of the cost of facilities and tooling.

9 Purchasing obtains firm quotes from outside vendors.

10 Cost analysis section of controller's department determines product costs, specific period costs, and allocated period costs. It also determines additional capital required for facilities, tools, inventory, and cash, if item is made, compared to outside purchase. Finally, it computes return on investment based both on average basis and a discounted cash-flow basis and prepares evaluation report.

11 Make-or-buy committee reviews all cases and makes decisions; returns problems to cost analysis section for additional data, or refers to top management for policy guidance.

12 Controller audits results of actions taken and reports deviations from estimates to the committee.

The above procedure is more involved than is usually necessary. However, the principles to be followed in all cases are demonstrated. With the four primary tools provided by the management accounting system, it is easy to establish a streamlined procedure for making such decisions.

In situations where capacity limits have been reached, the make-or-buy decisions require an additional analysis of alternate uses of available facilities. Such studies often result in decisions to purchase items at a price much higher than the direct cost to make them in order to free capacity to make other items that provide a better return on capital employed.

This whole area of utilizing management accounting data in order to maximize return on investment through selecting the most profitable items to make has tremendous potential. The most outstanding results have been obtained by the use of direct costing data with linear programming and computers. However, a great deal can be accomplished by simple arithmetic and operating know-how. In either case, the tools of management accounting provide the necessary information for precise decision making.

The use of the techniques described above will demonstrate clearly and concisely the savings made over the near term in each make-or-buy decision. It will show return on incremental capital employed and payback in terms of projected cash flow.

Two examples of analysis of cash flow and determination of payback period follow.

Appropriation Request I In this situation, the manufacturing unit proposes to spend $165,000 to buy a vertical boring mill to lower the level of work being subcontracted. Under cost to make, material costs are not listed since the material is furnished to a subcontractor on consignment. Cost to buy equivalent production includes the subcontractor's charges which were developed from actual invoices. See Table 8-1 for analysis.

Appropriation Request II The unit proposes to spend $210,000 for an N.C. checking lathe which will require EDP support in addition to all the period costs associated with the vertical boring mill. It is planned to use it full time over the next 5 years. See Table 8-2 for analysis.

Class II

Since Class II covers such a wide variety of projects, the procedure for evaluating them must have wide applicability. The DCF method (discounted cash flow) is therefore recommended as the most logical basis to be used for this class of capital expenditure. The DCF rate of return is the economic basis on which any given proposed project can be compared with all other proposed

Table 8-1
APPROPRIATION REQUEST I
Analysis of Cash Flow and Payback Period

Description	1976	1977	1978	1979	1980
Investment	$(165,000)				
Incremental net income	41,300	$ 35,700	$50,200	$50,600	$ 51,000
Depreciation	7,500	15,000	15,000	14,200	13,300
Reduction in inventory	1,500				
Cash flow	(114,700)	50,700	65,200	64,800	64,300
Cumulative cash flow	$(114,700)	(64,000)	1,200	66,000	130,300
Payback period 2.9 years					

Table 8-2
APPROPRIATION REQUEST II
Analysis of Cash Flow and Payback Period

Description	1976	1977	1978	1979	1980
Investment	$(210,000)				
Incremental net income	42,900	$31,600	$46,750	$47,275	$47,800
Depreciation	9,550	19,100	19,100	18,050	17,000
Reduction in inventory	1,500				
Cash flow	(156,050)	50,700	65,850	65,325	64,800
Cumulative cash flow	$(156,050)	(105,350)	(39,500)	25,825	90,625
Payback period 3.6 years					

projects.[1] A computer can be utilized to provide DCF computations (IBM System 3 is one such computer.) This requires a clear understanding of the cost of capital and the methods of converting capital expenditure costs and savings to "after tax" and "present value" bases.

The investments and benefits from a project should be based on the difference between making it and not making it. The important data are the incremental changes in sales, costs, and investments. The improvement resulting from an expenditure is not necessarily the gain from the present situation. There may be unused facilities, low prices, or poor distribution which may not prevail in the future. The required comparison is between the best possible solution which can be achieved with present facilities compared with the situation after proposed facilities are in place.

All capital employed should be included in the evaluation of a given project. Any increases in inventories should be included.

Existing facilities that can be used in a new project should be included at their equivalent *cash replacement value* without regard to their *book value* in accounting records. The equivalent cash replacement value is the amount of money that would have to be spent for facilities in comparable conditions had the existing facilities not been available.

The life of a project in years depends on its ability to continue to generate profits (savings).

In considering replacement of equipment, it should usually be assumed that maintenance costs applicable to the equipment to be replaced are what it would cost to keep the equipment one more year. Therefore, the comparison is between continuing with the old equipment for one more year compared with the total average annual cost of the new equipment based on its ideal economic life.

[1] See Maurice Gordon Wright, *Discounted Cash Flow,* 2d ed., McGraw-Hill, 1973, p. 10.

Class III

A sound program for expanding plant capacity is one of the most important ingredients for long-range profit and growth. In too many companies, a decision to build a new plant is made before it is decided just which products are to be produced in the new plant. Such action reflects poor long-range planning procedures. On the other hand, with the profit-planning procedures described in Chapter 10, the approach to plant expansion programs is product-oriented and ensures a careful evaluation of the effect any proposed plant expansion program will have on the rate of return on investment.

Decisions on substantial plant expansion programs are usually divided into two parts: the operating management decision and the financial management decision. The operating decision is based on a comparison of incremental operating profit to capital employed, whereas the financial decision is based on the financial operations ratio and the financial leverage factor as discussed in Chapter 10.

The first step is to determine whether or not a proposed plant expansion program will improve the return on capital employed. This is relatively simple for a company using the management accounting system described in Chapter 5. The present situation is set up in direct cost form along with the incremental change, and then the return is figured including the expanded facilities and sales. Table 8-3 shows such an analysis. As stated above under make-or-buy decisions, such comparisons should be checked by applying the

Table 8-3
ABC MANUFACTURING COMPANY
EVALUATION OF PROPOSED PLANT ADDITION

Description	Present facilities	Proposed addition	Proposed total
Net sales	$70,000	$25,000	$95,000
Direct cost	53,000	17,500	70,500
Profit contribution	$17,000	$ 7,500	$24,500
Per cent	24%	30%	26%
Period expense	12,100	2,000	14,100
Operating profit	$ 4,900	$ 5,500	$10,400
Cash	$ 4,000	$ 800	$ 4,800
Receivables	5,000	1,800	6,800
Inventories	8,000	2,000	10,000
Fixed assets	16,000	12,000	28,000
Capital employed	$33,000	$16,600	$49,600
Return on capital employed	15%	33%	21%

discounted cash-flow whenever there is a large immediate outlay, and a substantial period of time will elapse before the objective level of operations is reached.

After the expansion program is proved from an operating standpoint, the financial plans must be determined. This planning may sometimes result in curtailing the optimum expansion program because of inability to raise sufficient capital. In such cases, other projects requiring capital are reviewed to determine whether to eliminate some of them that fail to provide as good a return as that projected for the expansion program. The net effect is to determine the overall optimum application of available capital.

Class IV

Projects in this class do not have a measurable economic value. Therefore, the procedure does not include an economic evaluation of return. Here the proposal should show the proposed expenditure and how it will meet the requirements of the government regulation or how it will correct deficiencies, and that this is the most economical method of meeting those requirements. Other items in this class, such as a new cafeteria for improving employee relations, should show why the present situation is unsatisfactory and how the proposal is the least expensive way to meet the needs.

AVOIDING COST OVERRUNS

As soon as a specific capital expenditure is given final approval, a project identification number is assigned and the accounting department sets up an account to accumulate commitments and expenditures for this account. Quarterly reports are usually issued for each project from the time it is given final approval until it is completed and the post-completion audit is made. One of the greatest reasons for cost overruns in capital spending projects is due to failure to alert managers when commitments have reached the danger stage. By providing substantial rewards for cost reduction suggestions and the accuracy of projection of costs and benefits, the whole organization can become involved in the development of new and exciting proposals for capital expenditures.

POST-COMPLETION AUDIT

The post-completion audit provides an evaluation of actual performance by determining the extent to which proposals have achieved the results projected for them.

Advantages

1 Management can profit in the future by avoiding a repetition of past mistakes.

2 Management can focus attention on those individuals responsible for major or continuing errors. It can provide an incentive for improved performance.

3 The actual audit can provide a useful area for training younger executives.

Why then is the performance review resisted in a surprisingly large number of cases? Some executives believe that the operating personnel will express ideas less freely if subject to review. However, managers who use such reviews are enthusiastic about them. Almost all of them follow up projects in excess of $10,000 and wait until the project is completed before beginning the review.

Reports generally continue quarterly on projects that have failed in a major way to meet projections. Often a special task force is appointed to follow up on major projects that have failed to live up to projections. As stated above, providing substantial rewards for suggestions and accuracy of projections will give an incentive for more and more executives to participate in developing proposals for capital expenditures.

9
PROFIT GUIDELINES FOR MARKETING DECISIONS

Since the birth of the scientific management movement, the area of management that has made the least progress is the quality of data provided to managers for making pricing and other marketing decisions. As a result this area has the greatest potential for improving profit in today's competitive environment. The management accountant's greatest opportunity therefore is to help managers dispel the fog that shrouds most marketing decisions. The accountants complain bitterly that their cost data is ignored when marketing executives establish selling prices. Marketing executives argue that the cost data is of little value, because competition sets the selling prices.

That argument is only a half-truth. In a purely competitive environment, price is determined by the cost of the marginal producer. When the competitive price seems to be below out-of-pocket costs, prudent management should not wait for the competitor to go out of business but should restudy all product cost data developed by the management accountants. This restudy often leads to design changes, material substitutions, and methods improvements. The result is an adequate profit margin on the competitive price which seemed to be below out-of-pocket costs.

COST DATA FOR PRICING PRODUCTS

In manufacturing industries, the most prevalent method of determining costs for pricing products is as follows:

1 Production cost centers are established by machine or process.

2 All departmental labor and expense, service department expense, and fixed (or period) manufacturing expenses are distributed to the cost centers.

3 Costing rates per unit (usually work-hour or machine-hour) are set for each cost center based on either the normal level of activity or the forecast.

4 The cost estimate for a given product shows the work- or machine-hours for each cost center and the quantities of material required per unit.

5 The work- or machine-hours, extended by the costing rates, and the quantities of material extended by the estimated prices, are totaled to get aggregate manufacturing cost.

6 To that total, percentage is added to cover selling and administrative expenses and to provide for a profit.

In most cases, using full costing, the accounting department watches the overhead rates. Whenever volume of production fails to absorb the total cost of a given cost center, the rates are increased; when the volume overabsorbs the burden, the rates are reduced. Carrying the logic of this method of competitive pricing to an extreme, one of two situations results.

Case 1

The product is priced below the competitive level and volume is increasing. Burden rates are reduced because the factory burden is being overabsorbed. This results in lower prices, which causes volume to increase faster until the point is reached at which orders exceed capacity.

Case 2

The product is priced above the competitive level and volume is dropping. The costing rates are increased, to absorb the burden on the lower volume. This results in higher prices; the product becomes even less competitive and volume drops faster. Costing rates are increased again, and so on, until volume is zero and the costing rate is infinite.

In the first case, the company fails to maximize profits within the plant capacity; in the second, the company goes out of business. In the light of these results, it seems absurd to imply that any accountant would tell management to increase prices when the company is losing business to competitors and to reduce prices while taking business away from competitors. It is absurd when carried to extremes in a simple situation, but it is happening, to a limited degree, every day in thousands of complex businesses which use the whole-cost basis for the pricing of products.

Many companies solve this problem by using a long-range volume or capacity basis for setting burden rates. It has been stated in one of the National Association of Accountants' research reports:

> Over the long run, management's pricing objective is to obtain prices for the company's products which will return all costs and provide an adequate return on capital invested. For such a purpose, long-run normal or average cost of the product constitutes a better guide than does the cost which prevails in any given short period. One reason for this is that unit costs based upon short-period volume rise as volume declines and fall when volume rises. If management should follow short-period average costs in pricing, it might expect serious reduction in its share of the market potential if it increased selling prices in a time when activity in the industry was falling. On the other hand, to lower prices when a temporary rise in volume occurs destroys the opportunity to recover losses suffered in periods of low volume. These disadvantages can be minimized by developing product costs in which the fixed costs are spread evenly over the number of units produced during a period long enough to average out short-period volume fluctuations.[1]

For example, General Motors uses a level of activity based on a fixed percent of capacity in unitizing its period costs. Unit cost fluctuations from year to year therefore reflect changes in material costs, wage rates, and operating efficiency only. Accountants who use this long-range volume method of allocating fixed (or period) costs avoid the absurdity of telling management to raise prices when the volume of sales is shrinking. However, they still fail to give management cost data of most assistance in selecting the best price to meet a given competitive situation. Many go through extensive computations of comparative overall costs and profits with a given order at various selling prices. This is time-consuming and costly. Obviously, it can be justified only with large orders.

By using the flexible budget rates for costing products as described in Chapter 2, all this confusion and complexity can be avoided. Most pricing decisions can be made by nonaccounting executives, using simple arithmetic.

The advocates of absorption costing suggest that direct costs serve for a simple one-product business, but do not cost individual products fairly. They

---

[1] *NACA Bulletin,* Research Series no. 24, Section 2, August 1953, p. 1709.

point out that, in actual practice, one usually has many products that use different proportions of the time of costly facilities. They say, "How do you know that each product is carrying its fair share of burden if you do not allocate fixed manufacturing costs to products?"

As described in Chapter 3, period costs are allocated to products or product groups as part of the zero-base budgeting operation at least once a year. However, they are allocated in total for the planned volume and sales mix. They are never unitized. It is the unitizing of period costs that makes absorption costs confusing to operating managers because these unit costs are valid only with the assumed volume and mix. By showing the allocation in total, along with the forecasted volume and mix, confusion is avoided. Operating management can see clearly the true interrelation of prices, costs, and volume.

The profit plan for the XYZ Company (Table 9-1) demonstrates how this works. Not only are period charges allocated to product groups but capital employed is also allocated. This method permits a realistic appraisal of both short-term pricing and long-range planning. By carefully selecting the product groups, the profit plan will show not only whether each product is carrying its fair share of burden but also whether or not it is providing an adequate return on capital employed. According to most authorities, this is the true measure of profitability. It should be noted that the profit plan, shown in

Table 9-1
XYZ MANUFACTURING COMPANY
PROFIT PLAN
(000 Omitted)

Description	Total	Line X	Line Y	Line Z	Idle plant
Sales forecast	$70,000	$10,000	$20,000	$40,000	0
Direct cost					
Material	$30,000	$ 2,000	$ 8,000	$20,000	0
Direct labor and expense	23,000	3,000	6,000	14,000	0
Total	$53,000	$ 5,000	$14,000	$34,000	0
Margin	$17,000	$ 5,000	$ 6,000	$ 6,000	0
Percent of sales (P/V)	24%	50%	30%	15%	
Planned period	12,100	2,500	4,000	5,500	100
Net operating profit	4,900	2,500	2,000	500	(100)
Percent of sales	7%	25%	10%	1.3%	0
Capital employed	33,000	10,000	12,000	10,000	1,000
Percent return	15%	25%	16.7%	5.0%	(10%)

Table 9-1, has a column for idle plant, which permits the use of a long-range normal volume basis for product pricing while at the same time providing realistic profit plans for the coming year. This column shows a profit in any year in which the planned volume is above the selected normal percent of capacity and a loss when it is below normal. Product line Z helps the short-term picture because of the $6-million margin. However, the return on capital employed is so low that long-range plans must be made to improve the margin, or replace the line, because at no projected volume, with the present profit/volume ratio, would there be an adequate return on capital employed. (Computation of the profit/volume ratio is discussed in detail in Chapter 10.)

DIRECT COSTING AND DAY-TO-DAY PRICING DECISIONS

How does one arrive at a target selling price with direct costing data? One method is to divide the estimated direct cost of the item to be priced by the complement of the profit/volume ratio for that product line. Thus, the right price for a new product which is to become a part of product line Y (with a P/V of 0.30) and the direct cost of which is estimated to be $7.00 per unit would be as follows:

$$\text{Suggested price} = \frac{\$7.00}{1.00 - 0.30} = \$10.00$$

In actual practice, markup factors that also take into account the discount structure are usually computed in advance so that the suggested selling price is determined by multiplying the direct cost by the proper markup factor. For example, in a handmade glassware company that uses direct costs for pricing, the markup factor includes the dealer's markup so that when the direct cost is multiplied by the markup factor the "target" retail price is determined.

The merchandising and pricing executives then compare the new item with other items in the line and select a price that will look appropriate to the retail customer. If this price fails to provide an adequate ratio margin, consideration is given to either redesigning the piece or not adding it to the line.

This method works well if the material content is small or the proportion is relatively constant within a product division. However, in product divisions in which the relative material content varies widely, it is necessary to use a different markup on material from that used on direct conversion cost. For example, assume that two new products have been designed for line Y. Product A requires extensive machining processes using costly facilities. Product B

is an assembly of expensive purchased parts. Use of the same markup on material and conversion cost for these two products would result in a suggested price too low for the fabricated product and one that is too high for the assembly.

Companies using direct costs for pricing have various methods of solving this problem. For example, a well-known rubber company applies the markup to the direct conversion cost and then adds the material cost without markup. A manufacturer of upholstered chairs adds a markup to the material content based on the turnover rate and another markup to the direct conversion cost to provide a target return on capital employed. With this as a guide, the price is selected by comparing it with prices of other chairs in the line. Then the conversion markup for the selected price is computed. If this margin is below a certain minimum, the chair is redesigned or dropped. This method is believed to be most effective, and direct costing provides a simple procedure for selecting markup percentages that will provide a target return on capital employed for any relative ratio of conversion cost to material cost. This procedure can be used by any company that has direct product costs.

DEVELOPING THE PRICING FORMULAS

Consider, for example, the XYZ Company. As stated above, product line Y has a number of individual products which show a wide range of relative material content. Therefore, instead of dividing the direct cost of a product by the complement of the profit/volume ratio, the proper markup for material, as distinct from conversion cost, must be determined so as to give the same return regardless of relative material content.

Table 9-2 is illustrative. The present average return for line Y is 16.7 percent on capital employed. Assume that the pricing committee selects a 20 percent objective. By working back from the capital employed, it is easy to determine the objective margin ($6,400,000) and the objective sales income ($20,400,000).

The markup on the material content is determined by the objective return and the turnover rate. In the case of product line Y, the turnover was found to be twice a year, so that a markup factor of 10 percent on the material content should produce a 20 percent return on the capital employed in material ($8,000,000 multiplied by 1.10 is $8,800,000). The sales income required to provide a 20 percent return on capital employed in conversion is therefore: $20,400,000 less $8,800,000 is $11,600,000. This, divided by the direct conversion cost, gives the conversion markup factor ($11,600,000 divided by $6,000,000 is 1.93).

Table 9-2
XYZ MANUFACTURING COMPANY
DATA FOR PRICING FORMULAS
Product Line Y (000 Omitted)

Description	Profit plan	Objective
Net sales (S)	$20,000	$20,400
Direct cost		
Material (M)	8,000	8,000
Labor and expense (L)	6,000	6,000
Total direct cost	14,000	14,000
Margin	6,000	6,400
P/V	30%	32.3%
Period expense	4,000	4,000
Net operating profit	2,000	2,400
Percent of (S)	10%	11.8%
Gross assets employed	12,000	12,000
Percent return	16.7%	20%
S/M	2.50	2.55
L/M	.75	.75

The formula for competitive prices is determined as follows: A group of products that are believed to be competitively priced is selected. A list is made showing for each product the sales price(s), the direct material cost (M), and the direct conversion cost (L). The ratios S/M and L/M are computed and a graph using S/M as the ordinate and L/M as the abscissa is drawn. The line of best fit is selected by visual inspection or the method of least squares. This line represents the competitive pricing formula, and the objective pricing formula is then drawn. Such a comparison of competitive practices with objective return on capital employed provides a clear understanding of areas in which improvements can be made within the competitive structure. Figure 9-1 shows this development for the XYZ Company.

EXECUTIVE DECISIONS MADE EASY

Direct costing makes the interrelation of prices, costs, and volume crystal clear and so makes many difficult decisions easy. It avoids unnecessary complexity by simply keeping period and direct costs separate in accounting records and

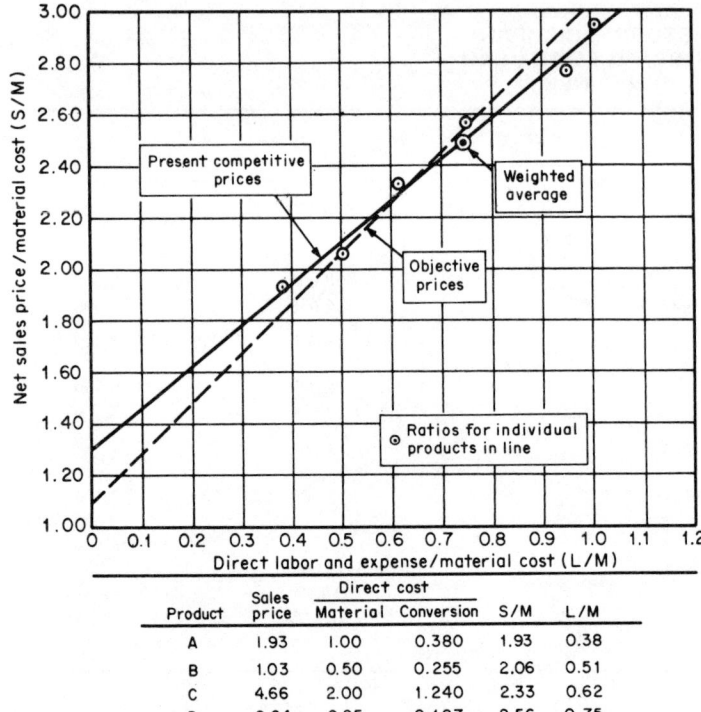

Product	Sales price	Direct cost Material	Direct cost Conversion	S/M	L/M
A	1.93	1.00	0.380	1.93	0.38
B	1.03	0.50	0.255	2.06	0.51
C	4.66	2.00	1.240	2.33	0.62
D	0.64	0.25	0.187	2.56	0.75
E	2.08	0.75	0.713	2.77	0.95
F	0.32	0.11	0.111	2.91	1.01

Present competitive prices:
Mark up on material = 1.30
Mark up on labor and expense
$$= \frac{2.50 - 1.30}{0.75} = 1.60$$

Objective pricing formula:
(20% return on total assets)
S/M = 1.1 (Turnover = twice/year)
$$S/L = \frac{2.55 - 1.10}{0.75} = 1.93$$

Figure 9—1 Development of competitive pricing formula and objective pricing formula for XYZ Manufacturing Company.

reports so that the cost for any actual volume of production and sales is stated clearly.

With this basic data, it is relatively easy for managers to understand true price-cost-volume relationships, which is the keystone of effective marketing decisions.

Table 9-3 shows a typical absorption cost product sheet. It is valid only for the planned sales volume of 5000 units and fails to show profit-volume relationships.

As soon as the volume level is changed, the overhead per unit is wrong because it includes fixed costs such as depreciation and rent, which will not

Table 9-3
CONVENTIONAL COST FORM
Cost Analysis—Product X

Pounds unit = 400	Dollars per unit	Profit plan
Planned volume—units		5,000
Net sales	$100.00	$500,000
Manufacturing cost:		
Direct labor	15.00	75,000
Material	30.00	150,000
Manufacturing overhead	30.00	150,000
Total manufacturing cost	$ 75.00	$375,000
Gross profit	25.00	125,000
Percent	25%	25%
Selling and administrative costs	15.00	75,000
Operating profit	$ 10.00	$ 50,000

change with the volume. Since, in most marketing problems, volume is the most important variable, cost data in this form tends to confuse the sales and marketing executives.

Table 9-4 shows the direct cost form of product cost sheet for this same product. The direct costs are kept separate from fixed costs. Therefore, the

Table 9-4
THE WRIGHT FORM
Cost Analysis—Product X

Pounds/unit = 400	Dollars per unit	Profit plan
Planned volume—units		5,000
Net sales	$100.00	$500,000
Direct cost:		
Material	30.00	150,000
Variable labor	20.00	100,000
Other direct expense	10.00	50,000
Total direct cost	$ 60.00	$300,000
Margin	40.00	200,000
Percent (P/V)	40%	40%
Specific period expense		100,000
Product contribution		$100,000
Allocated period expense		50,000
Operating profit		$ 50,000

profit results of marketing decisions can be computed from cost data shown on this form.

For example the following questions and computations show the kind of day-to-day decisions that can be made, based entirely on the concept of maximizing profit margins within committed period or capacity costs:

Question 1—If we cut the price by 15 percent, how much additional sales do we need to offset the price cut?

Amount of reduction per unit	$15.00
New margin per unit	$25.00
Present total margin	$200,000
New volume required—units	8,000
Percent increase	60

Question 2—If we increase the price 15 percent and drop 20 percent of our volume, what will be the effect on our profit?

Increase in margin per unit	$15.00
New margin per unit	$55.00
New volume—units	4,000
New total margin	$220,000
Less: present margin	200,000
Net change	+$ 20,000

Question 3—If we hire a special salesperson for $12,000 per year (including expenses) to promote product X, how much additional sales volume must be reached before profits begin to increase?

Margin per unit	$40.00
Additional units required	300

Question 4—How much must we raise the price of product X to make up for the 15 percent wage increase?

Increase in labor cost per unit	$3.00
Complement of P/V ratio	.60
Increase in price	$5.00

When your capacity is limited because of a bottleneck machine, you still can maximize profits by promoting products that have the greatest margin per hour of that machine's time. If your production is limited by your melting capacity, then you can maximize profits by promoting products with greatest margin per ton. If you have plenty of available capacity, then your profitability index is simply the P/V ratio.

LONG-RANGE POLICY DECISIONS

In the area of pricing, however, the day-to-day decisions have long-range implications. Guidelines for pricing must therefore show management both the short-term margin and the long-term return on investment.

In this connection, it is important to recognize that there is no such thing as a long-range pricing decision. Rather, there are long-range pricing policies, with a sequence of day-to-day pricing decisions within those broad policies.

Good pricing decisions call for instant knowledge of cost-price-volume relationships, which direct costing provides. Good pricing strategy requires profit guidelines which show the long-range implications of a given pricing decision in terms of return on investment. Many students of scientific management endorse the statement that pricing is the most neglected facet of modern management. For that reason, development of superior methods and strategies for pricing provides one of the best potentials for profit improvement.

Here is an actual example. A few years ago, we were installing a direct cost system for a clock company and the sales manager came to us with a competitive pricing problem. One of their models was listed in a certain premium catalog along with clocks from two other major producers.

Our client had a highly automated production line with high fixed overhead. They had experienced quality problems so that their share of the market had been declining over the prior 3 years until they had reached a level of only 10,000 units per year. With each decline, the accountants raised the burden rate so that the product looked less and less profitable.

At that point, the two competitors offered a substantial price reduction. The customer asked our client to quote the same price or they would have to drop them from the catalog. Because of a standing rule that prohibited pricing below full manufacturing cost, our client could not quote this competitive price.

The sales manager wanted to know what the decision would be if we based it on direct cost. We checked the direct cost and margin with this price and found that the P/V ratio was about the same as for some of their more profitable lines.

The decision was obvious. They would have automatic equipment sitting idle if they were dropped from the catalog. Based on the sales manager's forecast, we estimated that they should get at least a $150,000-per-year margin on this product if they met the competitive price.

We pointed out that since we had not yet developed our profit guidelines for long-term pricing policies, we couldn't be sure that they should accept orders that would require capital expenditures to increase capacity. Within their available capacity, however, there was no question but that they should meet the competitor's price.

Later, when we completed our pricing guidelines and computed return on capital employed for this clock, we found that even with the reduced price they had a good return when sales volume reached normal capacity. A few months ago, the president of this company told us that this product had grown in volume to 750,000 units per year and they now considered it one of the most profitable items in their line.

MARKETING EXECUTIVES SECOND-GUESS PRICES

A prime reason for the frustration and fog that shrouds most pricing decisions is the procedure of having the accounting and cost estimating people determine the price by formula and then have marketing executives second-guess the price based on their feel for the competitive climate.

Management accountants complain bitterly that their product costs are ignored when marketing executives set prices. Marketing executives, on the other hand, argue that costs are of little value for pricing because prices are fixed by competition.

It would seem that marketing executives would leave no stone unturned in finding out what the competitors are doing. Instead, many executives simply take a salesperson's word for something that might have been learned from a prevaricating purchasing agent.

DEVELOPING PROFIT GUIDELINES

With the Wright system of direct costing, profit guidelines are developed at least once a year. As described in Chapter 3, the planned sales are divided into appropriate product groups.

These groups are determined both by competitive marketing differences and the utilization of different facilities. For example, if part of a product line is produced on high-cost automated equipment, the automated items would be shown as a separate group.

For each group, direct costs are divided into material and conversion costs, and the margin and P/V ratios are determined. Then, period costs are allocated based on the data shown in the decision packages. These period costs are allocated in total. They are never unitized.

As we demonstrated in Table 9-3, it is the unitizing of period costs that confuses managers because these unit costs are valid only for the assumed volume. Then, total assets employed are allocated to product groups with the same care that is used with period costs.

Finally, the operating profit and return on capital employed are determined for each product group. It should be noted that when you have substantial idle plant, such as in the clock example, the excess capacity costs and capital employed are charged to an idle plant column. This technique permits the use of a normal capacity basis for evaluating the profitability of each product line while providing realistic profit plans for the coming year.

In cases where the material content is small or relatively constant for a product line, the pricing guidelines are determined by relating return on capital employed to margin per machine-hour, per ton, or per dollar of sales. For example, in the paper industry, guidelines are computed for each product group based on margin per paper machine-hour.

However, in product groups where the relative material content varies widely, it is necessary to develop guidelines which take into account the fact that to achieve a given return we must use a different markup on material cost than on conversion cost (see Figure 9-1).

In order to solve this problem, we have developed guidelines in the form of a grid which show at a glance the return on capital employed for any product in a given group regardless of relative material content.

Figure 9-2 shows this grid for Wright "widgets," and Figure 9-3 shows the procedure for constructing the grid based on the annual profit plan for this product group.

The concept is based on the theory that the price to determine a given return on capital employed can be determined by establishing a markup on material based on the period costs related to material and the annual turnover rate for material inventory. Then a markup for conversion cost is determined to achieve this same return.

By utilizing two ratios, the S/M and the L/M, one can easily determine these two markup rates.

Figure 9-2 shows pricing guidelines for Wright widgets based on the operating plan for the fiscal year. The y intercept, or the ratio at zero conversion cost, is the markup on material cost; and the slope of each line represents the

114 Management Accounting Simplified

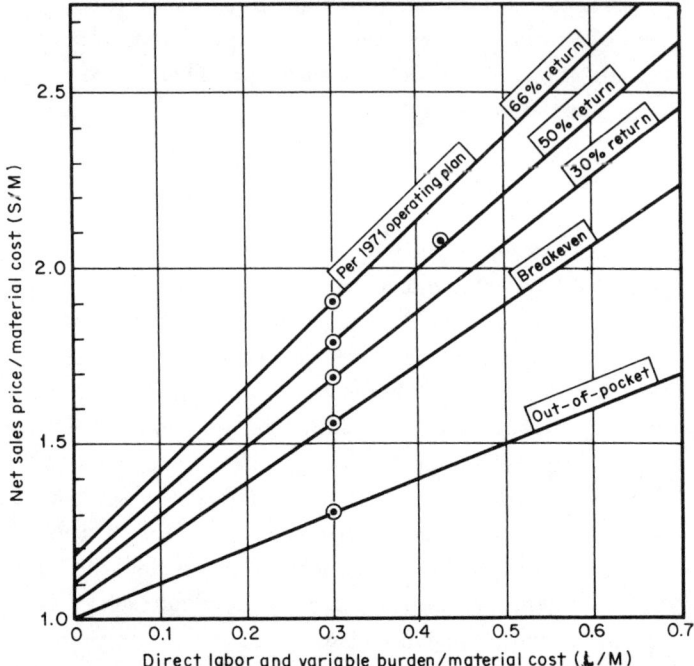

Figure 9—2 Pricing guidelines for Wright widgets based on the fiscal-year operating plan.

markup on conversion cost for each level of profitability. In other words, the slope is S/M less L/M, which equals S/L. This is the markup on conversion cost.

Utilizing the Guidelines

Having developed the pricing guidelines, how can they be used to improve profits? In the first place, the order in which accounting and marketing participate in the decision making should be reversed.

Our experience has shown that, when accountants determine a target price by formula, marketing executives will often accept it even when they have reason to believe they could get a higher price. When the formula price is above what marketing executives believe to be the competitive price, they refuse to accept it and suggest various reasons for quoting below the formula price.

Profit Guidelines for Marketing Decisions **115**

Marketing executives should establish the price they think they can get and then let the accountants predict what the long-range return would be if all products in the line were priced at that profitability level. This procedure accomplishes two goals. First, it forces marketing to do a better job of finding out what the competition is doing; second, it keeps them from missing the profit potential on products that the formula would price below the competitive level. In addition, it results in more weight being given to factors other than cost in making the final pricing decision.

ITEM		PLAN	CALCULATIONS FOR ALTERNATE RETURNS				PRODUCT "W" (PER UNIT)
			OUT-OF POCKET	BREAK-EVEN	30% RETURN	50% RETURN	
1 SALES	($)	15,159	10,427	12,543	13,724	14,512	2.300
3 DIRECT COST OF SALES							
4 MATERIAL	(M)	8,028	8,028	8,028	8,028	8,028	1.109
5 CONVERSION	(C)	2,399	2,399	2,399	2,399	2,399	.517
6 TOTAL DIRECT COSTS		10,427	10,427	10,427	10,427	10,427	1.626
8 MARGIN		4,732	0	2,116	3,297	4,085	.674
9 % (P/V)		31.2	0	16.9	24.0	28.1	29.3
11 PERIOD COSTS		2,116	2,116	2,116	2,116	2,116	
12 OPERATING PROFIT		2,616	(2,116)	0	1,181	1,969	
14 CAPITAL EMPLOYED							
15 MATERIAL		1,600	1,600	1,600	1,600	1,600	
16 OTHER ASSETS		2,337	2,337	2,337	2,337	2,337	
17 TOTAL ASSETS EMPLOYED		3,937	3,937	3,937	3,937	3,937	
18 % RETURN	(ROCE)	66.4%	(53.8%)	0	30.0%	50.0%	52%
20 INVENTORY TURNOVER: L4 ÷ L15 (T)							
22 MATERIAL MARKUP FACTOR:							
23 FORMULA: 1 + $\frac{R+H}{T}$		$1 + \frac{.664 + .25}{5}$	$1 + \frac{0}{5}$	$1 + \frac{0 + .25}{5}$	$1 + \frac{.30 + .25}{5}$	$1 + \frac{.50 + .25}{5}$	
25 FACTOR		1.18	1.00	1.05	1.11	1.15	
27 S/M: L1 ÷ L4		1.89	1.30	1.56	1.71	1.81	2.08
29 C/M: L5 ÷ L4		.30	.30	.30	.30	.30	4.24

WHERE R = RETURN OF CAPITAL EMPLOYED
H = PERIOD COSTS RELATED TO MATERIAL: ESTIMATED AT 25% FOR WRIGHT WIDGETS
T = INVENTORY TURNOVER: ESTIMATED AT 5 FOR WRIGHT WIDGETS

Figure 9—3 Based on the annual profit plan for Wright widgets, data for construction of grid shown in Figure 9-2.

In the widget example, here's how this procedure works: A new model of widget has just been designed, and marketing executives have compared it with other widgets in the line and with similar products being offered by competitors. They have determined they can get $2.30 each for the *W* widget. Then, the cost estimators and accountants determine that material cost is $1.109 and direct conversion cost is $0.517.

They then figure the S/M ratio, which is $2.30/$1.109, or 2.08; and the L/M ratio, which is $0.517/$1.109, or 0.424. They then plot this on the pricing guideline chart as shown on Figure 9-2 and tell marketing that this price represents a 52 percent return on capital employed and a 29.3 percent P/V ratio.

While these pricing guideline grids are easy to construct and use, in certain industries such as paper manufacturing and handmade glassware, direct reading charts may be used. In the paper manufacturing industry return on capital employed (ROCE) has been found to be directly related to margin per paper machine-hour. In the handmade glassware industry ROCE has been found to be directly related to the P/V ratios because the material cost factor is not a controlling factor. Thus, the pricing procedure in these two industries is as follows.

In order to analyze the competition, a paper company appoints an executive called the price coordinator whose full-time job is to keep track of what each of the competitors is doing with respect to cost effectiveness and pricing strategy. The marketing executive secures data from his sales representatives as to which companies are competing for a given order. After reviewing these reports with the price coordinator, the marketing executive states the price believed to be obtainable.

The accountants and cost estimators determine the margin per paper machine-hour that price would provide, and this determines the return on capital employed from a direct reading chart showing return on capital employed in terms of margin per hour. In case the ROCE is below a certain level, the final decision is referred to a pricing committee.

A handmade glassware company evaluates a new item for a product line by comparing it with other items in the line. They select the retail price that would look appropriate to a retail customer. The P/V ratio is determined, and the ROCE is selected from a direct reading chart that shows ROCE in terms of P/V. If the new piece does not provide an adequate return, consideration is given to redesigning the piece or not adding it to the line. The company has been using this procedure for years and has consistently improved profits in spite of fierce foreign competition while many of their domestic competitors have gone out of business.

OPPORTUNITY FOR MANAGEMENT ACCOUNTANTS

Since these are such simple procedures, why does the most difficult problem seem to be to educate people in the use of direct costs for pricing? By and large, this is because financial and operating executives have felt that direct cost data would be misused by sales executives and that prices would be quoted lower with direct cost data than with total cost data. Actually, a broad survey of companies which have converted to direct costs has shown that sales executives generally have held the line better with direct costs than they did before conversion.

There are two reasons for this. First, there is a general misconception about the behavior of burden rates in absorption costs. The average sales or operating executive considers that any price that absorbs some manufacturing overhead will help the profit picture. A survey of companies using direct costing showed an average of almost half of the manufacturing overhead to be direct or variable. When a sales executive is told that if the price is less than the direct cost, money will be lost out-of-pocket, the executive understands, and will act accordingly. With absorption costing, that point is not known. The sales executive thinks of all overhead as fixed; therefore, wishful thinking often rationalizes a price so low that it sometimes is below the out-of-pocket cost.

Second, with absorption costing, there is a confused picture with respect to responsibility in the profit-and-loss statement. This confusion is due to volume variances. With absorption costs, the price-volume results of policies and practices of the sales and merchandising people are mixed up with the manufacturing volume variance. For the short term, production volume is controlled by the manufacturing people. Thus, the profit-and-loss statement fails to show whether pricing policies are paying off as planned. With direct costing, the volume variances are eliminated so that the overall profit contribution achieved provides a clear measure of the effectiveness of pricing policies. The result: more mature and responsible pricing decisions.

In any pricing situation, it is the proper function of the management accountant to present to operating management the profit results of various alternatives. No matter whether the problem is simple or complex, direct costing provides the best basis for both short- and long-range decision making. Eliminating volume variances achieves a clear-cut separation of sales and manufacturing responsibilities and provides objective measurement of the quality of pricing decisions.

10
PRACTICAL LONG-RANGE PLANNING

Long-range planning in American industry has received the prime attention of sophisticated managers only since World War II. In less than 40 years it has emerged as the symbol of executive excellence and the pinnacle of achievement for professional managers. It has become one of the bywords of management jargon. In some respects, it has suffered from becoming a "fad" without enough knowledge from Kipling's "six honest serving-men": what, why, how, when, where, and who.

A review of existing management literature pertaining to long-range planning reveals very little before World War II. Then, in the following 15 years, there appeared a vast number of articles dealing with the subject, but often disguised under other titles. Since 1962, however, there have been at least six full-length books published and an avalanche of monographs dealing specifically with long-range planning.

Planning means looking ahead and anticipating problems and crises. It means planning action to avoid these anticipated problems instead of correcting them after they happen. It is a state of mind that causes managers to determine future courses of action instead of meeting each crisis as it occurs.

A fog of uncertainty shrouds the future, and this fog grows denser the further we try to look ahead. Grappling with the uncertainties looming in this fog is the essence of long-range planning. Selecting the probable certainties isolates and reduces the number of uncertainties. Provision in the plans may be made for some uncertainties and others may be ignored.

For example, consider the possibility of nuclear war. No one knows whether or not it will take place, or when. One must, therefore, decide whether this possibility should be taken into account in the long-range plans or whether it should be ignored. You might decide to make a long-range plan which would take this possibility into account. You could plan to move your central office away from a probable target area, and you could include civil defense shelters in all of your new offices. On the other hand, you could ignore the possibility of nuclear war. This is the assumption most companies have adopted because they have concluded that the probability is so small and the cost so great that there is no point in making plans which would be valid only in case of a nuclear war.

In peering into the fog-shrouded future, it is necessary to develop certain assumptions about the general environment in which a given company will operate during the span of the long-range strategic plan. In general industry, this is the most difficult of all areas of long-range planning. The planner must not only make many environmental assumptions but must consider and forecast technological changes.

Consider the case of General Wood and Sears, Roebuck and Company, as related by A. D. Chandler.[1]

After World War I General Wood joined Montgomery Ward and Company. Wood had developed a method of projecting population trends while he was stationed in Panama. He told his associates at Montgomery Ward that his projections showed that the United States was rapidly becoming an urban nation. Since the mail-order customers lived in rural areas, the company should adjust itself to these changes. Moreover, the mass-produced automobile was making it possible for the farmer to get to town more easily and to buy from a much broader assortment of goods than was available at the crossroads general store. In 1921, Wood pointed out to Montgomery Ward's president, T. Merseles, that chain stores such as J. C. Penney were already beginning to exploit this small-town market. He recommended that the company use its existing branch houses as distributing points to compete with these chain stores. With its highly developed purchasing organization and its long-established reputation, Wood insisted that they could walk away from these chain stores in any market.

President Merseles paid little attention to Wood's proposals and so in 1924 Wood resigned from Montgomery Ward and joined Sears, Roebuck and Company in a newly created post of vice president of factories and retail stores.

With Chairman Rosenwald's complete backing, Wood began immediately to implement his long-range strategic plan. The rest of it is well-known his-

---

[1] Alfred D. Chandler, Jr., *Strategy and Structure: Chapters in the History of the Industrial Enterprise*, MIT Press, Cambridge, Mass., 1962, pp. 225–237.

tory, and Wards is still trying to catch up with Sears in the retail store end of the business.

While the Sears story represents a relatively simple projection of a long-term trend and a sound interpretation of its business potential, most industry is faced today with a much more complex problem involving technological change and the life cycle of products.

Consider the case of the Martin Company of Baltimore, Maryland, as presented by Brian Scott.[2]

Through World War II and the Korean War, Martin was a major aircraft manufacturer. In 1952 sales were $144 million, consisting largely of B-57 jet bombers.

As a result of long-range strategic planning, Martin made some radical changes in their product line. They forecasted that the successful company of the 1960s would be oriented toward research and development. They proceeded to convert their business from a productive business to a research and development business and became the prime contractor and integrator of the Titan missile program. By the end of 1959 they had converted 80 percent of their production from airframes to rockets and electronics. Their sales for that year were $524 million and earnings were 16.8 percent of net worth, which was much higher than any other major aircraft manufacturer. Their competitors, who had failed to develop sound long-range plans, were struggling along with less than a third of their previous volume.

By 1961, long-range planning studies led the Martin executives to conclude that the missile business was going to drop because the United States and Russia had reached a stalemate. Therefore, their strategic long-range plans called for them to diversify into the field of astronautics. While this is still basically research and development work, it includes many features that are radically different from missile development and production.

Many firms give lip-service to long-range planning and develop very attractive programs. Many of these plans will not survive the experience of declining profits or even losses. Most long-range plans will be dumped when they interfere with short-term profit objectives. The firm that has the foresight to continue to implement its long-range plans during short-term periods of low volume will have a keen competitive advantage.

For example, several years ago, Seagrams developed a long-range plan for increasing distilling and warehousing capacity based on population projections and consumption per capita. The first year following development of the

---

[2] Brian W. Scott, *Long-Range Planning in American Industry*, American Management Association, New York, 1965, p. 75.

long-range plan, general business went into a recession and liquor sales fell sharply as marginal drinkers switched to beer. Seagrams held to its long-range expansion plan even though many of its competitors cut back on their expansion programs. Seven years later, as this extra production reached the age for bottling, the results of this decision paid off, and the company forged ahead of its competitors and has continued to stay ahead of them.

PLANNING THE PROGRAM

How does a company go about instituting a long-range planning program? There are four basic steps:

1 Establish a planning climate.

2 Evaluate current capabilities.

3 Develop alternate courses of action.

4 Establish the strategic plan.

Establish a Planning Climate

The first step, which is the establishment of a planning climate, is usually initiated with the appointment of a vice president of corporate planning and the holding of a top management seminar on the subject of long-range planning. During this seminar it is hoped that every member of the top management staff will become convinced that long-range planning is essential to the future profit and growth of the company.

Evaluate Capabilities

Before deciding where a given company wants to go, it is important to determine just where it is. Evaluation of a company's capabilities, both tangible and intangible, must play an important role in the development of long-range strategies.

One of the first questions to be answered is, "What business are we in, and what is the nature of that business?" The answer to this may seem obvious, but this is not the case. It is far from obvious and should be answered only after careful study and hard thinking.

A good illustration of the importance of a careful answer to this question is to be found in the history of the motion picture industry.[3] When commercial television was introduced after World War II, the motion picture companies did everything they could to retard its growth, even though they were well equipped to enter the new television industry. They had the skills and resources to beat all competition in this new field. However, they saw TV as a threat to rather than an enhancement of their established business. Hollywood has never recovered from this myopia. Many established firms got into financial trouble and some disappeared. Their self-appraisal had been too narrow.

Develop Alternate Courses of Action

Based on evaluation of "where we are," the next step in the planning process is to lay out various propositions as to "where we want to be" in view of projected potentials in the industry.

The focal point of all long-range planning should be to achieve a satisfactory return on investment along with a sound rate of growth. Many companies confuse their long-range goals by thinking primarily of expansion. Such a program of growth can lead to a decrease rather than an increase in profitability and is not a wise management objective. Sales, profit, and facilities plans provide the basis for rate of growth and return on capital employed. The long-range financing plan provides the financial leverage factor which converts return on capital employed to return on investment. We will consider long-range financing plans in detail below.

Establish the Strategic Plan

The final step is the establishment of the strategic long-range plan. In most companies this is delegated to a special task force. Utilizing data which will have been developed during the organization seminar, the planning task force develops a recommended strategic plan for submission to the chief executive officer and the board of directors. This plan should answer such questions as:

1 What business do we want to be in?

2 What customers do we want to serve?

---

[3] Scott, *Longe-Range Planning in American Industry*, p. 84.

3 What geographical areas do we want to reach?
4 What products and services do we want to provide?
5 What rate of growth do we want to achieve?
6 What level of profitability do we plan to achieve?
7 How is this growth and profitability to be achieved?
8 How is this growth and profit potential to be financed?
9 What organization and capital structure should we plan?
10 What facilities, personnel, and executive talent will be required to meet these objectives?

After revisions and final approval by the board of directors, it becomes official strategic plan. Each year it is revised and updated by the same procedure.

MEASURING MANAGEMENT EFFICIENCY

Students of scientific management have generally agreed that the most valid yardstick for measuring the overall effectiveness of management is *return on investment*, which is the ratio of *net profit* to *net worth*. However, this ratio has one weakness. It can be greatly distorted by the relative position of a given company in the cycle of financial growth or by the methods used for securing funds for expansion programs. For example, assume two companies with the same management capabilities. Company A has just built a new plant and has secured capital for expansion through a 20-year bond issue. Company B has just built a new plant and has secured funds by issuing common stock. Obviously, the comparison of these two companies would show a considerable difference in net profit to net worth. Or, assume the same method of financing, but one company has completed the new plant and has it operating at a profit while the other has just started operating its new plant.

In other words, this overall comparison of net profit to net worth is valid only when adjusted for the method of financing and the relative position in the cycle of financial growth. (See Table 10-1.)

In order to avoid this distortion, many companies have used net worth plus long-term debt as the investment base. This is the famous *duPont method*, which is expressed in the duPont formula:

$$\text{Investment} = \text{Fixed assets} + \text{working capital}$$

Other companies, with emphasis on operating management, have used *total assets* (which is net worth plus all debt). Still others have used *fixed assets* plus *inventories*.

The root of the problem has been the attempt to get a single benchmark for both operating and financial decisions. It therefore appears that if operating management were measured separately from financial management, it would be relatively easy to sort out the effect of the long-term cycle of financial growth in comparing overall results of a number of companies for a given period.

Since most management decisions are either of an operating or financial nature, this separation has proved entirely practical. Thus, overall management performance would be measured in two parts:

Operating management performance

Financial management performance

The product of these two performance ratios would equal return on investment or net profit to net worth. Thus, comparisons can easily take into account methods of financing and relative position in the cycle of financial growth.

What then would constitute the most accurate measure of these two facets of management? First, let's consider operating management.

OPERATING MANAGEMENT INDEX

Recent opinions of authorities on the subject have generally agreed that the most accurate yardstick for making operating decisions is the return on capital employed, whether it be furnished by stockholders, bond holders, banks, or vendors. Thus, the simplest index is *operating profit* to *capital employed*, which in most cases is simply total assets.

The exception occurs when there is an excess of funds on hand because of financial management problems. In such cases the excess should be excluded from capital employed in operations. In other words, the excess should not be charged to operating management but should be deducted from total assets. Thus, the *operating management ratio* equals operating profit to total assets employed, excluding excess funds.

The old profit-to-sales ratio for measuring operating performance fails to take into account degrees of integration and capital turnover. Profit to capital employed is not only a more accurate index but is also valid for comparing

Table 10-1
COMPARATIVE RATIOS
By Different Methods of Financing Expansion (000 Omitted)

Situation before expansion	U.S. average*	Description	Bond financing	Common stock financing	Situation after expansion†
$70,000		Net sales	$95,000	$95,000	$70,000
53,000		Direct cost	70,500	70,500	53,000
17,000		Profit contribution	24,500	24,500	17,000
.243	.312	P/V	.258	.258	.243
12,100		Period expense	14,100	14,100	14,100
4,900		Operating profit	10,400	10,400	2,900
.288	.259	Margin of safety	.424	.424	.171
		Less interest on bonds	2,000		
		Adjustment to period costs in inventory	(400)	(400)	
4,900		Profit before income tax	8,800	10,800	2,900
2,450		Provision for income tax	4,400	5,400	1,450
2,450		Net profit	4,400	5,400	1,450
4,000		Cash	7,000	7,000	7,000
5,000		Receivables	7,000	7,000	5,000
8,000		Inventories	12,000	12,000	12,000
16,000		Fixed assets	36,000	36,000	36,000
33,000		Total capital employed	62,000	62,000	60,000
16,500		Net worth and earned surplus	16,500	16,500	16,500
		Paid in capital		20,000	20,000
$16,500		Total net worth	$16,500	$36,500	$36,500
		Comparative ratios			
2.12	1.568	Capital turnover	1.532	1.532	1.166
.148	.127	Profit to capital employed	.167	.167	.048
.50	.488	Financial operations ratio	.50	.50	.50
2.00	1.894	Financial leverage	3.758	1.700	1.644
.148	.118	Return on investment	.267	.148	.040

*Ratios for U.S. manufacturing companies with asset size of $50 to $100 million.
†New plant completed but not yet shipping product. Present plant in full production.

companies in the same industry or in different industries regardless of the degree of integration, method of financing, or relative position in the cycle of financial growth. It is also just as valid for comparing divisions, plants, or products within a given company.

For analysis purposes this index may be broken down into three parts:

1. Profit/volume ratio   = P/V
2. Margin of safety (MS)   = OP/P
3. Capital turnover   = V/A
   (P/V) × (OP/P) × (V/A) = OP/A

The P/V Ratio

The profit/volume ratio is a most effective means of expressing cost-price relationships. It represents the part of each sales dollar that remains after paying all direct or out-of-pocket costs. For companies using direct costing it is the ratio of profit contribution or margin to net sales. The simplest method of determining this ratio for a company not using direct costing is by the use of the P/V breakeven chart.

As shown by Figure 10-1, a P/V breakeven chart can be drawn simply by plotting the monthly operating profit against sales, determining the y intercept by summarizing all period expenses, and then drawing the line of best fit.

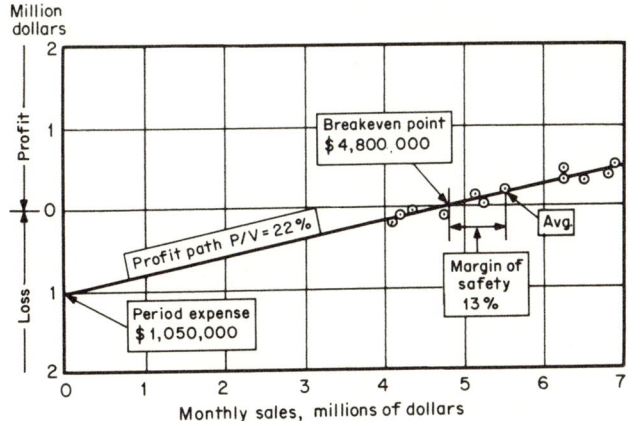

Figure 10–1 Profit/volume ratio (P/V) breakeven chart for the ABC Manufacturing Company.

Period expenses are those that do not vary with short-term fluctuations in production or sales volume but are a function of time or executive decision. They are sometimes called fixed or capacity costs. Advertising, rent, depreciation, and executive salaries are examples of period expenses.

The P/V ratio for Figure 10-1 can be figured as follows:

$$P/V = \frac{\text{Period expense}}{\text{Breakeven sales volume}} = \frac{1{,}050{,}000}{4{,}800{,}000} = 22\%$$

Margin of Safety

The *margin of safety* is the percent sales volume may drop before reaching the breakeven point. For Figure 10-1, it can be figured as follows:

$$\frac{5{,}500 - 4{,}800}{5{,}500} = \frac{700}{5{,}500} = 13\%$$

Figure 10-2 shows a way to figure margin of safety by even simpler arithmetic.

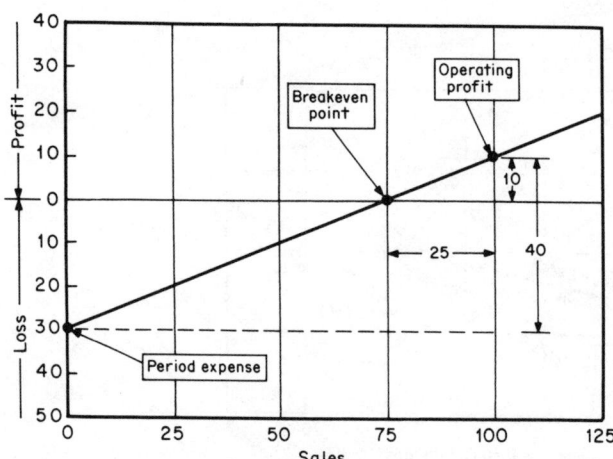

Figure 10–2 Profit/volume ratio (P/V) chart showing method for determining margin of safety.

$$\text{MS} = \frac{25}{100} = \frac{\text{Operating profit}}{\text{Period expense} + \text{Operating profit}} = \frac{10}{30 + 10} = 0.25 = 25\%$$

Note that the similar triangles make this ratio the same as the previously described method of computing margin of safety.

It should be noted that for companies using direct costing, these data are shown on the regular operating statements.

Sales-to-Assets Ratio

The third factor that determines the effectiveness of operating management is the intensity of use of capital. That is the number of dollars of sales secured for each dollar of capital employed. This is called the *sales-to-assets ratio* or the *capital turnover* (V/A).

The overall operating management index is therefore the product of the three parts: profit/volume ratio times margin of safety times capital turnover, which equals operating profit to capital employed, or

$$(P/V) \times (OP/P) \times (V/A) = OP/A$$

MEASURING FINANCIAL MANAGEMENT PERFORMANCE

Financial management performance can be measured accurately only over a long period. Comparative performance ratios should, therefore, be based on moving averages of from 3 to 5 years.

The *financial management performance ratio* is broken down into two parts:

Financial operations ratio

Financial leverage ratio

The *financial operations ratio* is simply the part of the operating profit that is brought down to net. It is the ratio of new profit after taxes to operating profit. Interest paid on loans, profit on security transactions, and income taxes are its main elements.

The *financial leverage ratio* is the measure of financial management's effectiveness in getting as much of the capital as practicable from sources other than common stock or retained earnings. It is the ratio of capital employed to net worth.

Table 10-2 shows the method of computing these ratios for both short-range and long-range comparisons.

Table 10-2
METHOD OF COMPUTING RATIOS

Assume the following financial data		Then	
Sales (V)	$100	Profit/volume ratio	$= \dfrac{P}{V} = \dfrac{40}{100} = .40$
Direct costs	60		
Profit contribution (P)	$ 40	Margin of safety	$= \dfrac{OP}{P} = \dfrac{10}{40} = .25$
Period expense	30		
Operating profit (OP)	$ 10	Profit to sales	$= \dfrac{OP}{V} = \dfrac{10}{100} = .10$
Other income and deductions	5		
(including Income Taxes)		Capital turnover	$= \dfrac{V}{A} = \dfrac{100}{50} = 2.00$
Net profit (NP)	$ 5		
Capital employed (A)	$ 50	Profit to Capital employed*	$= \dfrac{OP}{A} = \dfrac{10}{50} = .20$
Investment, or net worth (NW)	$ 40		
		Financial operations	$= \dfrac{NP}{OP} = \dfrac{5}{10} = .50$
		Financial leverage	$= \dfrac{A}{NW} = \dfrac{50}{40} = 1.25$
		Return on investment†	$= \dfrac{NP}{NW} = \dfrac{5}{40} = .125$

*Also: $\dfrac{P}{V} \times \dfrac{OP}{P} \times \dfrac{V}{A} = \dfrac{OP}{A}$

†Also: $\dfrac{OP}{A} \times \dfrac{NP}{OP} \times \dfrac{A}{NW} = \dfrac{NP}{NW}$

As stated before, long-range financial plans are required to provide the proper financial leverage and operating ratio to convert a good return on capital employed to optimum return on investment.

THE MASTER PROFIT PLAN

Consider the annual plan, which is called the master profit plan, as described in Chapter 3.

While the long-range plan specifies broad programs and projects by years, the master profit plan implements and details the specific long-range projects to be achieved in the current year. The annual master profit plan is set up in terms of return on capital employed rather than return on net worth.

By and large, the master profit plan is oriented in terms of product line and executive responsibility.

In addition to establishing the profit plan in terms of product line, similar analysis by market or channel of distribution provides a further insight into areas where sound planning can stimulate profit and growth. With multiplant operations, analysis by each production unit often is effective in revealing potentials for profit improvement.

Objectives

The first step in setting up the master profit plan is selecting an objective return on capital employed. The most effective way to select your objective return is to compare your company with a number of other companies in your industry. By making an appraisal of the relative strengths of each of the selected companies in terms of executive talent, product quality, production facilities, and distribution methods, your company may be slotted quite accurately. It is then a simple matter to select an objective return on capital employed that is ambitious enough to challenge your management but realistic enough to be attainable. Table 10-3 shows such an analysis for the ABC Casting Company and a group of competitive firms in the Gray Iron Foundry Industry.

These comparative ratios are developed from the annual survey made by Wright Associates. A copy of the 1977 comparative ratios is included as Figure 10-3, and a summary of all ratios since 1958 is included in Appendix III.

DEVELOPMENT OF OPERATING PLANS AND FEEDBACK

The development of specific operating programs to implement the strategic plans and to provide the mechanics for feedback determine the "when, where,

Table 10-3
COMPARATIVE RATIOS
(000 Omitted)

					Comparative data by company				
Description	ABC Castings Company	DEF Foundry Company	GHI Foundry Company	JKL Foundry Company	MNO Foundry Company	PQR Foundry Company	STU Foundry Company	VWX Foundry Company
Net sales	$ 70,000	$ 11,460	$ 6,275	$ 2,538	$ 1,977	$ 1,461	$ 1,055	$ 760
Direct cost	53,000	9,161	3,704	2,262	1,149	1,088	750	627
Margin	17,000	2,299	2,571	276	828	373	305	133
Profit volume (P/V) ratio	.243	.201	.410	.109	.419	.255	.289	.175
Period cost	12,100	1,232	1,339	160	591	247	172	122
Operating profit	4,900	1,067	1,232	116	237	126	133	11
Margin of safety (MS)	.288	.464	.479	.421	.286	.339	.436	.083
Operating profit to sales	.070	.093	.196	.046	.120	.087	.126	.015
Income taxes and other income and deductions	1,960	503	782	52	119	60	63	(1)
Net profit	2,940	564	450	64	118	66	70	12
Capital employed	33,000	6,088	4,305	1,468	860	232	595	501
Sales to capital employed	2,121	1,883	1,460	1,730	2,298	6,289	1,773	1,519
Operating profit to capital employed	.148	.175	.286	.079	.276	.545	.223	.022
Stockholder's investment	19,600	5,288	2,794	1,000	626	142	481	483
Financial operations ratio	.600	.529	.365	.552	.498	.523	.528	.1,083
Financial leverage	1,690	1,151	1,541	1,468	1,373	1,632	1,238	1,038
Return on investment	.150	.107	.161	.064	.188	.465	.146	.025

COMPARATIVE RATIOS 1977
U.S. Manufacturing Industries
(BASED ON FTC QUARTERLY FINANCIAL REPORT)*

CODE	CLASS	PROFIT VOLUME RATIO	MARGIN OF SAFETY	OPERATING PROFIT TO SALES	CAPITAL TURNOVER	PROFIT TO CAPITAL EMPLOYED	FINANCIAL OPERATIONS RATIO	FINANCIAL LEVERAGE	RETURN ON INVESTMENT
x	ALL MANUFACTURING CORP.	.372	.216	.081	1.440	.116	.658	1.873	.143
	BY ASSET SIZE:								
1	UNDER $5,000,000 ASSETS	.305	.195	.060	2.489	.148	.612	2.128	.193
2	5,000,000 TO 9,999,999	.286	.231	.066	2.146	.142	.484	1.991	.136
3	10,000,000 TO 24,999,999	.352	.196	.069	1.926	.133	.467	1.960	.121
4	25,000,000 TO 49,999,999	.341	.223	.076	1.775	.135	.487	1.897	.124
5	50,000,000 TO 99,999,999	.327	.244	.080	1.582	.126	.512	1.965	.127
6	100,000,000 TO 249,999,999	.334	.247	.082	1.560	.129	.531	1.891	.129
7	250,000,000 TO 999,999,999	.366	.234	.086	1.420	.122	.598	1.920	.140
8	1,000,000,000 AND OVER	.342	.256	.087	1.179	.103	.755	1.806	.141
	BY INDUSTRY CLASS:								
D	DURABLE GOODS	.407	.202	.082	1.441	.118	.642	1.922	.146
a	TRANSPORTATION EQUIPMENT	.409	.181	.074	1.719	.128	.675	2.046	.176
(1)	MOTOR VEHICLES & EQUIPMENT	.372	.210	.078	1.993	.156	.698	1.720	.187
(2)	AIRCRAFT	.395	.176	.067	1.372	.092	.609	2.632	.147
b	ELECTRICAL & ELECTRONIC EQUIPMENT	.422	.202	.085	1.436	.123	.628	2.006	.154
c	MACHINERY EXCEPT ELECTRICAL	.418	.256	.107	1.235	.132	.709	1.768	.165
d	FABRICATED METAL PRODUCTS	.328	.246	.081	1.681	.136	.593	1.960	.158
e	PRIMARY METAL INDUSTRIES	.261	.161	.042	1.149	.048	.543	1.997	.052
(1)	IRON AND STEEL	.226	.150	.034	1.220	.041	.421	1.962	.034
(2)	NON-FERROUS	.368	.158	.058	1.026	.060	.625	2.078	.078
f	STONE, CLAY & GLASS PRODUCTS	.431	.203	.087	1.407	.123	.621	1.830	.140
g	INSTRUMENTS & RELATED PRODUCTS	.544	.218	.119	1.179	.140	.750	1.606	.169
h	OTHER DURABLE MANUFACTURED PRODUCTS	.337	.236	.079	1.783	.142	.531	2.047	.154
N	NON-DURABLE GOODS	.314	.252	.079	1.439	.114	.671	1.826	.139
a	FOOD AND KINDRED PRODUCTS	.227	.241	.054	2.593	.140	.613	1.744	.150
b	TOBACCO MANUFACTURES	.552	.276	.153	.979	.150	.571	2.000	.171
c	TEXTILE MILL PRODUCTS	.234	.244	.057	1.837	.105	.400	1.900	.080
d	PAPER & ALLIED PRODUCTS	.361	.238	.086	1.259	.108	.611	1.866	.124
e	PRINTING & PUBLISHING	.394	.261	.103	1.618	.167	.563	1.895	.178
f	CHEMICALS & ALLIED PRODUCTS	.537	.199	.107	1.174	.125	.661	1.823	.151
(1)	INDUSTRIAL CHEMICALS & SYNTHETICS	.496	.215	.106	1.093	.116	.610	1.946	.138
(2)	DRUGS	.472	.303	.142	.959	.136	.870	1.594	.189
g	PETROLEUM & COAL PRODUCTS	.363	.233	.085	1.086	.092	.883	1.675	.136
h	RUBBER & MISC PLASTIC PRODUCTS	.335	.207	.070	1.535	.107	.565	1.955	.118
i	OTHER NON-DURABLE MANUFACTURED PRODS.	.292	.197	.058	2.337	.135	.500	1.969	.133

*SUPPLEMENTED BY SAMPLING TECHNIQUES APPLIED TO DATA FURNISHED BY REPRESENTATIVE COMPANIES TO OBTAIN "P/V" AND "MS" RATIOS.

Figure 10—3 Comparative ratios (1977) for U.S. manufacturing industries.

and who." These plans are primarily designed to specify action required during the current year to ensure adherence to the long-range strategic plan.

Here the critical path scheduling technique or PERT (see Chapter 6) can be used to good advantage. This technique not only ensures that implementational steps are planned for the right time but that feedback is provided to evaluate the effect of any failure to complete such steps on schedule.

The development and administration of the operational long-range plans and follow-up to see that they are carried out is usually assigned to a specific operating executive. It is no job for a committee. This executive usually reports to the chief executive officer and operates in a staff capacity.

The time span covered by the long-range operating plan is governed by the lead time required to achieve the strategic plan. In other words, if it requires 5 years to develop a specific part of the strategic plan, then the operating plan must cover a period of 5 years starting with the year when the first specific action must be taken.

For example, plans for opening new branches would require a 2-year span, automation a 3-year span, and the development of new services or lines of business might require 5 years.

Each year the long-range operating plan should be extended by one year and spelled out in detail on the PERT diagram and by executive responsibility.

And finally, feedback must be accurate and timely. Any breakdown of implementation of the plan must be reported immediately so that corrective action can be taken and so that the entire organization knows that management fully expects to achieve the long-range objectives.

So much for the theory of strategic long-range planning. When you come to the "how, when, and who," which is the implementation of the long-range plan, you must deal with the problems of human nature. Logan Cheek describes it in his excellent book, *Zero-Base Budgeting Comes of Age,* under the heading "The Politics of Rolling Up the Final Budget":

> At the top management level, there is quick recognition that the budget will have to be trimmed. The system now places that responsibility on the top men. Yet because activities are buried within function, executives lack the necessary understanding to know what to do or how to proceed. So an arbitrary task is edicted: to cut back 20 percent or to last year's level. Whether that is the appropriate amount is anyone's guess.
>
> The controller's staff now spend endless hours reviewing the submissions, suggesting tasks, and coordinating the rework. Theirs is a thankless task,

for lacking intimate knowledge of what the resources are for and why the spending is important, they must work in the dark—and their attention to detail, nurtured through many years in accounting, makes them least likely to enjoy this. They become increasingly frustrated and irritable, which leads to high turnover and morale problems. Extreme cases degenerate into ulcers and divorces. (I know of one situation where the controller came to work one morning faced with a nearly successful union organizing drive among his budget analysts!) As a last desperate move, the order is put out to cut, shave, chop, and trim.

If the order to cut is repeated over several planning cycles, a peculiar brand of gamesmanship develops among the cost center managers. On the one hand, an experienced cadre of clever men evolves. Each year they substantially overinflate their budget submissions, because they know that when their proposals have been cut, they will probably wind up with what they really needed anyway. The system implicitly rewards their behavior. On the other hand, those who made responsible submissions are penalized by the inevitable cuts. Few make the same mistake twice. The unfortunate result is that dishonesty is encouraged.

The end result of all this is that budgeting time becomes "dummy up" time, with few straightforward answers offered to critical business and planning issues and certainly not to the controller's staff. With that growing polarization between cost center manager, budget staff, and top management, there is often a total breakdown in communications.[4]

A PRACTICAL APPROACH

The procedure for the monthly report on profit plan, as described in Chapter 6, offers a practical solution to this problem. It is a simple matter for the chief executive officer to take responsibility for planning a favorable variance equal to the amount that the controller's staff believe the planned spending is overstated. (See Table 10-4.) This "gamesmanship" routine is therefore eliminated, the implementation plan can now be approved as submitted, and the directors can be assured that the strategic plan is attainable and managers at all levels can get back to the job of achieving the operating plan and developing a favorable overall variance equal to the amount for which the chief executive officer took responsibility.

[4]Logan Cheek, *Zero-Base Budgeting Comes of Age*, AMACOM, New York, 1977, p. 7.

Table 10-4
ABC CASTINGS COMPANY
REPORT ON PROFIT PLAN
($000 Omitted)

Actual February	Actual 2 months	Description	March forecast	April forecast	12 months forecast
		Net profit for period			
$612	$1,347	Master profit plan	$402	$550	$4,900
597	1,367	Actual and latest forecast	422	580	5,007
$(15)	$ 20	Variance	$ 20	$ 30	$ 107
		Analysis of variance			
		Sales			
$115	$ 150	Volume	$100	$ 75	$ 400
(85)	(70)	Price and Mix	(60)	(30)	(360)
(10)	(20)	Selling expense	(5)	......	10
$ 20	$ 60	Total sales	$ 35	$ 45	$ 50
		Manufacturing			
$(58)	$ (62)	Labor and expense	$(47)	$(40)	$ (250)
5	17	Material usage and scrap	8	10	85
10	11	Purchase price	10	5	120
$(43)	$ (34)	Total manufacturing	$(29)	$(25)	$ (45)
		Administration			
		General administrative			
		CEO cost reduction goal			
$ 6	$ (8)	Expense	$ 10	$ 7	$ 66
2	2	Idle plant	4	3	
$ 8	$ (6)	Total administration	$ 14	$ 10	$ 102

11
MEETING EXTERNAL REPORTING REQUIREMENTS

In 1955 the American Accounting Association's Committee on Concepts and Standards Underlying Corporate Financial Statements, was assigned the task of revising the 1948 statement of concepts and standards for the Association. Their report was issued in 1957 and covered a number of unresolved questions about the problem of matching costs against revenue for period income statements. Because of their impact on management accounting, Chapters III and IV of the report, reprinted in *The Accounting Review* (October 1957), are presented below.

III
Assets

Assets are economic resources devoted to business purposes within a specific accounting entity; They are aggregates of service-potentials available for or beneficial to expected operations. The significance of some assets may be uniquely related to the objectives of the business entity and will depend upon enterprise continuity.

Assets may be acquired in various ways; they may exist in numerous forms; and they may have different degrees and kinds of usefulness to the enterprise. Because of these facts, there are various criteria for asset recognition, classification and measurement.

Recognition

Typically, the initial appearance of an asset within an entity is the result of an exchange transaction in which terms and amounts established by negotiation are supported by documents and market data. This tends to make the transaction unambiguous and objective, and the requirements for measurement are met clearly and directly.

Assets may be converted from one form to another within the area of entity operations, and the amounts of assets may be reclassified as service potentials are converted. Even though reclassifications do not imply aggregate asset increase, they should be based upon objective data. The facts of production are the basis for cost assignments in inventory.

Any increase or decrease in the aggregate amount of assets should be corroborated by a market transaction or its equivalent. For example, discovery, gift or donation, the processes of accrual or accretion, and (under certain contractual arrangements) production, may entail recognition of new assets. In all cases the requirements of objective measurement should be met; the concept of realization provides general standards for the recognition of asset increases.

Measurement

The value of an asset is the money equivalent of its service potentials. Conceptually, this is the sum of the future market prices of all streams of service to be derived, discounted by probability and interest factors to their present worths. However, this conception of value is an abstraction which yields but limited practical basis for quantification. Consequently, the measurement of assets is commonly made by other more feasible methods.

Monetary assets—cash or claims to cash—should be expressed in terms of expected cash receipts adjusted for collection delay where significant. Cash on hand, demand deposits, and short-term government receivables are readily expressed in such terms because the force of interest and the uncertainty of collection are negligible. Other claims to cash may require adjustment to measure current realizable amounts. Accounts or notes receivable should be discounted for stated or implied interest factors, if material; they should also be reduced by allowances to cover shrinkage on collection. Still other cash claims may involve equitable considerations, as in the measurement of receivables arising from long-term construction contracts on a percentage of completion basis. In every case, however, the amount of monetary assets should be based on discernible, measurable, and reasonably certain collection and availability of cash.

Non-monetary assets—inventories, plant, long-term investments, and deferred items generally—are not as amenable to accurate money measurement. Such assets are typically stated at acquisition cost or some derivative thereof. Assuming a free market, acquisition cost expressed in the bargained price of an asset is presumed to be a satisfactory quantification of future service expectations at the time of acquisition. Bargained price is the objective and determinable result of a completed transaction, and it tends to reflect the unique relation of the asset to the entity at the time of the transaction.

Acquisition cost is the amount of cash or its equivalent stated or implied in the acquisition price, the amount given up for the items or services acquired. Assets that are acquired without a stated money consideration, or through transactions which do not result in an objective price, are measured by either the market price of the consideration given for the new asset or the exchange price of the new assets as established in the market. When there is no market price for either the consideration given or the asset acquired, appraisal by independent parties may be the best way to quantify the asset acquisition.

Acquisition costs derived from prices established in market transactions may be used to quantify events occurring within the entity in the process of transforming acquired goods and services into product for delivery to the market. *Thus the cost of a manufactured product is the sum of the acquisition costs reasonably traceable to that product and should include both direct and indirect factors. The omission of any element of manufacturing cost is not acceptable.*

Modification of acquisition cost may be occasioned by recognition of such factors as depreciation, depletion, or obsolescence. Any decline in the service potential of plant and other long-term assets should be recognized in the accounts in the periods in which such decline occurs. Unless they represent reasonable allocations of cost, neither traditional policies nor maximum charge-offs allowed under tax regulations should be permitted to control such estimates.

The aim of all measurements of assets is to state the amount of available service potential in the most objective and realistic terms. Amounts so stated should be carried forward unchanged, except for modifications as described, in order to provide a statistical base for comparison and interpretation. Adjustments for price level change, for instance, can be made meaningful only when the underlying asset amount is objectively stated.

When the service potential of a given asset is no longer available to the enterprise, whether transferred by sale, exhausted through use, or dissipated by obsolescence or damage, the acquisition cost of the asset, as modified by events subsequent to acquisition, should be eliminated from the accounts and any final gain or loss on disposition recognized.

IV
Income Determination

In modern accounting, income is determined for stated periods which are typically shorter than the life span of the enterprise. Since the useful lives of assets frequently extend over several periods, and since business transactions are not at uniform stages of completion at the ends of such periods, the determination of income is a complex accounting operation requiring the use of estimates and the exercise of judgment.

The realized net income of an enterprise measures its effectiveness as an operating unit and is the change in its net assets arising out of (a) the excess or deficiency of revenue compared with related expired cost and (b) other gains or losses to the enterprise from sales, exchanges, or other conversions of assets. Interest charges, income taxes, and true profit-sharing distributions are not determinants of enterprise net income.

In determining net income to shareholders, however, interest charges, income taxes, profit-sharing distributions, and credits or charges arising from such events as forgiveness of indebtedness and contributions are properly included. In financial reports and discussions alike, care should be exercised to indicate whether enterprise net income or net income to the shareholders is at issue.

Revenue

Revenue, the principal source of realized net income, is the monetary expression of the aggregate of products or services transferred by an enterprise to its customers during a period of time. In accounting for revenue, the two central questions are the timing of revenue recognition and the determination of amount.

If a tangible product is furnished by the enterprise to its customers, revenue should normally be recognized at the time of sale. An extended collection period or the necessity for substantial effort by the enterprise subsequent to sale may create problems of measurement without affecting the propriety of recognizing revenue on the basis of the sale. In the manufacture of special items on a contract basis, revenue may be recognized as appropriate to the progress of the work and the terms of the contract. If a service is furnished by the enterprise to its customers, revenue normally should be recognized at the time of performance. Performance may be identified with the passage of time, with a specific act, or with a combination of time and specific act.

Revenue is measured by the price established in the transaction with the customer after making appropriate allowance for any prolonged collection period. All discounts, trade allowances, or other reductions of billed prices should be treated as adjustments of the revenue figure to which they apply.

Expired Costs

Expired costs are those having no discernible benefit to future operations. They may be classified as "expense" or "loss." Expense is the expired cost, directly or indirectly related to a given fiscal period, of the flow of goods or services into the market and of related operations. Loss is expired cost not beneficial to the revenue producing activities of the enterprise.

The basic questions concerning cost expirations are the time of recognition and the determination of amount. Recognition of cost expiration is based either on a complete or partial decline in the usefulness of assets, or on the appearance of a liability without a corresponding increase in assets. The service potential of assets may decline because of transfer of title, gradual or abrupt physical deterioration, consumption of service potential through use even though no physical change is apparent, or economic deterioration because of obsolescence or change in consumer demand. The issuance of product guarantees, notice of adverse court rulings, and similar events establishing the existence of liabilities likewise call for recognition of cost expirations.

In the majority of companies, the most important category of expense is the cost of goods sold. Ideally, the measurement of this expense should accomplish three related objectives.

1 report in current terms the cost of products and services transferred to customers during the period;

2 report in current terms the costs present in inventories at the end of the period;

3 identify the gains or losses resulting from price changes.

The methods of inventory pricing in common use achieve these objectives in varying degrees. For example, LIFO usually reflects cost of goods sold in relatively current terms, but fails to do the same for inventories, and does not disclose the results of price changes. FIFO and average cost methods are reasonably satisfactory in many cases with respect to the pricing of inventories. They also reflect the effects of price changes but bury this information in the cost of goods sold figure, thereby failing to distinguish between trading profit or loss and the gains or losses from price movements. Standard cost methods can accomplish the objectives set forth above, but the results of these procedures typically are adjusted to historical outlay cost in published financial reports.

Income Tax

The law relevant to income taxation should conform as closely as practicable to accounting principles of net income determination. However, tax objectives are inevitably somewhat different from those of accounting, and continuing differences between reported and taxable business earnings are to be expected.

In any given period, some differences may be attributable to the inclusion or exclusion for tax computation of revenue or expired cost recognized under accounting principles as net income determinants in earlier or later periods. Since such differences are often significant, and since they may give rise to expectations of wholly or partially off-setting differences in later periods, they should be disclosed.

Disclosure is sometimes accomplished by recording the differences as prepayments (given an expectation of future tax savings) or accruals (given the opposing prospect). However, these items do not present the usual characteristics of assets or liabilities; the possible future offsets are often subject to unusual uncertainties; and treatment on an accrual basis is in many cases unduly complicated. Consequently, disclosure by accrual may be more confusing than enlightening and is therefore undesirable.

The following dissents are significant to management accountants.

The definition of product cost given in Section III is so framed as to deny the acceptability, with reference to published financial reports, of those procedures known as "direct costing." "Direct costing" does not exclude from product inventories those manufacturing costs directly attributable to current production, that is, varying with changes in the rate of manufacturing operations; it does exclude fixed manufacturing costs, on the ground that such invariant elements (like general administration costs) ought to appear as expense of the period in which they are incurred.

Mr. Hill and Mr. Vatter dissent from the majority position that direct costing is not an acceptable practice of accounting measurement. They believe that assets are indeed "service-potentials available for, or beneficial to, expected operations," and that asset measurement based on this definition need not include costs which must be incurred regardless of production or sale. They therefore conclude that direct costing is at least as acceptable in accounting theory as is the conventional "full costing" concept. Moreover, they believe that the use of direct costing procedures will, in many cases, yield results more useful to investors as well as to management.

Prior to publication of the 1957 report, public accountants based their certifications on consistency and materiality. In other words, if a company had used the same method of valuing inventory for a number of years without material change, it would not require a qualification on their certification. For example, a manufacturer of collapsible tubes had, for many years, taken into their inventory value only the metal content of the tubes, and all labor and manufacturing expenses were charged off in each period. When they converted to direct standard costs it was necessary to adjust their inventory to a higher value in order to be consistent with the values used in the management accounting system when making external reports.

Another example was the case of the Pittsburgh Plate Glass Company which had for many years used a "5200 account," which was called "noninventoriable manufacturing expense," and which included such items as depreciation and fringe benefits. When PPG converted to direct standard costs they eliminated all direct costs such as fringe benefits on direct labor from the 5200 account, and their public accountants certified their statements without qualification on the basis of consistency and materiality.

The case of the Fostoria Glass Company presents an unusual series of events. The company converted to direct standard costs in 1949 and wrote to

IRS and requested permission to use this basis for their tax returns because they had learned on good authority that IRS had given an informal approval for a midwestern company to convert and write off period costs in inventory over a period of 10 years. Another company had received an informal approval with the write-off of period costs in inventory over a 5-year period. When Fostoria had not received a reply to their request, they proceeded with their planned conversion and set up the period cost in inventory as a specific item on their balance sheet. A few months later they received a letter from IRS saying that their request had been referred to the Wheeling office of IRS. They never did hear from the Wheeling office. Therefore, they continued to keep these fixed costs in inventory on their balance sheet as a static item. Later they decided to employ one of the "big 8" public accounting firms to handle their audit. When the new accountants submitted their survey report they made a number of recommendations. Among them was one to the effect that the account, "Fixed Costs in Inventory," was not a good asset and should be written off. Needless to say, Fostoria implemented this recommendation.

The Dewey & Almy Chemical Company presents a very special case. The company had been using the direct cost method of pricing inventories since 1937, and there was no evidence of a qualification in their certification. In the meantime they had been acquired by W. R. Grace & Company, whose treasurer told an AMA seminar in 1958 that IRS was questioning their inventory valuation methods. It was his opinion that a "bright" revenue agent had come up with an idea to collect a large amount of taxes from corporations who were not pricing their inventories in accordance with the 1957 standards of the American Accounting Association. The treasurer stated that W. R. Grace tax authorities were confident that they could force the IRS to permit them to write up their last open year by the new method, which would result in a reduction in taxes for Dewey & Almy. As it turned out, the IRS never did implement this agent's proposed line of action, probably because they were afraid that W. R. Grace would win the case.

Then, on September 19, 1973, the IRS issued a new set of inventory regulations that required the use of the full absorption method of costing inventory and provide liberal transition rules to encourage taxpayers to adopt this method. Following promulgation of these new regulations, Fostoria changed their method of pricing inventory and PPG Industries converted to the LIFO method. Companies like Armstrong Cork, who had been adjusting inventory value to the full cost value, simply made certain that their adjustment procedure was in accordance with the 1973 regulations.

In view of the above, it is recommended that any company that converts its management accounting system to direct costing follow the Armstrong Cork Company example. This can be achieved very simply by utilizing the profitability analysis shown in Chapter 3, Table 3-1. Be sure to separate the period costs that can be inventoried (per 1973 IRS regulations) from the period costs that cannot be inventoried, such as selling and administrative costs.

For each product line determine the ratio of period costs that can be inventoried to total direct costs. This determines the percentage that the inventory priced at direct costs would have to be increased to meet the IRS regulations.

The following is an excerpt from the Armstrong Cork Company's accounting manual for making this adjustment.

PERIOD EXPENSE IN INVENTORY

When reports to stockholders, insurance companies and government agencies include a statement of inventories, such inventories will be valued at total manufacturing cost, which includes period expenses as well as direct costs. Responsibilities and procedures for the determination of period expense in inventory follow.

1 Determination of Period Expense Rates

(a) Operations Controllers will be responsible for the determination of period expense rates to the nearest 1/10th % for each plant by major product groups.

(b) Rates to be applied in any given year will be based on (1) the budgeted period expense for that year (Control 13400 only) related to (2) the current year standard direct production cost (at the inventory valuation point). Exclude period expenses applicable to unused production facilities.

(c) Operations Controllers will be responsible for the determination of budgeted period expense in the estimated inventory on hand at the end of each month during the budget year. This budgeted data, based on the Production Planning Department's estimates of inventories during the budget year, will be reported to the Corporate Accounting Department not later than the first week of December preceding the budget year.

(d) After the profit budget has been approved as the operating budget for the year, the estimated period expense rates used in developing the budgeted data will be reviewed and adjusted by the Operations Controllers, if necessary, to reflect changed conditions or costs.

The period expense rates to be applied to actual inventories throughout the year will be reported to the Corporate Accounting Department not later than the last week of January of the year of application. . . .

6 Adjust Account 110-02120—Period Expense Applied to Inventory—to the current amount. The Corporate Accounting Depart-

ment will make the following entry each month and at December 31. . . .
DR or CR 110-02120—Period Expense Applied to Inventory
CR or DR 110-13400-804-000-001-000—Mfg. Period Expense, Inv. Adjustments

This entry provides a very significant figure for top management reports. In case the adjustment is a credit (which improves the profit for the period), it tells management that inventory levels have increased, which is a bad sign and certainly not one on which to base future profit plans.

12
THE FUTURE OF MANAGEMENT ACCOUNTING

During the past two decades more and more major companies have selected their chief executive officers from the ranks of financial management executives. In fact, Charles Hornbostle, president of the Financial Executive Institute, has a list of over 300 CEOs who were members of the Financial Executive Institute. When you consider the training and experience the financial executives receive through their managerial accounting responsibilities, this trend is easy to understand. Here is a typical job description for a Chairman and CEO:

CHAIRMAN OF THE BOARD

The board of directors has created the office of chairman of the board as the chief executive officer of the Company. The chairman has sole responsibility to the board of directors for the administration of the Company.

The board of directors authorizes the chairman of the board to:

1 Determine basic policy other than that reserved to the board itself.

2 Redelegate administrative responsibility.

3 Exercise specific responsibility for:

(a) Acquisition and new business development. This refers to the development of new lines of product, whether by the acquisition of other companies or by development through the Company's own activities.
The president will provide for such assistance and cooperation as the chairman may need from within the Company in order to carry out this responsibility.

(b) Public relations and stockholder relations. This refers to formulation of practices and plans for the maintenance and improvement of relations with the public and stockholders and to provide advice and assistance, where required by the president, to divisions and departments under his supervision.

(c) Corporate and legal affairs. The chairman will provide for legal advice as required by the president and the divisions and departments under his supervision.

(d) Financial policy and general financial reports. Without limiting the president in specifying methods and procedure as an aid to the performance of his duties, the chairman reserves the power to prescribe additional financial activities, and the form and content of reports prepared for the board of directors, the chairman, the stockholders and the public.

(e) Capital expenditure budget and capital expenditures exceeding $25,000.

(f) Appointments, promotions, compensation, and termination of employment of persons receiving salaries of $12,000 or more per annum.[1]

According to Wayne Keller:

it is the function of the managerial accountant to aid management in setting optimum-profit objectives and in developing plans to meet these objectives, to provide control reports to guide management decisions, and to analyze and interpret performance to indicate where and what corrective action is necessary if the objectives are not being met. Standard costs and budgetary planning and control procedures are the tools of the managerial accountant, and co-ordinated periodic and special reports are his communication system.

To achieve the objective of management accounting the personnel of the accounting department must (1) have an interest in, and knowledge of, all phases of the management and staff functions of the enterprise, (2) believe implicitly in a "profit and loss" economic system, (3) rate above average as persons, (4) recognize the need for constant revision and improvement in the management accounting process, and (5) be skilled in the art and science of accounting.

Finally, the managerial accountant must be proficient in all branches of accountancy, and have a professional attitude in his work. . . . At no time may procedures be followed which are not in conformity with accepted

---

[1] Ernest Dale, *Planning and Developing the Company Organization,* American Management Association, New York, 1969, p. 254.

accounting practice. . . . Principles must be followed not only because statements will be published but more importantly because management must have the true facts and all the facts if they are to make intelligent, informed decisions. The entire organization for management accounting must be directed toward this objective.[2]

When you realize that it is the board of directors that elects chief executive officers, usually at the direction of the retiring CEO, then it is easy to see why the chief financial officer who has come up through the ranks of managerial accounting will have a decided advantage over other top executives when a new CEO is being selected.

John V. James, President and CEO of Dallas-based Dresser Industries, is a good example of such a case. James had been with a New York subsidiary and had taken an active part in converting that company to direct standard costs, and he was one of the early pioneers in the development of direct costing and long-range profit planning procedures. When he was transferred to Dallas, he brought with him his techniques of management accounting, and, even though he was a New York Yankee in southern territory, he immediately made many converts. One of his first major accomplishments was the introduction of a procedure which he called "profit planning in depth." This procedure was product-oriented and was very instrumental in the development of Dresser Industries.

It is easy to see how the directors were impressed with this young executive from New York with his fresh ideas about long-range planning and day-to-day control of operations. His background in managerial accounting had certainly equipped him to assume the duties of chief executive officer.

C. Robert Fay, who pioneered the flexible budget system at Westinghouse and directed the installation of the direct standard costing system at Pittsburgh Plate Glass Company, is another example. Although he was never elected CEO of PPG, he was a close runner-up.

L. Stanton Williams is a better example. He was selected by Bob Fay to be chairman of the task force that installed the direct standard cost system in the plate glass division of PPG. At that time, he was a fresh recruit out of Harvard Business School and did such an outstanding job as chairman of the task force that he was named controller when Bob Fay moved up in the organization. He is now vice chairman of PPG Industries. According to *Forbes* magazine (October 2, 1978, issue), he is given 6 to 5 odds to become the next CEO of

---

[2]Wayne Keller, *Management Accounting for Profit Control,* McGraw-Hill, New York, 1957, p. 12.

PPG Industries.[3] He credits his managerial accounting experience for training him to qualify for this position.

With the SEC requiring greater disclosures each year, such as replacement value accounting and profit by product line, it is reasonable to assume that the management accounting system will become recognized as the source of much of the data used in external reporting. For this reason companies will be sure that their young executives who have CEO potential are trained in management accounting and qualify for a certificate in management accounting (CMA).

With such a great infusion of talent into the ranks of managerial accountants, it is easy to predict that the great strides that have been made in recent years will be accelerated so that the techniques of management accounting will be refined and gain general acceptance by accounting authorities. In addition, these techniques will continue to provide managers with better tools for decision making, planning, and control for optimizing profit and growth.

---

[3] *Forbes* was right. On October 11, 1978, the Board of Directors of PPG Industries elected L. Stanton Williams Chairman and CEO to succeed Robinson F. Barker as of January 1, 1979.

APPENDIX I
TYPICAL FUNCTIONAL SPECIFICATIONS FOR AUTOMATION OF ROUTING FILES, BILLS OF MATERIAL FILES, PRODUCT COSTS, AND MANAGEMENT ACCOUNTING REPORTS

OBJECTIVES OF THE AUTOMATED PRODUCT COST SYSTEM

1 *GENERAL*

   A Design and develop an automated data base and product cost system to produce standard costs for parts and end-products of all active items in the line.

   B Design records to produce part and end-product costs at three different values:

   (1) FROZEN—or standard value in inventory.

   (2) CURRENT—or cost to replace at latest effective standard Labor Hours and rates for purchase price, outside processing, direct labor and variable factory overhead.

   (3) SIMULATED—or projected rates for a future period.

   C Design system to generate FROZEN values for new products and latest CURRENT or SIMULATED values for active products selectively at any time.

   D Design system so that cumulative costs for parts or end-products are available at the end of pre-selected critical fabricating operations or assembly points.

   E Update existing specifications for material, parts, product structure, outside processing, standard Labor Hours and rates for 100% coverage of active products.

2 *DATA BASE*

   A   Create records with high degree of accessibility to accommodate expanded "data base" of Product Structure, Routing File and Rates.

   B   PRODUCT STRUCTURE—End-product structure by part number and level in indented bill of materials format with end-product as Level "1."

   C   ROUTING FILE—Physical specifications by part number for raw material requirements including unavoidable loss allowance, standard Labor Hours by department and operation including description, outside processing and parts for assembly by operation.

   D   RATES—Standard values for elements of cost including Raw Material Purchase Price, Outside Processing Rates and Departmental Costing Rate for Direct Labor and Variable Factory Overhead.

3 *PRODUCT COSTS*

   A   Build up standard costs for all active end-products in format of indented bill of materials by part number and level corresponding with product structure above.

   B   Provide for greatest practical visibility of product cost elements.

4 *BY-PRODUCT APPLICATIONS*

   A   Design record lay-out and access techniques to provide for ultimate applications such as In-Process Inventory and Scrap Evaluation, Measurement of Variances For Length of Run, Alternate Method, Revisions of Standard and Labor Grade.

PHYSICAL SPECIFICATIONS
Product Structure (A)

DATA ELEMENT DESCRIPTIONS	Date: 3-15-78
Data Base: Product Structure	
Record: Bills of Material	By:
Item: General	WWA

DESCRIPTION

The Bills of Material record is a parts list of all purchased or fabricated parts used on each sub-assembly, and all parts and sub-assemblies used on each end-product. This listing contains the following items:

    Part Number
    Part Name
    Indented Level Number
    Quantity for next level
    Extended Quantity

For greatest flexibility in file maintenance, price information is kept in a separate record.

MAINTENANCE
A. (Who)
B. (When)
C. (How)

A   Engineering is responsible.

B   See below.

C   The initial input will be the present computerized file being prepared by Engineering. Key models will be reviewed and major changes will be made to update as appropriate.

A-1

	DATA ELEMENT DESCRIPTIONS	Date
Data Base: Product Structure		3-15-78
Record: Bills of Material		By
Item: Part Number		WWA

DESCRIPTION

The part number is a unique number assigned to each purchased or fabricated part, to each sub-assembly as required by manufacturing or engineering, and to each end-product. The numbers can be either numeric or a combination of alpha-numeric.

The system provides a field of twenty-two (22) digits for the Part Number.

MAINTENANCE
A. (Who)
B. (When)
C. (How)

A) Engineering is responsible

B)
) See "General"
C)

A-2

DATA ELEMENT DESCRIPTIONS	Date
Data Base: Product Structure	3-15-78
Record: Bills of Material	By:
Item: Part Name	WWA

DESCRIPTION

From Item Master

The system provides a field of twenty-five (25) digits for the Part Name.

MAINTENANCE
A. (Who)
B. (When)
C. (How)

A — Engineering is responsible.

B}
C} See "General"

A-3

	DATA ELEMENT DESCRIPTIONS	Date
Data Base: Product Structure		3-15-78
Record: Bills of Material		By
Item: Indented Level Number		WWA

DESCRIPTION

The Indented Level Number represents the stage at which the part or sub-assembly enters the manufacturing process in producing the specific end-product called for on the Bill. The end-product itself is Level 1. All sub-assemblies and parts coming together at final assembly are Level 2. Sub-assemblies and parts coming together in Level 2 sub-assemblies are Level 3, and so on.

The system provides a field of three (3) digits for the indented Level Number.

MAINTENANCE
A. (Who)
B. (When)
C. (How)

<u>A</u>   Engineering is responsible.

<u>B</u>
<u>C</u> } See "General"

A-4

DATA ELEMENT DESCRIPTIONS	Date
Data Base: Product Structure	3-15-78
Record: Bills of Material	By
Item: Quantity for Next Level	WWA

DESCRIPTION

    The quantity for next level represents the units of the part required to produce one unit of the next higher level of sub-assembly as shown on the indented bill.

    The system provides a field of three (3) digits for the quantity for next level.

MAINTENANCE
A. (Who)
B. (When)
C. (How)

  A Engineering is responsible.

  B)
) See "General"
  C)

A-5

DATA ELEMENT DESCRIPTIONS	Date
Data Base: Product Structure	3-15-78
Record: Bills of Material	By
Item: Extended Quantity	WWA

DESCRIPTION

The extended quantity represents the units of the part required to produce one unit of the Level 1 end-product.

The system provides a field of three (3) digits for extended quantity.

MAINTENANCE
A. (Who)
B. (When)
C. (How)

A Engineering is responsible.

B)
) See "General"
C)

A-6

PHYSICAL SPECIFICATIONS
Routing File—Labor Standards (B)

	DATA ELEMENT DESCRIPTIONS	Date
Data Base: Routing File		3-15-78
Record: Labor Standards		By
Item: General		WWA

DESCRIPTION

The Labor Standards Record of the Routing File specifies what work will be done on a part or model, where and how it will be done, and the time requirements for doing the work. This record consists of fifteen (15) key elements for expanded Routing File. Elements marked (*) are added for automated product cost purposes.

        Part Number
        Part Name
        Sequence Number
        Work Center
        Operation Number
        Operation and Tool Description
        Set-up Hours (per occurrence)
        Direct Hours/c
        Machine Hours/c
        Labor Type
*   Labor Grade
*   Outside Processing
*   Assembly Parts
*   Scrap
*   Lot Size

The above data will provide information for prompt and accurate measurement of labor performance, for recording variances in lot size, revisions of standard, and scrap, for automated accumulation of standard costs of parts, sub-assemblies and end-product, and for use in various advanced programs for manufacturing and inventory control.

MAINTENANCE
A. (Who)
B. (When)
C. (How)

This record is a physical file only, with no dollar values, thus providing for the greatest flexibility in file maintenance. In addition, the quantitative items (lot size, hours and scrap) are shown in (2) two fields:

    FROZEN (inventory standard)
    CURRENT (latest standard)

A.   The part number and part name are assigned by the Engineering Department. Lot size is the responsibility of Production Scheduling. Input to the Labor Standards Record of all other information listed above is the responsibility of Industrial Engineering.

B-1

DATA ELEMENT DESCRIPTIONS	Date
Data Base: Routing File (con't)	3-15-78
Record: Labor Standards	By
Item: General	WWA

DESCRIPTION

MAINTENANCE
A. (Who)
B. (When)
C. (How)

B. Entries are made to the record whenever new parts, sub-assemblies or products are engineered for processing; when methods are changed;, or when labor specifications are revised for any reason.

C. Input to the record is via a hand-written copy of the EDP input format.

B-1 (cont)

Appendix I **163**

DATA ELEMENT DESCRIPTIONS	Date
Data Base: Routing File	3-15-78
Record: Labor Standards	By
Item: Part Number	WWA

DESCRIPTION

See Product Structure.

MAINTENANCE
A. (Who)
B. (When)
C. (How)

A) Engineering is responsible
B)) See "General"
C))

B-2

	DATA ELEMENT DESCRIPTIONS	Date:
Data Base: Routing File		3-15-78
Record: Labor Standards		By
Item: Part Name		WWA

DESCRIPTION

From Item Master

MAINTENANCE
A. (Who)
B. (When)
C. (How)

A Engineering is responsible.

B)
) See "General"
C)

B-3

DATA ELEMENT DESCRIPTIONS	Date
Data Base: Routing File	3-15-78
Record: Labor Standards	By
Item: Sequence Number	WWA

DESCRIPTION

    An Operation Sequence Number is assigned to each operation performed on a part to indicate the sequence in which the work is done. The system provides a field of three (3) digits for this number.

    Where alternate operations may be used, the standard for preferred method is always identified by the alpha "P" as a suffix to the sequence number. Each alternate is coded with the alpha suffix "A", "B", "C", etc. The system provides a field of two (2) digits for this number.

MAINTENANCE
A. (Who)
B. (When)
C. (How)

<u>A</u>   Industrial Engineering is responsible.

<u>B</u>
<u>C</u>   See "General"

B-4

166 Management Accounting Simplified

DATA ELEMENT DESCRIPTIONS	Date
Data Base: Routing File	3-15-78
Record: Labor Standards	By
Item: Work Center	WWA

DESCRIPTION

    This number indicates the general work area where the specified operation is performed. A five (5) digit field is provided for this number.

MAINTENANCE
A. (Who)
B. (When)
C. (How)

  A Industrial Engineering is responsible.

  B)
      See "General"
  C)

B-5

	DATA ELEMENT DESCRIPTIONS	Date 3-15-78
Data Base: Routing File		
Record: Labor Standards		By
Item: Operation Number		WWA

DESCRIPTION

This is the number for the appropriate standard Labor Hours applying to the operation being performed. The system provides a three (3) digit field for this number.

MAINTENANCE
A. (Who)
B. (When)
C. (How)

A — Industrial Engineering is responsible

B)
C) See "General"

B-6

Management Accounting Simplified

	DATA ELEMENT DESCRIPTIONS	Date
Data Base: Routing File		3-15-78
Record: Labor Standards		By
Item: Operation Description		WWA

DESCRIPTION

      An explanation of the operation, whether performed in-house or by an outside processor, is shown in the operation and tool description field. This item also includes the tag number of the specific machine where this is available. This provides valuable supplemental information for the operator, foreman and scheduler in planning and organizing the work.

      This system provides a field of thirty (30) digits for this description.

MAINTENANCE
A. (Who)
B. (When)
C. (How)

A) Industrial Engineering is responsible.
B)
C) See "General"

B-7

	DATA ELEMENT DESCRIPTIONS	Date
Data Base: Routing File		3-15-78
Record: Labor Standards		By
Item: Set-Up Hours (per occurrence)		WWA

DESCRIPTION

  The set-up hours field, along with lot size, is provided for improved labor control, for more accurate product costing and for advanced scheduling techniques. Set-up hours represent the standard time to get ready for an operation with proper tooling and settings.

  By establishing standards for set-up per occurrence and lot size, it is possible to calculate standard set-up hours per piece (set-up hours per occurrence ÷ lot size) and thus charge set-up to the specific part and product.

  Set-up time is shown in four (4) decimal places. The system provides a field of six (6) digits for these hours.

MAINTENANCE
A. (Who)
B. (When)
C. (How)

A Industrial Engineering is responsible.

B)
) See "General"
C)

B-8

Data Base: Routing File	DATA ELEMENT DESCRIPTIONS	Date 3-15-78
Record: Labor Standards Item: Direct Hours/c		By WWA

DESCRIPTION

        The standard allowed labor hours for performing an operation. The figure is shown per 100 pieces.

        Time is shown in four (4) decimal places. The system provides a field of seven (7) digits for this number.

MAINTENANCE
A. (Who)
B. (When)
C. (How)

A Industrial Engineering is responsible.

B
C See "General"

B-9

DATA ELEMENT DESCRIPTIONS		Date: 3-15-78
Data Base: Routing File		
Record: Labor Standards		By: WWA
Item: Machine Hours/c		

DESCRIPTION

        This standard allowed machine hours for performing the operation where different from Labor Hours.

        For one-man/one-machine operation the machine hour standards are synonymous with labor hours. For one-man/multiple-machine operations machine hour standards can be converted to labor hours by dividing the machine hour standard by the number of machines included in the standard. The number of machines will be indicated by an identifying code.

        The system provides a field of seven (7) digits for this number.

MAINTENANCE
A. (Who)
B. (When)
C. (How)

A   Industrial Engineering is responsible.

B } See "General"
C

B-10

DATA ELEMENT DESCRIPTIONS	Date: 3-15-78
Data Base: ~~Routing File~~	
Record: Labor Standards	By:
Item: Labor Type	WWA

DESCRIPTION

The classification identifying the type of standard (i.e. stop watch, MTM, estimate, etc.)

The system provides a field of two (2) digits for this code.

MAINTENANCE
A. (Who)
B. (When)
C. (How)

A Industrial Engineering is responsible.

B)
) See "General"
C)

B-11

	DATA ELEMENT DESCRIPTIONS	Date: 3-15-78
Data Base: Routing File		
Record: Labor Standards		By: WWA
Item: Labor Grade		

DESCRIPTION

The classification of pay grade assigned to the operation.

The system provides a field of two (2) digits for this code.

MAINTENANCE
A. (Who)
B. (When)
C. (How)

A. Industrial Engineering is responsible.

B.
C. } See "General"

B-12

	DATA ELEMENT DESCRIPTIONS	Date
Data Base: Routing File		3-15-78
Record: Labor Standards		By
Item: Outside Processing		WWA

DESCRIPTION

      The incidence of outside processing, usually finishing operations, is denoted by an operation number in the proper sequence. The nature of the work is explained in the "Operation and Tool Description" item, including a unique code number to identify the specific processing service being provided. The standard cost per unit is included in the "Purchases" rate file.

MAINTENANCE
A. (Who)
B. (When)
C. (How)

A) Industrial Engineering is responsible.

B)
) See "General"
C)

B-13

	DATA ELEMENT DESCRIPTIONS	Date
Data Base: Routing File		3-15-78
Record: Labor Standards		By:
Item: Assembly Parts		WWA

DESCRIPTION

    For a sub-assembly or end-product, part numbers being assembled are enumerated and cross-referenced to the operation number where they are introduced to the manufacturing process. These are the same part numbers that appear on the bill of materials for the sub-assembly or end-product being produced.

    This cross-referencing technique makes it possible to accumulate an accurate cost for scrap evaluation, for in-process inventory valuation and for cost of sales pricing up thru the last operation performed.

MAINTENANCE
A. (Who)
B. (When)
C. (How)

A) Industrial Engineering is responsible

B)
   } See "General"
C)

B-14

	DATA ELEMENT DESCRIPTIONS	Date:
Data Base: Routing File		3-15-78
Record: Labor Standards		By:
Item: Scrap		WWA

DESCRIPTION

This item is expressed as a percentage and is cross-referenced to the operation number after which the standard allowance is applied.

The scrap percentage is applied to the accumulated value up through the operation indicated.

MAINTENANCE
A. (Who)
B. (When)
C. (How)

A) Industrial Engineering is responsible, with the assistance of Production Scheduling and Cost Accounting.
B)
C) See "General"

B-15

Appendix I **177**

DATA ELEMENT DESCRIPTIONS	Date: 3-15-78
Data Base: Routing File	
Record: Labor Standards	By:
Item: Lot Size	WWA

DESCRIPTION

This field is provided for more accurate product costing and for use in advanced scheduling and product control procedures. In conjunction with standard hours for set-up it makes it possible to establish a set-up cost per unit for each part number based upon pre-established order quantity targets. It also furnishes the basis for evaluating performance for the scheduling function by calculating a lot size variance.

MAINTENANCE
A. (Who)
B. (When)
C. (How)

A   Production Scheduling is responsible.

B
)   See "General"
C

B-16

PHYSICAL SPECIFICATIONS
Raw Material Usage (C)

	DATA ELEMENT DESCRIPTIONS	Date
Data Base: Raw Material Usage		3-15-78
Record: Raw Material Specifications		By:
Item: General		WWA

DESCRIPTION

The Raw Material Specifications record identifies the physical characteristics and quantitative requirements for raw material used on fabricated parts, sub assemblies and assemblies. These descriptions comprise the following items:

      Part Number
      Material Number
      Material Description
      Unit of Measure
      Net Quantity
      Allowance Factor
      Gross Quantity

For greatest flexibility in file maintenance, price information is kept in a separate record.

MAINTENANCE
A. (Who)
B. (When)
C. (How)

A   See Specific instruction for each data element.

B   Entries are made to the record whenever a new part or style is engineered for processing, when methods are changed, or when new materials are specified.

C   Data are entered into the record via the appropriate EDP input form.

C-1

	DATA ELEMENT DESCRIPTIONS	Date:
Data Base:	Raw Material Usage	3-15-78
Record:	Raw Material Specifications	By
Item:	Part Number	WWA

DESCRIPTION

See Product Structure.

MAINTENANCE
A. (Who)
B. (When)
C. (How)

A   Engineering is responsible.

B)
)   See "General"
C)

C-2

	DATA ELEMENT DESCRIPTIONS	Date 3-15-78
Data Base:	Raw Material Usage	
Record:	Raw Material Specifications	By
Item:	Material Number	WWA

DESCRIPTION

The material number is the unique number for the specific raw material as carried in inventory. This system provides fifteen (15) digits for the material number.

MAINTENANCE
A. (Who)
B. (When)
C. (How)

A   Engineering is responsible

B)
C)   See "General"

C-3

	DATA ELEMENT DESCRIPTIONS	Date
Data Base: Raw Material Usage		3-15-78
Record: Raw Material Specifications		By
Item: Material Description		WWA

DESCRIPTION

      The material description identifies the type of material called for by the material number including technical specifications where appropriate. The system provides thirty (30) digits for material description.

MAINTENANCE
A. (Who)
B. (When)
C. (How)

A Engineering is responsible.

B)
) See "General"
C)

C-4

Appendix I **183**

DATA ELEMENT DESCRIPTIONS	Date
Data Base: Raw Material Usage	3-15=78
Record: Raw Material Specifications	By
Item: Unit of Measure	WWA

DESCRIPTION

This unit of measure is the index used to inventory the specific raw material, i.e., pounds, feet, pieces, etc. The system provides six (6) digits for the unit of measure.

MAINTENANCE
A. (Who)
B. (When)
C. (How)

A   Engineering is responsible.

B)
) See "General"
C)

C-5

	DATA ELEMENT DESCRIPTIONS	Date
Data Base: Raw Material Usage		3-15-78
Record: Raw Material Specification		By
Item: Net Quantity		WWA

DESCRIPTION

The net quantity is the amount of raw material in the finished piece, before allowances for un-avoidable usage losses inherent in the process. The system provides six (6) digits for net quantity.

MAINTENANCE
A. (Who)
B. (When)
C. (How)

A) Industrial Engineering is responsible.

B)
C) See "General"

C-6

Appendix I

DATA ELEMENT DESCRIPTIONS	Date
Data Base: Raw Material Usage	3-15-78
Record: Raw Material Specifications	By
Item: Allowance Factor	WWA

DESCRIPTION

This factor, sometimes expressed as a percentage, indicates the allowance provided for unavoidable raw material losses inherent in the operation, such as ends of bar stock, skeletons of sheet metal, getting on specification with a new set-up and the like. The system provides five (5) digits for the allowance factor.

MAINTENANCE
A. (Who)
B. (When)
C. (How)

A Industrial Engineering is responsible.

B)
) See "General"
C)

C-7

	DATA ELEMENT DESCRIPTIONS	Date
Data Base: Raw Material Usage		3-15-78
Record: Raw Material Specifications		By
Item: Gross Quantity		WWA

DESCRIPTION

The gross quantity is the amount of raw material required to produce fabricated pieces, including an allowance for extra usage inherent in the work and caused by unavoidable losses represented by ends of bar stock, skeletons of sheet metal, running in a new set-up, and the like. The system provides six (6) digits for gross quantity.

MAINTENANCE
A. (Who)
B. (When)
C. (How)

A. Industrial Engineering is responsible.

B.
C. } See "General"

C-8

RATES FILE
General (D)

	DATA ELEMENT DESCRIPTIONS	Date
Data Base: Rates File		3-15-78
Record:		By
Item: General		WWA

DESCRIPTION	The Rates File consists of all dollar value records. These rates are combined with physical quantities and specs on the Routing File and Product Structure to calculate costs for the Parts Cost Listing and for Product Costs. These rates are maintained on separate records from the physical quantities for simplified maintenance since many changes can occur in rates without affecting physical characteristics.
	
	This data base is comprised of four (4) records as follows:
	
	    Raw Material Rates
	    Purchase Parts Rates
	    Outside Processing Rates
	    Labor/Expense Costing Rates
	
	Provision is made in all rates records for three (3) schedules:
	
	    Frozen (value in inventory)
	    Current (latest _effective_ value)
	    Simulation (projected _future_ value - not retained)

MAINTENANCE
A. (Who)
B. (When)
C. (How)
	<u>A</u> 1. <u>Purchasing</u> has primary responsibility for Raw Material, Purchase Parts and Outside Processing rates, with <u>Cost Accounting</u> exercising a review function and with Engineering and Industrial Engineering assisting as described in this section.
	    2. Cost Accounting is responsible for Labor/Expense <u>Costing</u> rates.
	
	<u>B</u> 1. Frozen rates are input usually once a year at the time of physical inventory. As a general practice these rates remain intact until the next inventory. At that time inventory is revalued at latest Current rates which then become the new Frozen rates.
	    2. Current rates for Raw Material, Purchase Parts and Outside Processing only, are input as actual experience dictates to reflect changes in vendor prices under <u>normal</u> purchasing conditions.
	
	<u>C</u> <u>Cost Accounting</u> will input all rates on EDP format.

	D-1

RATES
Raw Material Rates (E)

	DATA ELEMENT DESCRIPTIONS	Date 3-15-78
Data Base: Rates		
Record: Raw Material Rates		By:
Item: General		WWA

DESCRIPTION

   This record contains complete information on all Raw Material prices, expressed in terms of the unit of measure employed for the material as outlined under the Raw Material specifications File. Relating to the Frozen, Current and Simulation procedures, these rates consist of the following items:

   Raw Material Number
   Raw Material Description
   Purchase Price
   Conversion Factor
   Usage Price

MAINTENANCE
A. (Who)
B. (When)
C. (How)

A

B   See Rates File - General

C

E-1

Appendix I **191**

DATA ELEMENT DESCRIPTIONS	Date
Data Base: Rates	3-15-78
Record: Raw Material Rates	By
Item: Raw Material Number	WWA

DESCRIPTION

    See Raw Material Specifications record for description. The material number is the unique number for the specific raw material as purchased and as carried in inventory.

MAINTENANCE
A. (Who)
B. (When)
C. (How)

A

B See Raw Material Specifications.

C

E-2

DATA ELEMENT DESCRIPTIONS	Date
Data Base: Rates	3-15-78
Record: Raw Material Rates	By
Item: Raw Material Description	WWA

DESCRIPTION

See Raw Material Specifications record for description.

MAINTENANCE
A. (Who)
B. (When)
C. (How)

A.

B. See Raw Material Specifications.

C.

E-3

Appendix I

	DATA ELEMENT DESCRIPTIONS	Date
Data Base:	Rates	3-15-78
Record:	Raw Material Rates	By
Item:	Purchase Price	WWA

DESCRIPTION

Raw Material purchase price is the standard price at which the material is purchased from the vendor expressed in the unit of measure as purchased and inventoried.

The Frozen Schedule is used for valuing inventory and for calculating purchase price variances, by comparing with vendors' actual invoice billings.

The system provides seven (7) digits for purchase price.

MAINTENANCE
A. (Who)
B. (When)
C. (How)

A. Purchasing is responsible.

B.
C. } See "General"

E-4

DATA ELEMENT DESCRIPTIONS		Date
Data Base: Rates		3-15-78
Record: Raw Material Rates		By
Item: Conversion Factor		WWA

DESCRIPTION

      The Conversion Factor represents the factor used to convert the unit of measure on purchases to the unit of measure employed for inventory purposes. Plywood, for example, may be purchased by the piece from the vendor while entering inventory records in terms of square feet.

      This system provides a field of five (5) digits for this factor.

MAINTENANCE
A. (Who)
B. (When)
C. (How)

A) Material Control is responsible
B)
C) See "General"

E-5

DATA ELEMENT DESCRIPTIONS	Date 3-15-78
Data Base: Rates	
Record: Raw Material Rates	By
Item: Usage Price	WWA

DESCRIPTION

Raw Material usage price is the standard price at which the material is used in the manufacturing process expressed in the unit of measure employed for inventory purposes. This price will be the same as the Purchase Price whenever the Conversion Factor is "1".

The system provides seven (7) digits for usage price.

MAINTENANCE
A. (Who)
B. (When)
C. (How)

A. Cost Accounting is responsible for validating the Usage Price.

B.
C. } See "General"

E-6

RATES
Purchase Parts Rates (F)

	DATA ELEMENT DESCRIPTIONS	Date
Data Base: Rates		3-15-78
Record: Purchase Parts Rates		By:
Item: General		WWA

DESCRIPTION

This record contains all information on prices for Purchase Parts. The Frozen, Current and Simulation schedules consist of the following items:

> Part Number
> Part Name
> Purchase Price
> Purchase Part Override Code

MAINTENANCE
A. (Who)
B. (When)
C. (How)

A
B   See Rates File - General
C

F-1

DATA ELEMENT DESCRIPTIONS	Date
Data Base: Rates	3-15-78
Record: Purchase Parts Rates	By
Item: Part Number	WWA

DESCRIPTION

See description under Product Structure. This part number is the number of the part that is being <u>purchased</u>.

MAINTENANCE
A. (Who)
B. (When)
C. (How)

<u>A</u>

<u>B</u> See Rate File - General.

<u>C</u>

F-2

DATA ELEMENT DESCRIPTIONS	Date: 3-15-78
Data Base: Rates	
Record: Purchase Parts Rates	By:
Item: Part Name	WWA

DESCRIPTION

From Item Master.

MAINTENANCE
A. (Who)
B. (When)
C. (How)

A

B See Rates File - General.

C

F-3

Data Base: Rates	DATA ELEMENT DESCRIPTIONS	Date 3-15-78
Record: Purchase Parts Rates		By
Item: Purchase Price		WWA
DESCRIPTION	The price per purchase part is the standard price at which the part is purchased from the vendor. The Frozen schedule is used for valuing inventory and for calculating purchase price variances by comparing with vendors' actual invoice billings. The system provides a field of seven (7) digits for the price.	
MAINTENANCE A. (Who) B. (When) C. (How)	**A** Purchasing is responsible. **B** } See "General". **C** }	
		F-4

		DATA ELEMENT DESCRIPTIONS	Date
Data Base:	Rates		3-15-78
Record:	Purchase Parts Rates		By
Item	Purchase Part Override Code		WWA

DESCRIPTION

    This code is used in the Product Cost build-up program to indicate that the purchase cost should be used in place of the manufactured cost. This technique makes it possible to retain the manufactured cost in the record.

    The system provides a field of one (1) digit for this code.

MAINTENANCE
A. (Who)
B. (When)
C. (How)

A) Industrial Engineering is responsible.

B)
C) See "General"

F-5

RATES
Outside Processing (G)

	DATA ELEMENT DESCRIPTIONS	Date: 3-15-78
Data Base: Rates		
Record: Outside Processing Rates		By:
Item: General		WWA

DESCRIPTION

This record contains information on the cost of operations performed by outside processors. These are usually finishing operations. They are identified on the Routing File by an appropriate sequence number indicating when they take place. As with other rates, Outside Processing is recorded in terms of cost per 100 units. The Frozen, Current and Simulation schedules consist of the following items:

      Processing Number (Service Number)
      Service Description
      Cost per 100

MAINTENANCE
A. (Who)
B. (When)
C. (How)

A

B   See Rates File - General.

C

G-1

DATA ELEMENT DESCRIPTIONS	Date: 3-15-78
Data Base: Rates	
Record: Outside Processing Rates	By:
Item: Processing Number (Service Number)	WWA

DESCRIPTION

See Routing File for description. This number is the identification number for the particular service being performed.

MAINTENANCE
A. (Who)
B. (When)
C. (How)

A) Industrial Engineering is responsible.

B))
) See Rates File -- General.
C))

G-2

Appendix I

DATA ELEMENT DESCRIPTIONS	Date: 3-15-78
Data Base: Rates	
Record: Outside Processing Rates	By:
Item: Cost per 100	WWA

DESCRIPTION

Cost per 100 is the price paid to the vendor for the outside operation. The Frozen schedule is used for valuing inventory and for calculating purchase price variances by comparing with vendors' actual invoice billings.

The system provides seven (7) digits for "cost per 100".

MAINTENANCE
A. (Who)
B. (When)
C. (How)

A. Purchasing is responsible.

B. }
C. } See Rates File - General.

G-3

RATES
Labor/Expense Costing Rates (H)

Appendix I

	DATA ELEMENT DESCRIPTIONS	Date
Data Base: Rates		3-15-78
Record: Labor/Expense Costing Rates		By
Item: General		WWA

DESCRIPTION

This record contains information about the rates applied to earned direct labor hours (SALH) in production departments to calculate the standard value added for conversion as product passes through operations. These rates are applied in two (2) parts: Direct Labor and Direct Expense. Although the same rates are used for all operations in a department, the record provides for later breakdown by machine center should the need arise. The Frozen, Current and Simulation schedules consist of the following items:

        Department Number
        Planned Efficiency
        Direct Labor Rate
        Variable Factory Overhead Rate

The system provides a field of five (5) digits for these rates.

MAINTENANCE
A. (Who)   A. Cost Accounting is responsible for these rates.
B. (When)
C. (How)   B. } See Rates File - General
            C. }

H-1

DATA ELEMENT DESCRIPTIONS	Date: 3-15-78
Data Base: Rates	
Record: Labor/Expense Costing Rates	By
Item: Department Number	WWA

DESCRIPTION

See Routing File for description and responsibility.

MAINTENANCE
A. (Who)   <u>A</u>
B. (When)   <u>B</u>
C. (How)   <u>C</u>

H-2

Appendix I

	DATA ELEMENT DESCRIPTIONS	Date
Data Base: RATES		3/15/78
Record: LABOR/EXPENSE COSTING RATES		By
Item: PLANNED EFFICIENCY		WWA

DESCRIPTION

This is the target performance level of the department for the fiscal period usually twelve (12) months. During which the costing rates will be used. It is expressed as a percentage (earned hours ÷ actual hours) for direct labor. In developing the costing rates, projected actual hours are first multiplied by this percentage to arrive at projected earned hours. Projected Direct labor dollars and projected direct expense dollars are then divided by projected earned hours to establish the costing rates.

The system provides for four (4) digits for planned efficiency.

MAINTENANCE
A. (Who)
B. (When)
C. (How)

A. Industrial engineering and manufacturing managers are jointly responsible

B.
C. } See Rate File - General

H-3

Data Base: Rates	**DATA ELEMENT DESCRIPTIONS**	Date: 3-15-78
Record: Labor/Expense Costing Rates		By:
Item: Direct Labor Rate		WWA

DESCRIPTION

The Direct Labor Rate represents the standard cost per earned hour for direct labor. A Direct Labor Rate is established for each department. This rate is applied to earned hours for each operation performed on each part in that department. The sum of earned hours for the month for each department extended by the Direct Labor Rate determines the standard Direct Labor Dollars for the month for spending control and is the same value transferred to inventory for value added. For each fabricated part or assembly, labor hour standards for each operation extended by the Direct Labor Rate for the department performing the operation and then added to the extensions for all other operations results in The Standard Direct Labor Cost for the part or assembly.

The system provides for six (6) digits for direct labor rate.

MAINTENANCE
A. (Who)
B. (When)
C. (How)

A. Cost Accounting is responsible.

B. See rate file "General".

C.

H-4

Appendix I **211**

| DATA ELEMENT DESCRIPTIONS | Date: 3-15-78 |

Data Base: **Rates**

Record: **Labor/Expense Costing Rates**

Item: **Variable Factory Overhead Rate**

By: **WWA**

DESCRIPTION

The Variable Factory Overhead rate represents the standard cost per earned hour for factory overhead that varies with volume. A rate is established for each department. This rate covers all variable overhead charged to the department. It is applied to earned hours for each operation performed on each part in that department. The sum of earned hours for the month for each department, extended by the direct expense rate, determines the flexible budget dollars for the month for overhead spending control and is the same value transferred to inventory for value added. For each fabricated part or assembly labor hour standards for each operation extended by the variable factory overhead rate for the department performing the operation and then added to the extensions for all other operations results in the standard variable factory overhead cost for the part or assembly.

The system provides a field of six (6) digits for this rate.

MAINTENANCE
A. (Who)
B. (When)
C. (How)

A) Cost Accounting is responsible.

B) See Rate File - General

C)

H-5

REPORTS
General (I)

Appendix I

Report	REPORT DESCRIPTIONS Reports from the Product Cost System	Date 3-15-78
Line (Title, Detail, Summary)	General	By WWA

ITEM	DESCRIPTION AND SOURCE

	The Edwards computerized Product Cost System provides the data for a number of key management reports. One of these was covered in the functional specifications relating to the Routing File and the Labor Reporting Procedure. The Product Structure, expanded Routing File and Rate Files now being specified make it possible to furnish additional reports. Certain basic reports are identified below. This is only a partial listing since requests for further reports will naturally arise as soon as management becomes familiar with information that is available.
	
	SHORT RANGE:
	
	The following five reports will be obtained from the Automated Product Cost System as it becomes operative:
	
	    Routing Sheet
	    Product Cost Accumulation
	    Part Cost Listing
	    Operation Cost Listing
	    Data Base Listings:
	
	        Physical Specifications
	        Rates
	
	LONG RANGE:
	
	A number of operating reports can be designed and programmed by use of information in the Data Base. Some of these are:
	
	    Lot Size Variance
	    Revision of Standard & Cost Reduction
	    Cost of Sales
	    Scrap Variance
	    Usage Variance by Department
	    Labor Variance by Department,
	        Operation or Operator.

REPORTS
Routing Sheet (J)

REPORT DESCRIPTIONS		Date: 3-15-78
Report: Routing Sheet (Operation Sheet)		
Line: General		By: WWA
(Title, Detail, Summary)		

ITEM	DESCRIPTION AND SOURCE
	This is a hard-copy printout of all information relating to physical information required for calculating a standard cost for each part. The Routing Sheet stands alone as a permanent record.
	A variation of the Routing Sheet is the Routing Card, a travelling envelope which accompanies the factory order through the plant and contains order number, due dates, order quantity and various extensions of standards by the order quantity to project thruput time.

J-1

	REPORT DESCRIPTIONS	Date
Report **Routing Sheet**		3-15-78
Line **Title and Detail Lines**		By
(Title, Detail, Summary)		WWA

ITEM	DESCRIPTION AND SOURCE
Report Title	Routing Sheet
Part Number	Number of part or assembly being manufactured.
Part Name	Corresponding name from Item Master.
Raw Material Number	Number of raw material being used.
Raw Material Description	Description of raw material being used.
Unit of Measure	Unit of measure used to carry raw material in inventory.
Raw Material Quantity	Net quantity, allowance factor and gross quantity of material required.
Lot Size	Standard lot size.
Report Date	Date Routing Sheet printout was requested.
Requested By	Name of individual and/or department requesting printout.
Run Date	Date printout is run in EDP.

J-2

REPORTS
Indented Product Cost (K)

218 Management Accounting Simplified

REPORT DESCRIPTIONS	Date 3-15-78
Report: Indented Product Cost	
Line: General	By WWA
(Title, Detail, Summary)	

ITEM	DESCRIPTION AND SOURCE
	The Product Cost is the standard direct cost per unit for a fabricated part, sub-assembly or end-product. These costs are expressed in dollars and cents, being carried to the nearest penny. At physical inventory time product counts are priced at Frozen standards to verify ledger balances. In-process product is valued at the cumulative cost through the last completed operation.
	The same physical counts are then re-priced at Current standards and inventory is revalued accordingly. These Current standards then become the Frozen standards until the next inventory revaluation, usually twelve (12) months. Any changes in standards during the intervening period are recorded as Current standards.
	Frozen product costs are available for all product in inventory or being produced.
	During the year Current product costs are developed selectively, upon request, as needed for marketing decisions, make/buy considerations and other management planning.
	Simulation product costs are only developed selectively upon request for special planning and analysis projects. Normally the simulated data base is not maintained although the company may want to retain the product cost output for various purposes.
	The product cost system is designed to yield a hard copy listing in the format of an indented parts list explosion. This provides for an in-depth visibility of cost build-up from lowest level parts to top level end-product.
	Assembly parts are identified as to whether they are fabricated or purchased. Direct labor hours are fully stated throughout. An allowance for scrap is included as a separate line item at the appropriate point in the operation sequence.
	Provision is made to show lot size and set-up hours separately.

K-1

REPORT DESCRIPTIONS

Report	Indented Product Cost
Line	Title and Detail Lines
(Title, Detail, Summary)	
Date	3-15-78
By	WWA

ITEM	DESCRIPTION AND SOURCE
Report Title	Indented Product Cost.
Sub Title	For Sub-assemblies and assemblies. Note: This listing is used for all sub-assemblies and assemblies that are inventoried as unique part numbers. Standard costs for fabricated parts are calculated from Routing Files, Raw Material Specifications and rate files by operation sequence.
Description	Description of sub-assembly or end-product being assembled. From Item Master.
Part Number	Part number of sub-assembly or end-product being assembled.
Code	F = Frozen Cost C = Current Cost S = Simulated Cost
Requested By	Name of individual and/or department requesting listing.
Request Date	Date request received in EDP.
Run Date	Date of listing run in EDP.

K-2

	REPORT DESCRIPTIONS	Date
Report Indented Product Cost		3-15-78
Line Column Heading		By
(Title, Detail, Summary)		WWA

ITEM	DESCRIPTION AND SOURCE
General	**For Purchase or Fabricated Parts in Listing** One line is shown for each purchase or fabricated part going into assembly. These are identified in the listing by Code I indicating inventory value. **For Sub-Assemblies in Listing and for each End-Product Assembly** Two lines are shown for each sub-assembly going into the assembly and for each end-product assembly. These are identified by the code on each line. The first line (Code I) represents the cumulative cost or inventory value. The second line (Code A) represents the value added in the assembly process. **For All Line Items** The description below applies to all line items appearing in the listing:
Level	The level for the part in the assembly process. (From Product Structure)
Quantity Extended	The units of the line item required to assemble one unit of top level part being assembled. (From Product Structure)
Quantity Per (Optional)	The units of the line item required to assembly one unit of the next higher level of assembly on the listing. (From Product Structure).
Part Number	The number of the part, sub-assembly or top-level assembly.
Type	The identity of the line item as to whether it is (F) a fabricated part, (P) a purchased part or (A) Assembly. (From Product Structure).
Date Up-Date	The date of the latest engineering or rate change affecting the line item.
Lot Size	The standard order quantity for evaluating fabricated parts on the list (See Routing File).

K-3

Appendix I **221**

Report	Indented Product Cost	REPORT DESCRIPTIONS	Date	3-15-78
Line	Column Heading		By	
(Title, Detail, Summary)				WWA

ITEM	DESCRIPTION AND SOURCE
	Note: For all quantities and values shown for items below the data represents figures for the extended quantity required for the top level assembly. Thus, the figure per piece is determined first and then is multiplied by the extended quantity.
Metal Pounds	The pounds of metal in raw material used in fabricated parts. (See Material Specification File)
Metal Dollars	Standard cost of raw material used for fabricated parts. (See Material Specification File and Rate File)
Other Raw Materials	Standard cost of other raw materials used for fabricated parts. (See Material Specification file and rate file)
Purchased Parts Dollars	Standard purchase price of each purchase part. (See Rate File)
Purchase Services Dollars	Standard purchase cost of outside services. (See Routing File and Rate File)
Set-Up Labor Hours	Standard hours to set-up for fabricated part. Standard set-up hours per piece = standard hours per occurrence ÷ standard lot size. (From Routing File)
Set-Up Labor Dollars	The Standard Cost for set-up labor for the fabricated part. (See Routing File and Rate File)
Direct Labor	The Standard run hours for each fabricated part or assembly. (See Routing File)
Direct Labor Dollars	The Standard cost of direct run labor for the fabricated or assembled part. (See Routing File and Rate File)
Variable Factory Overhead Dollars	The Standard Cost of variable overhead for fabricated or assembled part. (See Routing File and Rate File)
Total Manufacturing Cost Dollars	The total direct standard manufacturing cost for the part sub-assembly or assembly. (Total of all dollar columns)

K-4

222 Management Accounting Simplified

REPORT
Parts Cost Listing (L)

REPORT DESCRIPTIONS	Date
Report: Parts Cost Listing	3-15-78
Line: General	By
(Title, Detail, Summary)	WWA

ITEM	DESCRIPTION AND SOURCE
	This is a one-line list of the standard cost for each raw material, part or service purchased, for each part number fabricated, and for each sub-assembly and end-product inventoried or shipped. The listing is in sequence by the appropriate identifying number.
	This listing has many uses. Among them are marketing decisions, make/buy considerations, other planning applications, pricing physical inventory, valuing scrap and calculating cost of sales.
	Normally this listing is at "Frozen Value". However, it may well be a valuable reference if run periodically, say quarterly, at Current Value.
	All data for quantities and dollars are shown for the number of units of the line item used for cost purposes, whether per 100 or per each.

L-1

Appendix I **225**

REPORT DESCRIPTIONS	Date
Report: Parts Cost Listing	3-15-78
Line: Title and Column Headings	By
(Title, Detail, Summary)	WWA

ITEM	DESCRIPTION AND SOURCE
Report Title	Parts Cost Listing
Run Date	Date Listing was run in EDP.
Code	F = Frozen Cost C = Current Cost S = Simulated Cost

	<u>Column Headings</u>
	
	The Parts Cost Listing utilizes the same column headings as the Indented Product Cost, except that the following two columns would be omitted:
	
	    Level
	    Quantity
	
	and the following two columns would be added:

Part Name	The description of the Line Item (From Item master)
Standard Units	The number of units used for cost purposes (i.e. per 100 or per each)

L-2

REPORTS
Operation Cost Listing (M)

Appendix I

REPORT DESCRIPTIONS	Date
Report: Operation Cost Listing	3-15-78
Line: General	By
(Title, Detail, Summary)	WWA

ITEM	DESCRIPTION AND SOURCE
	This listing is at Frozen inventory value only and is normally run just once a year after inventory has been repriced. The column headings are the same as on the parts cost listing.
	For each fabricated and assembled part, this listing shows the accumulated standard quantities and values through each operation on the Routing File. In the case of assemblies, the data at the end of each operation includes the figures for the next lower level assembly parts brought into the assembly process at that operation.
	This listing will have broad application in the valuing of scrap and in the pricing of in-process inventory.

M-1

REPORTS
Data Base Listings (N)

Appendix I

REPORT DESCRIPTIONS		
Report: Data Base Listings		Date: 3-15-78
Line: General (Page 1 of 2)		By: WWA
(Title, Detail, Summary)		

ITEM	DESCRIPTION AND SOURCE
General	To assure full visibility and complete understanding on the part of all users, the information stored on data base records is printed out in hard copy report form. These listings are run periodically during the year. They are always run immediately after inventory has been re-priced at the new Frozen values. In addition they are run at intervals during the year, say quarterly or whenever there have been significant changes in physical or rate standards. Printouts always show both Frozen and Current standards. Data base listings include the following:
Raw Material Specifications	This listing is presented as an addition, or a possible alternate to the Routing Sheet Report previously described in another section. The Routing Sheet Report serves to group all physical data relating to a fabricated part on one sheet. A separate Raw Material Specifications Report, however, lists in Part Number sequence all quantitative and descriptive information about raw material consumed in the manufacturing process.
Raw Material Rates	This report lists the standard purchase price in raw material number sequence. Prices paid to vendors are compared with the Frozen standard as invoices are vouchered during the year. The standard value of purchases is carried into inventory. Any difference is recorded as a variance against income for the month. The variance for the month is analyzed by type of material. The magnitude of the variance is determined by a cost ratio (actual ÷ standard).
Purchase Parts Rates	This listing shows the standard purchase price of parts in number sequence. As with raw materials, actual price paid vendors are compared with the Frozen standard; the standard value is transferred to inventory and the difference is charged off as variance which is analyzed by type of part and magnitude.
Outside Processing Rates	This report is in processing number sequence and lists the standard price from the vendor. Again, as with raw materials, actual prices paid to vendors are compared with the Frozen standard. The standard value is carried into inventory and the difference is charged off as a variance which is analyzed by type of processing and magnitude.

N-1

	REPORT DESCRIPTIONS	Date 3-15-78
Report **Data Base Listings**		
Line **General** (Page 2 of 2)		By WWA
(Title, Detail, Summary)		

ITEM	DESCRIPTION AND SOURCE
Current Standards for Purchases	Where there are permanent changes in prices paid for raw material, purchase parts or outside services, the new price is entered in the Current file. Before recognizing the latest price as the Current standard, however, a review is made by Purchasing and Cost Accounting to assure that the change is a valid one and does not merely reflect a one-time local condition.
Labor/Variable Factory Overhead Rates	This is a listing by Department Number showing separately the applicable costing rates for Direct Labor and Variable Factory Overhead for each production department. These rates are applied to standard or earned direct labor hours to determine standard value added as a result of production for the month. The standard value added is transferred to inventory each month and is also used as the flexible budget for the department. In the product cost build-up, the standard value added is calculated for each operation sequence. These values are then accumulated to provide the standard cost for direct labor and direct expense for each part number.

APPENDIX II
GLOSSARY OF TERMS

Absorption costs   A cost system which includes *all* manufacturing expenses in cost of sales and inventory values whether based on actual or standard costs. The terms *full costs* or *total costs* are also used to describe this system.

Under this system fixed or capacity costs such as supervision, depreciation, and rent are assigned to products on some logical basis and are absorbed on the basis of production. The simplest method is to estimate manufacturing direct labor and expense for a forecasted level of production represented by direct labor dollars and then develop an overhead costing rate per labor dollar expressed as a percentage.

Direct Labor	$100,000
Overhead	$200,000
Overhead Rate =	200%

Thus overhead is absorbed by productive labor at this rate.

More sophisticated systems organize manufacturing estimates by departments or cost centers. Most operating costs such as labor, operating supplies, and tooling can be charged directly to the department using them. But fixed or capacity costs and services must be allocated to each producing department. A unique overhead rate for each department is then calculated by dividing assigned and allocated overhead by projected direct labor dollars.

The problem with any absorption cost system is that fixed or period costs remain virtually the same month by month regardless of volume unless changed by management decision. On the other hand, actual volume is rarely the same as the forecast volume. Therefore, overhead costing rates compared to true costs can be very misleading.

Attainment factors   A rate used to adjust standard hours produced to a reasonable level which can and should be achieved. Actual hours are compared with earned hours, and the difference is reported as a variance.

Cost centers The organizational groups of a unit used to control operating costs and expenses. A cost center should be under the direct supervision of a person who has the delegated responsibility for costs and expenses incurred.

Direct cost centers Cost centers are points of management control. The budget allowances, against which actual expenses are measured, are based upon units of production volume (both actual and standard) with which the expenses vary. Measurement units can be standard machine-hours, standard work-hours, product units, and so on. Every direct cost center will have an individual person who is responsible to top management for the costs incurred and the productivity performances of the center.

Direct costing An accounting method whereby period expenses are kept separate from direct costs in the accounting records and in all internal management reports and operating profit is stated in terms of a P/V breakeven chart.

Direct cost of sales The dollar result of multiplying the units of each product shipped to an outside customer times the actual or standard direct cost per unit. Direct cost of a product consists of (but is not limited to) raw materials and conversion cost, which includes direct labor and fringes and other direct expenses such as operating supplies, maintenance labor, maintenance parts, and power for processing.

Direct costs Those expenses that vary more or less automatically with changes in volume of production or sales. Examples are: raw materials, packaging materials, direct labor wages, fringe benefits on direct labor, operating supplies, perishable tools, and sales commissions.

Direct labor Hourly-paid personnel working directly on the product and who are instrumental in physically changing it.

Direct manufacturing cost variances This applies when the direct manufacturing cost of sales defined previously is at standard. The difference between actual and standard is called a *variance*. When the actual is greater than standard, it is usually shown as a negative or unfavorable variance; and when the actual is less than standard, it is usually shown as a positive or favorable variance.

Direct margin The dollars remaining to cover all period expenses and then provide a profit. Also called profit contribution, direct margin is equal to sales income less direct cost.

Direct margin—standard The dollar result of subtracting standard direct manufacturing cost of sales (defined above) from net sales. This is margin (meaning dollars remaining) to cover other direct costs as well as all period costs and then provide a profit.

Direct standard costing This accounting procedure introduces standards into the direct cost system against which actual performances are measured and reported out as variances from standard. The records are set up in such a way that these variances can be traced back through the organization structure. Thus, with responsibility accounting and direct standard costs, any variance can always be assigned to the person responsible for that variance and suitable action can be taken.

Direct standard product costs Using the techniques of direct standard costing (measurement of input to inventory by responsibility and measurement of output from inventory to cost of sales by product), the basic standards used to measure performance in a given cost center are used to establish the direct standard value added to each product going through that cost center. In a similar fashion, the same standard prices and material requirements used to measure variances are applied to the product cost sheets. This results in the ability to measure the direct standard cost of any product at any stage of its manufacture; hence, inventory pricing at both beginning and end of a period is simplified.

Flexible budgets A system of reporting and controlling costs in a direct cost center though volume varies substantially from "normal" operation. An activity unit is determined, and both "budget" and "actual" costs are reported at that particular level of activity. Thus, the budget reports measure performance against standard for the level of production actually achieved.

Fringe benefits The compensation which an employee receives over and above his or her salary or wages. Such benefits include but are not limited to: FICA, retirement or pension plans, workmen's compensation, group insurance, vacation, holidays, and so on.

Gross profit Sales income less absorption cost.

Head count The number of persons assigned to a direct cost center or to a period department. The *force report* provides this head count and is a valuable budget building and control tool.

Indirect labor Hourly-paid labor which is not specifically related to the production of any product.

Labor standards A part of the direct standard cost system. Direct labor standards are established in each direct cost center. Depending on need, daily or weekly reports are issued which compare actual labor performance credited or charged against the standard. Any variances are charged to the statement of income.

Material standards Part of a standard cost system. Standard prices are set for each material purchased. When material is received, actual price is compared with standard. The difference is charged or credited to the income statement for the period as the purchase price variance. Usage and scrap are measured and compared with standard, and these variances are also charged or credited to the income statement.

Operating supplies Supplies used in direct cost centers which vary with production volume. On reports to production supervisors, operating supplies are usually shown in detail so that each production or first-line supervisor can see the quantity and cost charged to the account.

Overhead In general, that portion of the costs which are not directly traceable to volume. In an absorption cost system, overhead consists of some direct and some period costs and is transferred from point to point by allocation. The term *overhead* is not used in any of the management accounting procedures; instead, we refine our separation of all costs into direct or period.

Period departments Points of control are charged with costs as defined under *period expenses*. These departments follow lines of responsibility as established by management.

Period expenses Those expenses which vary primarily with the passage of time or by executive decision are called period expenses. Examples of these types of expenses are: salaries; depreciation; rent; postage, telephone, office supplies, etc.; and advertising. These period expenses perform in a step fashion relative to activity level and are budgeted based upon a "normal volume" activity level. They are manageable costs which are incurred as a result of management decisions.

Product costs   The collection and summarizing of all the various cost factors determine the cost of manufacturing a specific product. Various methods are in use in industry today such as job costs, standard costs, and direct standard costs.

Profit/volume ratio   The rate by which sales volume contributes to profit. It is determined by dividing direct margin by sales income.

Responsibility accounting   One of the basic elements of the management accounting system. All costs are assigned on a responsibility basis, that is, to the one person who is committed to and can best control such costs. A clear-cut organization structure and the assignment of costs to the lowest level of responsibility possible are crucial elements for this system to work properly.

Standards   Measures (established by those given this responsibility by management) of quality, quantity, price, volume, time, extent, performance output, or methods. They become the benchmarks or goals used for control and analysis. Standards can be engineered or historical. They should be attainable so that unfavorable variances will represent unnecessary excess costs about which something should be done. Standards are the basis for the development of plans and standard unit product costs.

Variances   The result of comparing actual with standard. Variances assist management in looking for areas for profit improvement.

APPENDIX III
THE WRIGHT COMPARATIVE RATIOS FOR U.S. MANUFACTURING INDUSTRIES 1961–1977

Class	1961	1962	1963	1964	1965	1966	1967	1968	1969	1970	1971	1972	1973	1974	1975	1976	1977
All manufacturing corporations																	
Profit/volume ratio	.335	.335	.337	.339	.345	.345	.342	.343	.341	.330	.333	.330	.337	.330	.327	.338	.372
Margin of safety	.222	.236	.243	.256	.269	.269	.242	.256	.246	.212	.221	.237	.251	.235	.221	.239	.216
Capital turnover	1.350	1.384	1.391	1.410	1.432	1.436	1.364	1.352	1.325	1.249	1.259	1.323	1.425	1.460	1.349	1.419	1.440
Financial operations ratio	.579	.575	.577	.604	.603	.603	.608	.577	.568	.577	.561	.549	.556	.704	.636	.663	.658
Financial leverage	1.530	1.551	1.564	1.573	1.624	1.676	1.704	1.758	1.808	1.849	1.860	1.869	1.907	1.871	1.866	1.861	1.873
Return on investment	.089	.098	.103	.116	.130	.134	.117	.121	.114	.093	.097	.106	.128	.149	.116	.142	.143
Durable goods																	
Profit/volume ratio	.350	.350	.352	.355	.360	.360	.358	.360	.355	.346	.350	.354	.356	.350	.344	.350	.407
Margin of safety	.221	.243	.250	.262	.283	.278	.242	.257	.247	.194	.210	.230	.246	.217	.195	.227	.202
Capital turnover	1.309	1.370	1.386	1.410	1.454	1.464	1.365	1.363	1.325	1.215	1.230	1.307	1.407	1.387	1.292	1.389	1.441
Financial operations ratio	.507	.516	.514	.549	.555	.560	.557	.532	.522	.528	.516	.520	.536	.614	.610	.657	.642
Financial leverage	1.577	1.600	1.616	1.629	1.677	1.732	1.763	1.814	1.874	1.926	1.935	1.941	1.985	1.941	1.936	1.913	1.922
Return on investment	.081	.096	.101	.117	.138	.142	.117	.122	.114	.083	.090	.107	.131	.125	.102	.139	.146
Non-durable goods																	
Profit/volume ratio	.300	.300	.301	.305	.310	.310	.305	.305	.305	.300	.300	.294	.309	.300	.300	.304	.314
Margin of safety	.238	.244	.250	.262	.267	.271	.258	.271	.261	.242	.245	.254	.305	.263	.258	.270	.252
Capital turnover	1.391	1.399	1.397	1.409	1.408	1.406	1.364	1.340	1.326	1.287	1.289	1.341	1.307	1.538	1.408	1.450	1.439
Financial operations ratio	.654	.643	.652	.672	.668	.661	.667	.635	.626	.624	.608	.582	.536	.787	.656	.670	.671
Financial leverage	1.485	1.504	1.513	1.519	1.571	1.621	1.643	1.698	1.739	1.770	1.793	1.796	1.985	1.801	1.798	1.802	1.826
Return on investment	.096	.099	.104	.115	.122	.127	.118	.119	.115	.103	.103	.105	.131	.172	.125	.144	.139
Under $1000 assets*																	
Profit/volume ratio	.225	.230	.225	.230	.235	.240	.250	.245	.240	.235	.237	.243	.252	.252	.245	.252	N/A
Margin of safety	.110	.137	.138	.163	.188	.217	.183	.177	.184	.127	.131	.178	.189	.227	.190	.181	
Capital turnover	2.441	2.478	2.490	2.544	2.577	2.619	2.511	2.530	2.532	2.442	2.405	2.524	2.693	2.662	2.541	2.732	
Financial operations ratio	.482	.560	.545	.623	.636	.645	.617	.604	.579	.515	.474	.618	.610	.601	.526	.625	
Financial leverage	1.911	1.921	1.966	1.954	1.976	1.992	1.940	2.012	1.992	2.078	2.073	2.102	2.150	2.158	2.133	2.112	
Return on investment	.056	.084	.083	.116	.143	.175	.137	.134	.129	.078	.074	.142	.168	.198	.133	.164	

*Assets size groups, 000 omitted.

$1,000 to $5,000*																
Profit/volume ratio	.260	.265	.270	.275	.280	.285	.285	.285	.280	.273	.283	.283	.283	.288	.277	.291	.305
Margin of safety	.159	.177	.166	.196	.213	.221	.199	.205	.203	.167	.164	.183	.217	.220	.206	.222	.195
Capital turnover	2.022	2.053	2.004	2.047	2.058	2.113	2.097	2.090	2.068	2.013	2.144	2.104	2.236	2.359	2.236	2.406	2.489
Financial operations ratio	.450	.483	.476	.522	.540	.527	.518	.511	.487	.464	.488	.505	.547	.506	.474	.529	.612
Financial leverage	1.622	1.676	1.694	1.705	1.754	1.786	1.798	1.777	1.795	1.822	1.777	1.937	2.016	2.070	2.023	2.069	2.128
Return on investment	.061	.077	.073	.098	.116	.126	.111	.111	.103	.078	.086	.107	.151	.157	.123	.170	.193
$5,000 to $10,000*																
Profit/volume ratio	.280	.280	.280	.290	.300	.305	.305	.305	.295	.288	.293	.275	.287	.287	.284	.293	.286
Margin of safety	.211	.222	.222	.225	.240	.254	.237	.236	.224	.182	.213	.230	.250	.252	.235	.241	.231
Capital turnover	1.649	1.682	1.741	1.750	1.793	1.873	1.792	1.817	1.777	1.718	1.671	1.931	1.951	2.055	1.957	2.167	2.146
Financial operations ratio	.475	.485	.483	.520	.535	.528	.523	.493	.467	.440	.475	.496	.503	.475	.444	.469	.484
Financial leverage	1.485	1.552	1.573	1.619	1.662	1.716	1.662	1.668	1.748	1.762	1.771	1.713	1.788	1.893	1.882	1.963	1.991
Return on investment	.069	.079	.082	.096	.115	.130	.113	.108	.096	.070	.088	.104	.126	.134	.109	.140	.136
$10,000 to $25,000*																
Profit/volume ratio	.290	.295	.305	.310	.305	.305	.315	.315	.310	.323	.338	.370	.350	.350	.300	.364	.352
Margin of safety	.226	.238	.235	.243	.269	.275	.241	.239	.231	.180	.185	.179	.199	.216	.239	.210	.196
Capital turnover	1.478	1.522	1.493	1.554	1.608	1.663	1.600	1.628	1.630	1.542	1.558	1.661	1.880	1.868	1.784	1.855	1.926
Financial operations ratio	.485	.495	.492	.521	.543	.531	.525	.481	.469	.445	.472	.490	.516	.473	.487	.511	.467
Financial leverage	1.488	1.522	1.544	1.593	1.659	1.712	1.706	1.717	1.758	1.754	1.722	1.732	1.803	1.911	1.906	1.910	1.960
Return on investment	.070	.080	.083	.097	.119	.127	.109	.101	.096	.070	.079	.093	.122	.127	.119	.139	.121
$25,000 to $50,000*																
Profit/volume ratio	.320	.325	.320	.325	.335	.335	.330	.330	.330	.312	.314	.317	.309	.309	.304	.311	.341
Margin of safety	.232	.246	.241	.254	.269	.275	.248	.252	.238	.200	.197	.211	.245	.249	.239	.254	.223
Capital turnover	1.356	1.401	1.399	1.436	1.477	1.512	1.478	1.529	1.474	1.470	1.474	1.531	1.590	1.632	1.555	1.684	1.775
Financial operations ratio	.508	.504	.493	.532	.552	.552	.544	.518	.494	.463	.467	.502	.511	.458	.464	.471	.487
Financial leverage	1.498	1.525	1.557	1.576	1.594	1.659	1.673	1.689	1.751	1.807	1.840	1.874	1.912	2.023	1.960	1.910	1.897
Return on investment	.077	.086	.083	.100	.117	.127	.110	.111	.100	.077	.078	.096	.118	.117	.103	.119	.124

*Assets size groups, 000 omitted.

Class	1961	1962	1963	1964	1965	1966	1967	1968	1969	1970	1971	1972	1973	1974	1975	1976	1977
$50,000 to $100,000*																	
Profit/volume ratio	.330	.335	.335	.345	.345	.350	.340	.340	.340	.327	.335	.328	.321	.315	.300	.312	.327
Margin of safety	.242	.238	.236	.251	.257	.269	.241	.241	.249	.208	.209	.229	.244	.263	.239	.259	.244
Capital turnover	1.359	1.380	1.412	1.442	1.487	1.497	1.392	1.391	1.377	1.298	1.329	1.423	1.548	1.609	1.529	1.568	1.582
Financial operations ratio	.500	.502	.508	.538	.544	.540	.532	.500	.486	.479	.478	.506	.513	.510	.500	.488	.512
Financial leverage	1.533	1.551	1.533	1.566	1.633	1.696	1.760	1.835	1.866	1.877	1.842	1.812	1.908	1.931	1.890	1.894	1.965
Return on investment	.083	.086	.089	.105	.117	.129	.107	.105	.106	.079	.082	.098	.119	.132	.104	.118	.127
$100,000 to $250,000*																	
Profit/volume ratio	.340	.340	.355	.360	.355	.360	.355	.360	.350	.342	.335	.331	.331	.320	.317	.319	.334
Margin of safety	.232	.251	.248	.256	.271	.275	.264	.259	.268	.227	.223	.228	.240	.249	.246	.260	.247
Capital turnover	1.312	1.335	1.343	1.356	1.396	1.421	1.360	1.340	1.355	1.254	1.313	1.402	1.730	1.523	1.427	1.483	1.560
Financial operations ratio	.518	.520	.522	.553	.561	.557	.548	.512	.495	.498	.500	.520	.513	.523	.515	.494	.531
Financial leverage	1.564	1.583	1.606	1.613	1.668	1.709	1.698	1.743	1.814	1.906	1.896	1.866	1.650	2.011	1.958	1.917	1.891
Return on investment	.084	.094	.099	.112	.125	.133	.119	.112	.114	.093	.093	.103	.116	.128	.112	.117	.129
$250,000 to $1,000,000*																	
Profit/volume ratio	.360	.355	.350	.360	.360	.360	.355	.360	.350	.347	.347	.341	.348	.338	.332	.345	.366
Margin of safety	.245	.235	.246	.257	.273	.270	.242	.262	.257	.231	.226	.241	.256	.245	.237	.256	.234
Capital turnover	1.227	1.252	1.265	1.276	1.302	1.321	1.301	1.291	1.299	1.257	1.244	1.296	1.372	1.386	1.287	1.374	1.420
Financial operations ratio	.538	.539	.546	.569	.569	.570	.576	.549	.540	.533	.533	.527	.533	.622	.583	.598	.598
Financial leverage	1.605	1.631	1.632	1.632	1.697	1.755	1.794	1.806	1.855	1.917	1.895	1.904	1.940	1.949	1.947	1.920	1.920
Return on investment	.094	.092	.097	.110	.123	.129	.116	.121	.117	.103	.099	.107	.126	.139	.115	.139	.140
$1,000,000* +																	
Profit/volume ratio	.350	.342	.340	.335	.340	.330	.320	.315	.315	.303	.307	.309	.319	.310	.310	.322	.342
Margin of safety	.323	.361	.380	.379	.389	.367	.324	.347	.321	.272	.291	.303	.314	.265	.249	.275	.256
Capital turnover	.932	1.005	1.027	1.060	1.078	1.067	1.023	1.058	1.027	.974	1.013	1.057	1.168	1.172	1.079	1.144	1.179
Financial operations ratio	.744	.686	.678	.695	.675	.682	.697	.641	.642	.672	.622	.575	.580	.918	.777	.789	.755
Financial leverage	1.388	1.407	1.421	1.434	1.482	1.551	1.614	1.720	1.774	1.817	1.844	1.853	1.879	1.766	1.783	1.790	1.806
Return on investment	.109	.119	.128	.134	.143	.136	.119	.127	.118	.098	.104	.105	.128	.156	.116	.143	.141

*Assets size groups, 000 omitted.

Transportation equipment																	
Profit/volume ratio	.350	.345	.345	.340	.345	.340	.330	.330	.325	.315	.329	.322	.317	.312	.315	.332	.409
Margin of safety	.228	.301	.311	.299	.324	.274	.225	.276	.245	.130	.225	.247	.236	.139	.134	.208	.181
Capital turnover	1.532	1.641	1.645	1.643	1.709	1.644	1.521	1.561	1.455	1.305	1.433	1.476	1.570	1.441	1.434	1.576	1.719
Financial operations ratio	.510	.512	.496	.547	.544	.557	.557	.522	.471	.576	.513	.504	.526	.629	.580	.691	.675
Financial leverage	1.701	1.732	1.735	1.726	1.774	1.829	1.893	2.001	2.015	2.051	2.062	2.078	2.116	2.015	2.091	2.084	2.046
Return on investment	.106	.150	.152	.158	.184	.156	.119	.149	.110	.063	.112	.123	.130	.079	.074	.157	.176
Motor vehicles & equipment																	
Profit/volume ratio	.390	.380	.375	.365	.360	.350	.340	.340	.330	.309	.340	.340	.325	.275	.270	.295	.372
Margin of safety	.269	.351	.372	.347	.368	.311	.254	.317	.279	.136	.261	.274	.255	.124	.134	.251	.210
Capital turnover	1.413	1.565	1.582	1.570	1.685	1.617	1.511	1.619	1.592	1.394	1.949	1.703	1.780	1.575	1.532	1.796	1.993
Financial operations ratio	.526	.518	.496	.551	.547	.562	.566	.524	.516	.623	.523	.511	.553	.775	.667	.765	.698
Financial leverage	1.468	1.501	1.582	1.539	1.597	1.598	1.582	1.647	1.666	1.686	1.447	1.783	1.840	1.664	1.752	1.738	1.720
Return on investment	.114	.163	.167	.169	.195	.159	.117	.151	.126	.061	.131	.144	.150	.069	.065	.177	.187
Elec. Mach., equip., & supp.																	
Profit/volume ratio	.345	.355	.355	.370	.370	.365	.365	.365	.365	.350	.351	.355	.360	.350	.342	.355	.422
Margin of safety	.201	.211	.205	.213	.236	.247	.224	.233	.222	.194	.200	.217	.234	.202	.179	.211	.202
Capital turnover	1.548	1.572	1.548	1.547	1.583	1.619	1.503	1.467	1.417	1.311	1.285	1.334	1.398	1.363	1.345	1.435	1.436
Financial operations ratio	.498	.503	.515	.530	.544	.537	.535	.502	.479	.491	.504	.504	.511	.547	.521	.603	.628
Financial leverage	1.668	1.699	1.730	1.734	1.797	1.887	1.942	1.942	2.023	2.076	2.083	2.095	2.168	2.107	2.079	2.039	2.006
Return on investment	.089	.100	.101	.113	.135	.148	.128	.122	.111	.091	.095	.108	.131	.111	.089	.132	.154
Other machinery																	
Profit/volume ratio	.345	.350	.355	.365	.370	.375	.370	.365	.370	.359	.350	.355	.360	.350	.354	.365	.418
Margin of safety	.238	.253	.263	.303	.312	.315	.291	.297	.295	.262	.241	.269	.288	.252	.251	.281	.256
Capital turnover	1.218	1.280	1.300	1.349	1.394	1.415	1.327	1.300	1.262	1.152	1.129	1.198	1.277	1.239	1.173	1.204	1.235
Financial operations ratio	.501	.509	.504	.522	.536	.540	.530	.506	.498	.492	.500	.535	.540	.672	.697	.709	.709
Financial leverage	1.551	1.568	1.573	1.597	1.641	1.668	1.706	1.725	1.779	1.848	1.827	1.809	1.870	1.796	1.825	1.766	1.768
Return on investment	.078	.091	.096	.125	.141	.150	.129	.123	.122	.098	.087	.110	.134	.132	.132	.154	.165

Class	1961	1962	1963	1964	1965	1966	1967	1968	1969	1970	1971	1972	1973	1974	1975	1976	1977
Fabricated metal products, metalworking mach. & equip.																	
Profit/volume ratio	.350	.330	.335	.335	.340	.345	.340	.335	.320	.290	.290	.305	.330	.300	.297	.306	.328
Margin of safety	.187	.231	.246	.299	.318	.339	.306	.300	.290	.230	.139	.188	.266	.279	.268	.270	.246
Capital turnover	1.281	1.382	1.378	1.467	1.520	1.587	1.504	1.454	1.422	1.321	1.231	1.356	1.521	1.750	1.565	1.678	1.681
Financial operations ratio	.496	.543	.524	.562	.560	.558	.538	.519	.512	.512	.429	.503	.570	.549	.521	.582	.593
Financial leverage	1.440	1.449	1.461	1.510	1.568	1.659	1.659	1.642	1.711	1.835	1.766	1.667	1.773	2.063	2.010	1.941	1.960
Return on investment	.060	.083	.086	.124	.144	.171	.140	.124	.116	.083	.038	.065	.135	.167	.130	.156	.158
Other fabricated metal prod.																	
Profit/volume ratio	.270	.275	.280	.285	.295	.300	.305	.300	.295	.294	.294	.304	.304				
Margin of safety	.204	.231	.231	.243	.272	.290	.267	.267	.257	.216	.214	.228	.256				
Capital turnover	1.556	1.609	1.623	1.660	1.710	1.743	1.629	1.602	1.604	1.451	1.452	1.592	1.704	N/A	N/A	N/A	N/A
Financial operations ratio	.449	.493	.498	.537	.564	.560	.549	.512	.496	.477	.458	.503	.519				
Financial leverage	1.487	1.562	1.589	1.641	1.708	1.736	1.739	1.785	1.869	1.943	1.982	1.990	2.014				
Return on investment	.059	.079	.083	.101	.132	.147	.127	.117	.113	.085	.083	.110	.138				
Primary metal industries																	
Profit/volume ratio	.310	.300	.310	.315	.320	.330	.325	.315	.320	.310	.306	.314	.314	.325	.310	.312	.261
Margin of safety	.296	.273	.297	.322	.338	.345	.276	.273	.275	.205	.162	.202	.264	.316	.204	.188	.161
Capital turnover	.898	.931	.965	1.024	1.069	1.091	.976	.960	.976	.913	.869	.945	1.119	1.285	1.238	1.113	1.149
Financial operations ratio	.527	.541	.545	.582	.580	.587	.624	.613	.610	.645	.581	.520	.554	.643	.667	.659	.543
Financial leverage	1.488	1.491	1.493	1.516	1.569	1.635	1.637	1.754	1.825	1.880	1.912	1.927	1.963	1.931	1.877	1.918	1.997
Return on investment	.065	.062	.072	.091	.105	.119	.090	.089	.096	.070	.048	.060	.101	.164	.083	.082	.052
Primary iron & steel																	
Profit/volume ratio	.315	.305	.315	.315	.315	.320	.315	.305	.305	.284	.293	.302	.311	.320	.300	.294	.226
Margin of safety	.288	.245	.289	.310	.313	.313	.245	.256	.243	.148	.161	.192	.236	.323	.241	.201	.150
Capital turnover	.902	.938	.971	1.047	1.094	1.090	.987	.977	.983	.930	.938	1.025	1.187	1.377	1.184	1.229	1.220
Financial operations ratio	.505	.518	.530	.571	.580	.578	.626	.590	.593	.599	.552	.535	.559	.616	.656	.667	.421
Financial leverage	1.488	1.493	1.490	1.506	1.557	1.625	1.618	1.689	1.763	1.842	1.862	1.901	1.958	1.923	1.833	1.865	1.962
Return on investment	.061	.054	.070	.088	.098	.102	.077	.076	.076	.043	.045	.061	.096	.169	.103	.090	.034

Primary nonferrous metals																	
Profit/volume ratio	.300	.305	.305	.315	.325	.335	.325	.305	.315	.315	.291	.300	.308	.320	.209	.313	.368
Margin of safety	.283	.311	.308	.345	.387	.409	.337	.319	.326	.292	.185	.244	.318	.318	.162	.171	.158
Capital turnover	.890	.919	.954	.982	1.026	1.092	.960	.937	.966	.891	.777	.828	1.023	1.149	.834	.946	1.026
Financial operations ratio	.630	.579	.570	.599	.581	.597	.623	.638	.641	.671	.621	.498	.548	.691	.636	.692	.625
Financial leverage	1.489	1.480	1.500	1.534	1.590	1.650	1.668	1.850	1.915	1.929	1.980	1.965	1.973	1.942	1.949	1.986	2.078
Return on investment	.071	.075	.076	.098	.119	.148	.109	.108	.122	.106	.051	.059	.108	.157	.051	.069	.078
Stone, clay & glass prod.																	
Profit/volume ratio	.400	.395	.395	.400	.405	.395	.390	.395	.390	.380	.393	.393	.393	.385	.382	.395	.431
Margin of safety	.273	.261	.251	.248	.251	.241	.210	.234	.220	.177	.199	.212	.216	.187	.163	.209	.203
Capital turnover	1.077	1.120	1.134	1.161	1.163	1.145	1.079	1.106	1.168	1.127	1.185	1.264	1.313	1.311	1.230	1.295	1.407
Financial operations ratio	.534	.540	.534	.569	.582	.590	.592	.559	.549	.532	.571	.566	.572	.613	.412	.583	.621
Financial leverage	1.410	1.422	1.451	1.462	1.490	1.536	1.565	1.607	1.675	1.717	1.732	1.702	1.760	1.814	1.835	1.836	1.830
Return on investment	.089	.089	.087	.096	.103	.099	.082	.092	.092	.069	.092	.101	.112	.105	.058	.115	.140
Furniture & fixtures																	
Profit/volume ratio	.230	.235	.235	.230	.235	.235	.253	.235	.235	.233	.242	.238	.238	N/A	N/A	N/A	N/A
Margin of safety	.169	.209	.220	.237	.285	.292	.268	.284	.289	.218	.245	.287	.279	N/A	N/A	N/A	N/A
Capital turnover	1.964	2.091	2.036	2.147	2.177	2.198	2.052	2.143	2.121	1.940	1.938	2.089	2.042	N/A	N/A	N/A	N/A
Financial operations ratio	.405	.481	.483	.526	.564	.561	.562	.515	.513	.490	.512	.532	.543	N/A	N/A	N/A	N/A
Financial leverage	1.587	1.605	1.623	1.645	1.640	1.682	1.660	1.664	1.711	1.644	1.621	1.709	1.798	N/A	N/A	N/A	N/A
Return on investment	.049	.080	.083	.101	.134	.142	.121	.122	.126	.079	.095	.130	.133	N/A	N/A	N/A	N/A
Lumber & wood products																	
Profit/volume ratio	.230	.230	.230	.240	.240	.240	.235	.245	.245	.235	.255	.255	.271	N/A	N/A	N/A	N/A
Margin of safety	.143	.172	.219	.245	.247	.242	.224	.344	.332	.197	.289	.332	.392	N/A	N/A	N/A	N/A
Capital turnover	1.324	1.609	1.460	1.466	1.430	1.425	1.365	1.491	1.433	1.207	1.269	1.484	1.710	N/A	N/A	N/A	N/A
Financial operations ratio	.591	.619	.651	.668	.665	.647	.652	.634	.591	.530	.600	.603	.588	N/A	N/A	N/A	N/A
Financial leverage	1.583	1.644	1.716	1.723	1.784	1.863	1.840	1.840	1.893	1.997	2.032	2.099	2.085	N/A	N/A	N/A	N/A
Return on investment	.041	.056	.082	.099	.101	.100	.086	.146	.130	.059	.114	.159	.223	N/A	N/A	N/A	N/A

Class	1961	1962	1963	1964	1965	1966	1967	1968	1969	1970	1971	1972	1973	1974	1975	1976	1977
Instruments & related products																	
Profit/volume ratio	.485	.490	.490	.500	.500	.510	.510	.510	.505	.510	.510	.510	.510	.505	.512	.518	.544
Margin of safety	.225	.235	.240	.262	.309	.333	.302	.298	.300	.276	.272	.277	.297	.240	.218	.214	.218
Capital turnover	1.313	1.352	1.321	1.307	1.316	1.394	1.340	1.286	1.244	1.165	1.127	1.150	1.183	1.137	1.115	1.174	1.179
Financial operations ratio	.499	.513	.510	.546	.559	.558	.552	.531	.513	.521	.522	.547	.557	.758	.692	.700	.750
Financial leverage	1.482	1.503	1.525	1.538	1.545	1.579	1.584	1.594	1.610	1.665	1.661	1.613	1.596	1.546	1.583	1.597	1.606
Return on investment	.106	.120	.121	.144	.175	.209	.180	.166	.156	.143	.136	.143	.159	.162	.136	.146	.169
Other durable misc. mfg. & ordnance																	
Profit/volume ratio	.290	.285	.290	.300	.300	.305	.305	.310	.300	.293	.293	.295	.295	.300	.293	.302	.337
Margin of safety	.252	.233	.219	.220	.234	.272	.245	.248	.240	.221	.224	.232	.231	.227	.204	.248	.236
Capital turnover	1.500	1.434	1.400	1.426	1.471	1.613	1.606	1.638	1.593	1.530	1.462	1.552	1.656	1.613	1.481	1.647	1.783
Financial operations ratio	.509	.524	.521	.540	.539	.590	.557	.516	.528	.525	.483	.498	.467	.514	.464	.575	.531
Financial leverage	1.814	1.900	1.907	1.866	1.916	1.950	1.957	1.910	1.917	1.927	1.955	2.060	2.200	2.073	2.052	2.031	2.047
Return on investment	.099	.095	.088	.095	.107	.154	.131	.124	.116	.100	.090	.109	.116	.117	.084	.145	.154
Food & kindred products																	
Profit/volume ratio	.250	.245	.245	.245	.245	.245	.245	.245	.245	.245	.246	.242	.242	.225	.231	.237	.227
Margin of safety	.187	.189	.195	.206	.206	.200	.197	.207	.209	.207	.212	.206	.213	.223	.246	.239	.241
Capital turnover	2.408	2.371	2.351	2.332	2.333	2.375	2.338	2.248	2.246	2.196	2.154	2.208	2.408	2.495	2.217	2.173	2.593
Financial operations ratio	.496	.496	.495	.524	.544	.552	.538	.512	.501	.498	.500	.516	.509	.535	.565	.615	.613
Financial leverage	1.593	1.614	1.618	1.622	1.668	1.740	1.778	1.839	1.886	1.954	1.956	1.970	2.015	2.093	2.030	2.016	1.744
Return on investment	.089	.088	.090	.100	.107	.112	.108	.107	.109	.108	.110	.112	.127	.141	.144	.152	.150
Alcoholic beverages																	
Profit/volume ratio	.350	.350	.350	.350	.350	.350	.355	.355	.360	.350	.355	.352	.352				
Margin of safety	.198	.200	.205	.207	.214	.224	.225	.235	.238	.226	.235	.231	.246				
Capital turnover	1.486	1.496	1.528	1.509	1.525	1.521	1.482	1.471	1.459	1.429	1.387	1.397	1.416				
Financial operations ratio	.468	.468	.481	.528	.520	.539	.533	.497	.485	.534	.502	.505	.504	N/A	N/A	N/A	N/A
Financial leverage	1.527	1.525	1.502	1.528	1.560	1.630	1.636	1.657	1.716	1.744	1.825	1.853	1.747				
Return on investment	.074	.075	.079	.088	.093	.105	.103	.101	.104	.105	.106	.106	.108				

Tobacco manufactures																	
Profit/volume ratio	.500	.500	.510	.510	.520	.520	.525	.520	.515	.525	.529	.517	.510	.510	.530	.534	.552
Margin of safety	.258	.253	.252	.235	.225	.227	.232	.237	.231	.239	.250	.238	.239	.222	.320	.313	.276
Capital turnover	1.515	1.466	1.503	1.554	1.536	1.539	1.539	1.589	1.435	1.349	1.338	1.326	1.273	1.177	.884	.952	.979
Financial operations ratio	.444	.452	.456	.494	.503	.501	.486	.451	.437	.461	.461	.486	.472	.602	.529	.500	.571
Financial leverage	1.576	1.557	1.512	1.459	1.491	1.545	1.583	1.639	1.946	2.015	1.937	1.945	2.020	1.944	1.948	2.000	2.000
Return on investment	.136	.131	.134	.134	.135	.141	.144	.144	.145	.157	.158	.154	.148	.156	.155	.159	.171
Textile mill products																	
Profit/volume ratio	.250	.245	.245	.250	.260	.255	.250	.245	.245	.234	.236	.230	.234	.230	.224	.235	.234
Margin of safety	.180	.211	.204	.241	.282	.271	.229	.272	.259	.203	.221	.232	.255	.269	.188	.250	.244
Capital turnover	1.576	1.643	1.639	1.671	1.691	1.662	1.557	1.607	1.567	1.482	1.530	1.579	1.641	1.634	1.551	1.784	1.837
Financial operations ratio	.465	.473	.469	.517	.524	.523	.506	.471	.449	.403	.467	.481	.474	.411	.416	.450	.400
Financial leverage	1.512	1.546	1.579	1.624	1.667	1.681	1.687	1.737	1.772	1.798	1.791	1.848	1.934	1.946	1.887	1.900	1.900
Return on investment	.050	.062	.061	.085	.109	.101	.076	.088	.079	.051	.067	.075	.090	.081	.051	.090	.080
Apparel & other finish. prod.																	
Profit/volume ratio	.230	.230	.225	.230	.230	.230	.240	.235	.235	.245	.233	.225	.229	N/A	N/A		
Margin of safety	.119	.138	.133	.162	.176	.186	.180	.200	.188	.160	.197	.205	.190				
Capital turnover	2.701	2.655	2.652	2.659	2.577	2.436	2.322	2.337	2.271	2.135	2.150	2.250	2.299				
Financial operations ratio	.464	.511	.450	.573	.573	.551	.541	.521	.521	.492	.515	.514	.471				
Financial leverage	2.109	2.121	2.098	2.061	2.127	2.291	2.214	2.271	2.281	2.255	2.199	2.252	2.297				
Return on investment	.072	.091	.077	.117	.127	.131	.120	.130	.119	.093	.111	.120	.108				
Paper & allied products																	
Profit/volume ratio	.340	.345	.345	.350	.350	.355	.350	.350	.350	.332	.320	.347	.375	.372	.364	.372	.361
Margin of safety	.266	.261	.253	.259	.244	.265	.235	.245	.242	.186	.150	.211	.262	.315	.239	.247	.238
Capital turnover	1.165	1.192	1.203	1.220	1.213	1.212	1.128	1.150	1.155	1.090	1.099	1.191	1.288	1.375	1.189	1.302	1.259
Financial operations ratio	.514	.509	.517	.564	.581	.571	.573	.554	.564	.551	.476	.550	.553	.604	.643	.667	.611
Financial leverage	1.449	1.482	1.497	1.496	1.567	1.638	1.714	1.779	1.836	1.877	1.911	1.878	1.844	1.823	1.888	1.881	1.865
Return on investment	.079	.081	.081	.093	.094	.106	.091	.097	.102	.070	.048	.090	.129	.178	.126	.150	.124

Class	1961	1962	1963	1964	1965	1966	1967	1968	1969	1970	1971	1972	1973	1974	1975	1976	1977
Printing & publishing																	
Profit/volume ratio	.300	.305	.305	.315	.320	.325	.325	.320	.325	.325	.322	.327	.327	.330	.330	.336	.394
Margin of safety	.190	.211	.209	.250	.262	.280	.240	.241	.274	.245	.244	.264	.265	.255	.261	.291	.261
Capital turnover	1.677	1.621	1.562	1.588	1.597	1.632	1.575	1.578	1.515	1.462	1.429	1.440	1.485	1.540	1.504	1.612	1.618
Financial operations ratio	.499	.530	.495	.550	.576	.568	.564	.536	.524	.529	.522	.540	.549	.552	.516	.512	.563
Financial leverage	1.792	1.868	1.861	1.831	1.835	1.854	1.879	1.918	1.780	1.808	1.835	1.809	1.819	1.845	1.846	1.857	1.895
Return on investment	.085	.103	.092	.126	.142	.156	.130	.125	.126	.112	.107	.121	.128	.132	.123	.150	.178
Chemicals & allied products																	
Profit/volume ratio	.500	.495	.495	.500	.505	.500	.495	.495	.495	.487	.495	.501	.510	.505	.503	.505	.537
Margin of safety	.255	.265	.269	.272	.274	.272	.242	.257	.248	.226	.228	.235	.242	.234	.227	.221	.199
Capital turnover	1.098	1.136	1.145	1.194	1.188	1.164	1.141	1.161	1.155	1.114	1.115	1.162	1.233	1.255	1.129	1.188	1.174
Financial operations ratio	.575	.565	.564	.578	.573	.575	.573	.533	.528	.538	.539	.543	.552	.708	.657	.658	.661
Financial leverage	1.457	1.476	1.504	1.538	1.575	1.661	1.666	1.689	1.709	1.735	1.740	1.729	1.766	1.732	1.778	1.795	1.823
Return on investment	.118	.124	.129	.144	.149	.151	.131	.133	.128	.114	.118	.128	.148	.182	.150	.157	.151
Basic chemicals																	
Profit/volume ratio	.530	.525	.525	.525	.525	.520	.510	.505	.505	.495	.482	.490	.508	.500	.497		
Margin of safety	.248	.268	.269	.275	.277	.267	.218	.232	.221	.186	.195	.211	.238	.247	.236		
Capital turnover	.874	.910	.937	1.010	1.006	.983	.953	.978	.974	.934	.942	1.002	1.080	1.166	1.041	N/A	N/A
Financial operations ratio	.622	.600	.598	.600	.574	.581	.587	.538	.535	.541	.529	.527	.543	.986	.583		
Financial leverage	1.478	1.519	1.558	1.603	1.706	1.763	1.749	1.784	1.800	1.831	1.843	1.824	1.859	1.820	1.863		
Return on investment	.105	.117	.123	.140	.143	.140	.109	.110	.105	.085	.086	.100	.129	.258	.133		
Drugs																	
Profit/volume ratio	.450	.445	.445	.445	.445	.440	.435	.435	.440	.432	.432	.441	.435	.432	.435	.441	.472
Margin of safety	.416	.419	.436	.444	.457	.443	.417	.425	.418	.401	.398	.414	.417	.326	.316	.323	.303
Capital turnover	1.233	1.240	1.214	1.238	1.282	1.311	1.270	1.279	1.261	1.205	1.187	1.148	1.144	1.035	.930	.949	.959
Financial operations ratio	.526	.527	.521	.542	.554	.555	.559	.525	.525	.541	.553	.562	.561	.862	.833	.762	.870
Financial leverage	1.375	1.370	1.369	1.372	1.407	1.434	1.457	1.477	1.508	1.559	1.583	1.573	1.625	1.535	1.578	1.592	1.594
Return on investment	.167	.167	.168	.182	.203	.203	.187	.183	.184	.176	.178	.186	.189	.187	.167	.163	.189

	1	2	3	4	5	6	7	8	9	10	11	12	13	14	15	16	17
Petroleum refining & related																	
Profit/volume ratio	.350	.350	.350	.350	.355	.360	.360	.360	.355	.355	.351	.345	.366	.366	.366	.374	.363
Margin of safety	.249	.248	.270	.274	.290	.306	.301	.290	.274	.262	.249	.239	.281	.232	.231	.250	.233
Capital turnover	.755	.770	.788	.789	.786	.791	.790	.757	.750	.750	.779	.801	.921	1.122	1.039	1.060	1.086
Financial operations ratio	1.166	1.105	1.117	1.115	1.053	.996	1.003	1.007	1.035	.993	.936	.802	.739	1.378	.886	.894	.883
Financial leverage	1.344	1.357	1.357	1.352	1.387	1.427	1.455	1.528	1.555	1.581	1.618	1.643	1.664	1.602	1.588	1.641	1.675
Return on investment	.103	.101	.113	.114	.118	.124	.125	.122	.117	.110	.103	.087	.116	.210	.124	.145	.136
Rubber & misc. plastic prod.																	
Profit/volume ratio	.345	.345	.345	.350	.345	.350	.350	.360	.345	.345	.359	.363	.357	.319	.312	.316	.335
Margin of safety	.212	.201	.203	.213	.213	.223	.199	.239	.196	.166	.201	.221	.220	.265	.169	.223	.207
Capital turnover	1.837	1.579	1.556	1.539	1.542	1.530	1.427	1.433	1.369	1.254	1.289	1.333	1.434	1.465	1.307	1.456	1.535
Financial operations ratio	.522	.538	.513	.552	.581	.568	.566	.523	.554	.478	.502	.495	.513	.578	.615	.524	.565
Financial leverage	1.328	1.616	1.651	1.683	1.776	1.808	1.832	1.901	2.008	2.065	2.057	2.039	2.100	2.011	1.969	1.950	1.955
Return on investment	.093	.095	.092	.106	.117	.122	.103	.122	.103	.071	.096	.108	.121	.144	.083	.110	.118
Leather & leather prod.																	
Profit/volume ratio	.250	.250	.250	.255	.255	.255	.260	.265	.255	.255	.255	.258	.253	N/A	N/A	N/A	N/A
Margin of safety	.111	.152	.149	.192	.205	.218	.217	.242	.207	.210	.205	.204	.199				
Capital turnover	2.182	2.144	2.156	2.165	2.199	2.253	2.192	2.161	1.957	1.937	1.918	2.021	2.026				
Financial operations ratio	.403	.464	.480	.535	.542	.544	.526	.518	.485	.470	.423	.455	.485				
Financial leverage	1.789	1.814	1.819	1.854	1.868	1.890	1.831	1.811	1.850	1.928	1.917	1.876	1.895				
Return on investment	.044	.069	.069	.105	.116	.129	.119	.130	.093	.094	.082	.091	.094				
Other nondurable																	
Profit/volume ratio														.257	.260	.262	.292
Margin of Safety														.207	.215	.200	.197
Capital turnover														2.226	2.264	2.444	2.337
Financial operations ratio														.459	.523	.500	.500
Financial leverage														2.150	2.022	1.968	1.969
Return on investment														.117	.133	.128	.133

INDEX

INDEX

Absorption costing:
  method of least squares, 35-36
  origin and development of, 3-4
  pricing and, 101-104, 108-109, 117
  standards, 3-4, 10, 11, 33, 35-36, 45
Accounting Review, The, 137
Acquisition costs, 138-139
American Accounting Association, 6, 137, 143
American Can Company, 5
Armstrong Cork Company, 4-5, 143-145
Arrow diagrams, 90, 92
Asset recognition and measurement, 137-138
Audit, post-completion, 99-100
Automation of management accounting:
  functional specifications, 151-230
    data base listings, 228-230
    indented product cost, 217-222
    labor/expense costing rates, 207-211
    objectives, 151-152
    operation cost listing, 226-227
    outside processing, 203-205
    parts cost listing, 223-225
    physical, 153-186
    product structure, 153-159
    purchase parts rates, 196-201
    rates, 189-211

Automation of management accounting, functional specifications (*Cont.*):
    rates file, 187-188
    raw material rates, 189-195
    raw material usage, 178-186
    reports, 212-230
    routing file—labor standards, 160-177
    routing sheet, 214-216
  models for, 87-92

Balances, verification of, 53
Barry, Gregg, 3
Bedaux incentive plan, 21-22
Bell & Howell Corporation, 82
Beyer, Robert, 5
Bills of material, 53, 62, 69
Bin tickets, 53
Bittel, Lester R., 84
Blackstone, Henry, 75
Book value, 97
Budget data sheets, 11-15, 39, 40
Budget summary sheets, 15, 34
Budgetary control:
  "dictatorship" approach vs. "democratic" approach, 9-10
  (*See also* Flexible budgeting; Zero-base budgeting)
Burden rates, 102, 117

249

Burns, Arthur, 37
Business Week, 86

Capital employed, allocation of, 46
Capital expenditures, 93-100
  classification of, 93-99
    Class I, 93-97
    Class II, 93, 96-97
    Class III, 93, 98-99
    Class IV, 93, 99
  cost overrun avoidance, 99
  post-completion audit, 99-100
Capital turnover (V/A), 129
Carter, Jimmy, 37, 38, 47
Case, Ralph E., 2
Cash discounts, 50
Cash-flow analysis, 96, 97
Cash replacement value, 97
Certificate in Management Accounting (CMA), 6-7
Chairman of the board, 147-148
Chandler, A. D., 120
Cheek, Logan, 134-135
Chief executive officers, 147-150
Competitive pricing, 101-103, 108, 112
Computers, 97
  management by exception and, 85-86
  models for automation of management accounting, 87-92
Continental Can Co., 3-5
Cost-and-variance statement, 16
Cost distribution sheet, 66
Cost of goods sold, 141
Cost overrun avoidance, 99
Costing rates, development of, 65-71
Critical path method (CPM), 77-78, 90-92, 134
"Cycle count" physical inventories, 53

Daily report on productivity, 80-82
DCF method (discounted cash flow), 96-97
Decision package form, 40
Decision packages, 37, 38, 45
Depreciation, allocation of, 46
Dewey & Almy Chemical Co., 4, 143
Direct costing:
  external reporting requirements and, 142-145

Direct costing (*Cont.*):
  flowchart for, 21
  make-or-buy decisions and, 94, 95
  management by exception and, 77
  origin and development of, 4-6
  pricing with, 103-117
    advantages of, 117
    day-to-day decisions, 105-106
    long-range policy decisions, 111-112
    price-cost-volume relationships, 107-111
    pricing formulas, 106-108
    profit guidelines, 112-116
  product cost determination with, 61-73
    case study, 72-73
    computation of, 69, 72
    costing rates, development of, 65-71
    maintenance of, 72
    material specification, 62-64
    process sheets, 64-65
  standards, 4-6, 10, 11, 33-35, 43-45, 77
  temporary costs, 28-30
Direct labor, 10, 19
Direct material costs, 49-59
  material usage variances, 52-53, 59
  procedures tailored to special needs, 53-59
  purchase price variances, 50-52, 54-58
  standard material prices, 49-51
duPont method, 124

Electronic data processing (EDP), 87-92
Element time standards, 18, 26-28, 69
Emerson, Harrington, 2, 61, 76
Engineering estimates, 31
Equipment, replacement of, 97
Exception principle of management (*see* Management by exception)
Expired costs, 140-141
Exponential smoothing, 41
External reporting requirements, 137-145
  asset recognition and measurement, 137-138
  conversion to direct costing and, 142-144
  income determination, 139-142

Index **251**

Farrell Steamship Lines, 5
Fay, C. Robert, 4, 149
Financing plans (*see* Long-range planning)
Finished goods, 53
Flexible budgeting, 2, 9-36
  absorption costing (*see* Absorption costing)
  approval of standards, 14-19
  budget data sheets, 11-15, 39, 40
  direct costing (*see* Direct costing)
  origin and development of, 3-6
  performance reports, 31-33
  simple, 10-11
  standard data, use of, 26-31
    element time standards, 26-28
    engineering estimates, 31
    temporary standards, 28-30
  standards for measuring productivity (*see* Productivity measurement, standards for)
Forecast, sales, 41-42
Fostoria Glass Co., 5, 142-143
Fringe benefits, 10

Gee, George D., 6-7
General Motors Corporation, 103
General Wood, 120
Grace, W. R., & Co., 143

Halsey incentive plan, 23, 24
Harris, Jonathon, 4, 6, 77
Harrison, G. Charter, 2, 4, 6, 76-77
Hawthorne study, 17-18
Hornbostle, Charles, 147
Hughes Aircraft Co., 85

Income determination, 139-142
Income tax, 141-142
Indirect labor, 10
Institute of Management Accounting, 7
Inventory:
  material usage variances, 52-53
  materials specification, 62-64

James, John V., 149
Job cost system, 61

Keller, I. Wayne, 4-6, 34, 148

Least squares, method of, 35-36
Line production report, 33
Lockheed Aircraft Co., 86
Long-range planning, 39, 119-136
  alternate course of action, 123
  capabilities, evaluation of, 122-123
  management efficiency measurement, 124-130
    financial management, 129-130
    operating management, 125, 127-129
  master profit plan and, 131, 133
  monthly report on profit plan and, 135-136
  operating plans, development of, 131, 134-135
  planning climate, 122
  strategic plan, 123-124
Long-range pricing policies, 111-112

Machine-hours, standard, 19
Make-or-buy decisions, 94-96
Management accounting:
  automation of (*see* Automation of management accounting)
  future of, 147-150
  origin and development of, 1-7
Management Accounting, 6
Management Accounting for Profit Control (Keller), 6
Management by exception, 75-86
  advantages of, 80, 82-83
  applications of, 77-82
    critical path method (CPM), 77-78
    daily report on productivity, 80-82
    monthly report on profit plan, 78-80
  computers and, 85-86
  defined, 76
  pitfalls of, 83-85
Management by Exception (Bittel), 84
Margin of safety, 128-129
Markup, 105-106, 113-116
Marple, Raymond, 4
Martin Company, 121
Martino, "Rocky," 77-78, 92
Master profit plan, 39, 41-46, 132
  allocation of capital employed, 46
  allocation of decision package costs, 45

252 Management Accounting Simplified

Master profit plan (*Cont.*):
  format, 43-45
  objectives, 131, 133
  preliminary statement of objectives, 42-43
  review and approval, 46
  sales forecast, 41-42
Material costs (*see* Direct Material costs)
Merseles, T., 120
Monetary assets, 138
Montgomery Ward & Co., 120-121
Monthly report on profit plan, 39, 78-80, 135-136
Moving average sales, 41

NAA Bulletin, 6
NACA Bulletin, 2
National Association of Accountants, 6-7, 103
National Association of Cost Accountants, 2, 4
New Wine in Old Bottles (Harrison), 4
Nonmonetary assets, 138
Nonproductive cost centers, 65

Olin Mathieson Corporation, 77-78, 92
Operating management index, 125, 127-129
Operating plans, development of, 131, 134-135
Operating supplies, 10
Otis Elevator Co., 83
Overhead, 2, 10, 102

Payback period determination, 96, 97
Percy, Charles H., 82
Performance reports, 31-33
Period costs, allocation of, 20, 43-45, 69, 94, 103, 104, 113
Perpetual inventory records, 52-53
Piecework plan, 19-21
Pittsburgh Plate Glass Company, 4-5, 28-30, 142
Planning (*see* Long-range planning; Profit plans)
Plant expansion programs, 98-99
Post-completion audit, 99-100
PPG Industries, 149-150

Preliminary statement of objectives, 42-43
Price index card, 50, 51
Prices, material:
  procedures tailored to special needs, 53-59
  purchase price variances, 50-52, 54-58
  standard, 49-51
Pricing, 101-117
  absorption costing and, 101-104, 108-109, 117
  direct costing and (*see* Direct costing, pricing with)
  grid, 113
  guideline development, 112, 114
  by marketing executives, 112
Prime Costs Keeping for Engineers, Ironfounders, Boiler and Bridge Makers, et cetera, Practically Explained with the Method of Arriving at All the General Averages Required (Walker), 2
Process sheets, standard, 64-65
Product cost sheets, 66-72
Product costs, standard, 61-73
  case study, 72-73
  computation of, 69, 72
  costing rates, development of, 65-71
  maintenance of, 72
  material specification, 62-64
  process sheets, 64-65
  (*See also* Direct material costs)
Productive cost centers, 65
Productivity, daily report on, 80-82
Productivity measurement, 17-26
  common denominators of production and, 18-19
  Hawthorne study, 17-18
  standards for, 19-26
    Bedaux plan, 21-22
    Halsey plan, 23, 24
    Rowan plan, 23-24
    standard-hour plan, 24-26
    straight piecework, 19-21
Profit guidelines, 112-116
Profit planning in depth, 149
Profit plans, 104-105
  zero-base budgeting and, 39, 40
  master (*see* Master profit plan)
  monthly report on, 39, 78-80, 135-136
Profit/volume (P/V) ratio, 72, 127-130

Program evaluation and review technique (PERT), 77-78, 134
Purchase price summary, 52
Purchase price variances, 50-52, 54-58
Pyhrr, Peter, 37

Ratios:
　comparative, 235-245
　computation of, 130
Raw materials, 52-53
Regional sales forecasts, 42
Requisitions, 53
Research Institute of America, 5-6, 37-38
Responsibility accounting, 10, 61
Return on investment, 124
Revenue, 140
Robert Beyer Medal awards, 7
Rowan incentive plan, 23-24

Sales forecast, 41-42
Sales-to-assets ratio, 129
Scattergraph, 13
Scott, Brian, 121
Seagrams Co., 121-122
Sears, Roebuck and Co., 120-121
Shop Management (Taylor), 76
Spool Cotton Co., 4
Standard costs:
　origin and development of, 2-7
　(*See also* Flexible budgeting; Product costs, standard)
Standard-hour incentive plan, 24-26
Standard material price card, 50, 51
Standard material prices, 49-51
Standard process sheets, 64-65
Standard product cost sheet, 68
Standard product unit cost card, 70
Statement of objectives, preliminary, 42-43
Straight piecework plan, 19-21

Strategic long-range plan, 123-124

Taylor, Frederick Winslow, 76, 85
Temporary cost standards, 28-30
Time standards, 18, 26-28, 69

Universal Cyclops Steel Co., 5

Volume variance, 2
Volume variance accounts, 11

Wage incentive plans, 19-26
　Bedaux plan, 21-22
　Halsey plan, 23, 24
　Rowan plan, 23-24
　standard-hour plan, 24-26
　straight piecework, 19-21
Walker, John, 2
Western Electric Co., 17-18
Westinghouse Co., 2, 77
Williams, L. Stanton, 149-150
Work-hours, standard, 18
Work-in-process records, 53

Zero-base budgeting, 37-46
　defined, 37-38
　integration of planning with, 39, 40
　master profit plan, 39, 41-46, 131
　　allocation of capital employed, 46
　　allocation of decision package costs, 45
　　format, 43-45
　　objectives, 131, 133
　　preliminary statement of objectives, 42-43
　　review and approval, 46
　　sales forecast, 41-42
Zero-Base Budgeting Comes of Age (Cheek), 134-135